A Personal Touch On...™ Adoption

Written by:
People Touched By Adoption
Sharing Stories To Help You

edited by:
Peter R. Berlin
Jerry Stone

A Personal Touch Publishing, LLC.
Los Angeles, California

APT Publishing

9-30-05

Printed in the United States of America

ISBN 0-9748566-1-4

Library of Congress Control Number: 2004098395

Publisher: A Personal Touch Publishing, LLC.
1335 La Brea Avenue #2
Los Angeles, California 90028
www.aptbooks.com

We would like to thank the following individuals for allowing us to reprint their pieces:

"A Reason For Everything" Reprinted by permission of Barbara James. ©2004 Barbara James

"Interview With An Adoptee" "Questions To Ask A Potential Birthmother" and "To Tell Or Not To Tell (The School) That Is The Question" Reprinted by permission of Karen Ledbetter. ©2004 Karen Ledbetter

"Alison's Journey-Home Journal" Reprinted by permission of Nicole Sandler. ©2004 Nicole Sandler

"A Mother's Thoughts On Cultural Pride" "Unsolicited Comments" Reprinted by permission of Leceta Chisholm Guibault. ©2004 Leceta Chisholm Guibault.

"Of Band-Aids And Such" "He's Yours" Reprinted by permission of Cheryl L. Dieter. ©2004 Cheryl Dietter

"Thoughts On Adopting Older Children" Reprinted by permission of Linda Belles ©2004 Linda Belles

"Thoughts On Loving A Helpless Child" "Building A Child's Self-Esteem" Reprinted by permission of Rosemary Gwaltney.©2004 Rosemary Gwaltney

"Our Journey Through Attachment Disorder" Reprinted by permission of Nancy Geoghegan. ©2004 Nancy Geoghegan.

"The Toothbrush Monster And Other Silly Strategies For Parenting Success" Reprinted by permission of Mollie McLeod. ©2004 Mollie McLeod.

"Enhancing Attachment and Bonding With Your Child" Reprinted by permission of Karin Price ©2004 Dillon International.

To Michael and Ciara, we hope we've enriched your lives as much as you've enriched ours.

To all those who have traveled the road to adoption: birthmothers, adoptive parents, adoptees. May your love keep growing.

"If during the course of your own life, you have saved one life, it is as if you have saved all humankind."

- The Talmud

Table Of Contents

1. Moving Past Infertility
Adoption: The Light At The End Of The Tunnel

2. Roads To Adoption
Bumpy But Worth It

3. Adoptee Stories
It's Great To Be Wanted

4. Birthmother Stories
A Loving Decision

5. Open Adoption
No Whispering Needed

6. International Adoption
A World Of Love Waiting For You

7. Special Needs
All Children Need Love!

8. Many Ways To Make A Family
Breaking the Mold

9. Special Moments
Our Lives Will Never Be The Same!

10. What's Worked For Us
The School Of Experience

Acknowledgements

by Jerry Stone

I have been an entrepreneur since moving to California nearly three decades ago. My businesses have encompassed leading-edge communications, finance, and property management. When Peter Berlin approached me about starting a publishing company, I decided to tackle that world as well. We realized there are many solutions to a situation and what works for one is not always right for another. The Personal Touch On... series offers varied approaches to different situations. We hope you'll find it helpful and inspirational.

This is the second book of our *Personal Touch On...*™ series. Our first, on celiac disease, the number one misdiagnosed intestinal disorder, showed us that books written solely by people willing to share their first-hand experiences can inform, inspire, encourage, present options, and give hope to others. So the first note of thanks goes to all of the generous people who contributed to this "support group in a book" on adoption. Your effort will provide comfort and inspiration to others, and we are extremely grateful.

Several individuals and organizations were extremely helpful and supportive in getting the word out about our project. We'd like to thank Gloria Hochman of the National Adoption Center (www.adopt.org), John Harrah of Harrah's Family Services (www.hfsadopt.com), and Cindy Haftner of the Adoption Support Centre of Saskatchewan (www.sasktelwebsite.net/adoption/) for posting messages on their websites and helping us expand our network.

Several agencies put us in contact with adoptive parents, birthmothers, and adoptees who contributed stories. They are: Maxine Chalker and Alexandra Kane-Weiss of Adoptions From The Heart (www.adoptionsfromtheheart.org), Shawn Kane of American Adoptions (www.americanadoptions.com), Sharon Fitzgerald of Independent Adoption Center (IAC, www.adoptionhelp.org), and Dawn Degenhardt of Maine Adoption Placement Service (MAPS, www.mapsadopt.org).

Special thanks to Nicole Strickland, co-founder of BirthMom Buds (www.birthmombuds.com), who not only wrote several pieces for the book but helped us obtain stories from birthmothers. You are doing a remarkable job to help others.

Special thanks to Jillian Barberie who enthusiastically agreed to write the forward. We appreciate you fitting the time into your busy schedule as co-anchor of the Los Angeles FOX morning news show, "Good Day LA." Thanks to Lisa Blum, Rosie Pinto, and Loren Ruch for bringing the book to Jillian's attention.

Thanks to Bradley Stone for your work in building our website.

Thanks as always to Beverly Berlin and Donna Stone for your love, support, faith, and hard work.

One last note. The Internet is a tremendous resource for all things concerning adoption. There are articles, bulletin boards, and chat rooms, on thousands of sites. We encourage everyone to learn from people who have experienced what you are going through and then share your experiences with those who come after you. The benefits to you and others will be tremendous.

Foreword

by Jillian Barberie

One of the benefits of being a television personality is it allows me to bring attention to topics that are important to me. Having been given up for adoption, related issues quickly gain my attention and efforts. I am proud to have been a part of "America Works for Kids," working with foster girls in Los Angeles County, and I hope sharing my personal story helps people who are going through similar times.

When I was asked to write the foreword for this book, what made me immediately want to be involved is that it is a compilation of writings by real people who have real experiences with adoption. I was adopted, and before deciding to find my birthmother I read every book on the subject I could get my hands on. I am proud to share my story and am lucky it is a positive one. While I realize that my experience is unique, I can identify with anyone who has ever had questions about who they are and where they come from.

My birthmother gave me up for adoption when I was born and meeting her was something I always wanted to do. I spent so many years of my life wondering about my background and my biological history. Finally, at age 34, I hired a detective. It was the best 500 bucks I ever spent.

Before I decided to find my blood ties, I tried to seek advice from every outlet. People told me the worst-case scenario would be I would find my birthmother but she would be deceased. I disagreed. I thought the worst-case scenario would be that I would find her and she would reject me. In spite of that fear I decided to look for her, because rather than viewing it as possible rejection I saw it as finally getting closure.

Soon after she was hired, the detective called me at home and asked if I was ready to hear about my family. She found out my birthmother and birthfather had gotten married after they gave me up for adoption. They went on to have two other daughters, my sisters. I had looked for my birthmother because I wanted closure, but what I ended up with was a new family and finding them was the best thing I have ever done.

Of course, I didn't want to be a burden to the family. My birthparents had since gotten divorced and my birthmother was remarried. I wasn't sure if her new husband knew I had ever been born. I decided to contact her by writing her a letter. In it, I thanked her for doing the right thing and she later told me my letter alleviated years of guilt and uncertainty that had built up in her throughout the years. Meanwhile, I found a new appreciation for what she had been through and the sacrifice that she made.

There is nothing like the bond between a mother and her child. We began our bond when she gave birth to me. We finally met again when she walked in my door 34 years later. We were even in a whole different country!

For anyone out there who may feel alone in the process, whether you've been adopted or want to adopt, this book is a wonderful way to realize there is a world of support available from those who have been through it. It is my hope that in these pages, we are providing comfort and inspiration, for people whose lives have been touched by adoption, and I am honored to be part of something that can help someone learn more about adoption, about other people's experiences, and even about themselves.

Introduction
by Peter R. Berlin

I founded Personal Touch Publishing a year ago with Jerry Stone. We realized that when facing life's challenges, the best information received was from others who had been down the same road before. This book offers inspiration, hope, and encouragement to those now on the path to adoption.

I am an adoptive parent and have been for over 15 years. After years of unsuccessful treatment for infertility, my wife and I decided what we really wanted was to have children and a family, whether they carried our genes or not. So we decided to adopt. There has not been a day where we have regretted that decision or a day we don't feel blessed. We are the proud parents of two tremendous children, a boy and a girl. To answer the question, "Can you love adopted children like your own?" let me assure anyone who might ask (and it is a perfectly normal question) that they are your own. I couldn't imagine loving a child any more than I love them.

I realize not every story will turn out as well as ours. Perhaps one of the reasons for our success was the knowledge we obtained going in. We researched and talked to everyone we knew or we could find who had an adoption story. It's much easier to do this today than it was in the 1980's. The Internet has opened a whole new way of obtaining information. But in order to ask the right questions you still need to have background information. The dictionary defines adoption as: *"to take into one's family through legal means and raise as one's own child."* Though a simple definition, the process of adoption is both emotional and complex. There are many options for prospective parents and birthmothers. My hope is this book will present many of the options and emotions from the point of view of those who have experienced them. We have collected pieces written by birthmothers, adoptive parents, and adopted children. We cover many different aspects of adoption: adopting newborns, international adoption, older child adoption, open adoption, single parent adoption, adopting special needs children, and more. We've focused on the positive side to give options and to show how lives can be enriched through the process. We have organized the stories into chapters, but as you will see, adoption is so multifaceted that many of the pieces could easily fit in several different places.

The process of adoption can be long and hard. As Jessica Ritter says in her piece "People In Our Path," *"Adoption is not a process for the faint of heart. It is an emotional roller coaster."* But knowing this at the start of your journey and reading about the life-changing results of those who succeeded should inspire you when things get tough. Knowing what to expect is a great way to prepare and Richard Gold, in "The Home Study: Baring Your Soul," will give you an idea of what you will go through during *"an inspection that puts every aspect of your life under a microscope."* But if you ask Jessica and Richard if it was worth it, they'll both say yes.

Our book will give you a better understanding of the unselfish birthmothers who give up their children for adoption in order to secure a better life for their child. You'll meet birthmothers like Lisa Scheen who expresses her feelings by saying, in "A Pregnant

Teen's Choice," "*Today's society often tries to make birthmothers look bad . . .What they don't understand is that it's because we loved them so much we let them go.*" Understanding what a birthmother goes through is essential for adoptive parents as well as for the children they give up. I also hope the birthmother stories will let women who are giving a child up for adoption, or those considering this option, realize they are not alone and there is support out there.

Adopted children have a voice in our book and you can see how, as an adoptive parent, you have the power to change lives forever. Richard Lockwood gives a wonderful sense of what it's like being adopted in "On Being Adopted." "*My 'real' parents are the ones that, when I hit 'mom and dad' on my speed dial, I expect to answer. I appreciate them. I love them.*"

Many come to adoption after years of battling infertility. Your questions and concerns about adoption will be answered by others who have been there before and who share their anxieties and feelings. Carla King, in "A Love We'd Never Felt Before," poignantly states, "*All the years and heartache of longing to be a family is erased the second you hold your baby. You no longer look in the past. Instead, you look in your arms and see the future.*"

Adoption isn't only about newborns. Older children and children of all races and colors need homes too. If you are considering adopting an older child, it is important to have information. Linda Belles provides many thought-provoking questions and strategies in her piece "Thoughts On Adopting Older Children." Moreover, Courtney Rathke talks about the rewards of adopting a toddler in her piece, "But Why Not A Baby?" "*The interaction and learning are fascinating to watch and to participate in as a parent. It is such a joyous thing to offer a child a new experience and to see how they absorb it.*"

Maybe the road you will travel will take you to a foreign country to save the life of a child. Read "My Long Amazing

Journey" by Russian adoptee, Sera McManus, who writes, *"At the age of almost ten, my adoption was a miracle. I was so happy to finally go home."* And Caitlin Chun, born in Vietnam, tells in "About Me" of her adjustment: *"I had trouble learning to trust and love others. I gradually matured and learned about genuine love. My adoptive parents taught me everything."* You'll also read pieces by adoptive parents who talk about their trips and prepare you for what to expect.

Not all children are born with perfect health and not all children adjust easily. But all children need homes. Rosemary Gwaltney is the mother of 26 children, most of whom were adopted and have disabilities. In her piece "Building A Child's Self-Esteem" she explains, *"I don't see my children's handicaps when I look at them. To me, they are simply children. Children with strengths and weaknesses like everybody else."* She goes on to explain how she handles her remarkable family.

Adoption isn't just for married couples. Single mom, Bonnie Loomis, in "Brooke's Bridge," describes her decision-making process: *"For three years I went back and forth about my ability to be a mom. I knew instinctively I'd be a good mom, I just didn't know how to make it happen."* In her heartwarming piece, she tells you how she made it happen.

These examples are just the tip of the iceberg of what you will find within these pages. We have collected over 80 pieces covering a wide range of experiences. Read, enjoy, learn, and realize adoption in whatever form is really all about one thing: making the best life for a child that needs a family

Good luck and best wishes to all of you!

Moving Past Infertility

Adoption:
The Light At The End Of The Tunnel

*"Our children are not ours because they share our genes . . .
They are ours because we have had the audacity to envision them.
That, at the end of the day . . . or long sleepless night,
is how love really works."*

- Unknown

A Child Born In Our Hearts

by Alison Vivona

We are Michael and Alison. We are in our early 30's and have been married for seven years. We suffered through four years of infertility and finally decided to adopt. It was the best decision we ever made. We are now parents to a beautiful little angel named Michael. He was born in May 2004. Dreams can come true. Patience and a strong belief that you will achieve your ultimate dream is all you need. I wish I could help each and every one of you. Good luck! Stay strong! Most importantly, when you feel you have nothing left to believe in, remember you always do.

"A Child Born In Our Hearts" is the title we gave our adoption profile. It took a long time to come up with something that expressed how we felt about adoption. How do you put these feelings into just a few words without writing forever? We believe we found a way in that statement.

Michael and I had been trying to conceive since 2000. We have suffered the trials and tribulations of infertility, having been through tests, surgery, never-ending specialty doctor visits, shots, drugs, and six IUI's (Intrauterine Inseminations). It was consuming our lives. We fought, we went to counseling, we ignored the problem, but it didn't get any better. Unfortunately, we have male-factor infertility, so there is little hope that we were to conceive on our own. We came to the conclusion it was not fair to

. . . we kept asking ourselves, when is enough, enough? When do we accept the fact that we may never have biological children?

me to have to go through the Gonal-F shots again. We also couldn't bear the thought of more heartache from finding out we weren't pregnant AGAIN (what sealed the deal was we found out on Christmas Eve we weren't pregnant). It became harder to see women who were pregnant and harder to talk to friends with children. Suddenly, we had less in common with them. I always say it isn't fair people could practically use the same soap and get pregnant. It's hard to deal with these feelings but it gets easier. Because of all this we stopped trying to conceive in December 2002.

We needed a break. If you feel depressed or sad, or find you are arguing with your spouse about the stupidest things, step back from the situation. Take some time to straighten things out between yourselves. Realize a child will not solve all the problems you have and work on being happy without a child. That way you can enjoy the time when you are blessed with one. We refused to become a statistic.

Yet we kept asking ourselves, when is enough, enough? When do we accept the fact that we may never have biological children? Enough is enough when you realize having a child is more important than being pregnant. It is more important than worrying about the time frame or the cost of having a baby. It is more important than everything else. That is when we said enough is enough.

After a few months of talking about it, soul searching, crying, and A LOT of research we decided to adopt. The love we have to give a child should be shared with a child, biological or not.

Even after researching adoption, we still didn't know where to start. Then we discovered a friend's daughter had adopted two children. He suggested we speak with her and we did. It was the most enlightening yet overwhelming thing we had done so far. Would we be able to afford it? How long would it take? Did we really want to give up on the chance of a biological child? We knew whatever we needed to do to become parents we would do. It didn't matter.

Through her referral we are adopting through an agency in Texas, even though we live in New York. It is a lot of paperwork, background checks, and home studies. It is even more waiting around but the end result is worth it, don't you think?

We had to make a "Dear Birthmother Book," which is how the biological mother chooses who she wants to raise her child. It is basically a family photo album the birthmother looks through to get an idea of who we are. It was difficult to show a person who we are, what we believe in, and how we live. How do you prove to someone you are good enough to raise her child? What is the birthmother looking for in a family? Does she want someone rich? Thin? Blonde hair? Brown hair? Vacations a lot? Is into sports? Has a pet? Who knows? We agonized over this for months until we decided we just had to be totally honest about who we are and hope something clicks in her heart. Something that makes her see we are the ones for her.

We are scared that no one will like us. No one will choose us. We will never become parents.

We are now waiting for the call to tell us we are parents. It could come at any time. We don't leave the house without forwarding the phone to our cell phones. We are scared that no one will like us. No one will choose us. We will never become parents. But that goes away. There is a child for us. We just have to wait to be chosen.

Fate has already decided what it wants for you. It is about the child, not about you. I believe we were given the infertility issue because all the love we have for a child is supposed to go to a child that otherwise wouldn't have that love. Even though the child is not born unto you, this child is one that is born unto your heart.

You are strong. You will get through this. You may have taken the first step in exploring adoption, or you may just be thinking about it. The hardest step to take is yet to come: raising a child.

You are never alone in how you feel about adoption. There are many resources to utilize that can help you through whatever you are feeling. There are message boards with other people who are experiencing what you are. There are also books and websites. Never feel you are alone or the only person who has ever experienced the pain or hurt. There are many of us out there; you just have to look for us.

It took me a long time to get to this place and I am a full supporter of anyone who is considering adoption. It takes time to get to this mind frame but it's worth the trip. I want others to know there is a light at the end of the tunnel and it is full of smiles as well as dirty diapers and 3 a.m. feedings!

There are many gifts we wish for in this world. Riches, health, a better job, but the best gift in the world is the gift of the selfless words "you are parents."

Good luck.

A Blessing In Disguise
by Kara Funk

Hello. Our names are Kara and Gary. We adopted two beautiful boys, Sam in 2001 and Joey in 2003. Both experiences had a profound effect on our families, our close friends, and us. We feel as if adoption has not only made us stronger people, but has made us feel love like no other love.

We must first tell you we now look at our infertility, which once caused so much pain, as something we feel immensely grateful for. If it had not been for that, we would have never had Sammy and Joey, our treasures. Our entire family supported us through this even though we think they were silently terrified for us in the beginning.

Sam's adoption happened very fast; there were no delays. We were matched quickly and the birthmother was very positive, as she had decided about adoption from the beginning. She proceeded quickly with the paperwork to surrender both her and the birthfather's rights. Joey's was quite different. We had two failed adoptions before his and in both failed cases, the birthmothers changed their minds and decided to parent.

In the first failed adoption, the birthmother barely spoke to us, never said phrases like "when you take your baby home" or referred to the child as "your baby." We met her at the hospital and had a prior conference call with a social worker. However, we never felt she wanted to talk to us or really understood what was going on. When we were at the hospital following the birth of the child, her family was constantly in the room with her. This was a definite red flag because the family was so involved and this is when things went bad for us. Don't confuse this with a birthmother who has a strong support system and family members who approve of her plan.

In the second failed adoption, there were a couple of indications which we see now as we look back. The nurses didn't look at us when we arrived at the hospital. The birthmother and birthfather were both feeding the baby and sitting together. This was the evening the child was born. It wasn't as if they were saying goodbye before she was being discharged from the hospital. She changed her mind one day after the birth, which made things easier for us because it didn't drag on for several days.

Even though both experiences were heartbreaking, we look back with a sort of comfort and sense of unexpected growth because we would have never have had Joey had it not been for those two failed adoptions. We would take the risk and do it all over again to have Sam and Joey forever.

In both adoptions, we had the privilege of meeting our children's birthmothers and in Sam's case, his birthfather too. We cannot express how grateful we were for this opportunity to meet, thank, and see our children's genetic link. We love every part of our children, even the part that we could not create: their genetics. This doesn't mean we want future relationships with the birthparents; instead it means that we simply respect those responsible for choosing life for our boys.

In retrospect, we wish we knew not to be nervous about the birthmother/birthparents asking where we live and if they could come visit. We now know this is a very normal and common fear among prospective adoptive families. What we wish we knew was simply that there is a huge myth about birthparents. In our experience, for the most part, they do not want to be a part of your life. They want to get on with their lives as much as you do. If you have a birthparent that asks for future visits right before she is giving up her rights, the best thing to do is speak from your instincts and never ever sway from that.

The driving force that led us to adoption is the belief there were these children out there who would not be raised by their genetic links and we would never be able to create a genetic link. We felt connected to these children. We stuck with faith (adoption) and it took us where we needed to be.

We hope this story has brought both comfort and hope in your journey. Adoption is beautiful! Good Luck!

Most sincerely,

Kara, Gary, Sam, and Joey

Experiencing Life To The Fullest

by Jenny Galiani

My husband David and I are both so happy to be included in this special book. The road to adoption has brought us our two beautiful girls, who I can't imagine our lives without. They are both true miracles from God. God bless you in your journey of adoption.

Dave and I were married in 1995 and had dreams of having a large family with lots of children. We began trying to have children within the first two years of marriage. After years of fertility treatments, surgeries for both of us, miscarriages, and shattered hearts, it was clear our children were going to come to us via another way, through people we now affectionately call our birthmoms. Two very selfless and caring individuals who have given us the family we've always dreamed of.

We registered with a domestic adoption agency in July 2001 and by September our home study and all of our paperwork was complete. We were officially "waiting" to be matched. I remember the phone call like it was yesterday. Our social worker simply left a message saying, "Congratulations! You've been matched with a birthmother; please call as soon as you can." I remember playing it and my heart flip-flopping! Our oldest daughter Grace was born just a little over two weeks later.

Grace brought us so much joy that we wanted to adopt again. We anxiously awaited her first birthday so we could put our paperwork in for our next baby. We became activated again and within six days we were matched! What a wonderful whirlwind! On April 17, our second angel, Sophia, was born.

To say we've been incredibly blessed sounds cliché and is an understatement. We've received two miracles from God through adoption and by the brave hearts of the girls' birthmothers.

We arrived within hours of both of our children's birth and got to meet their birthparents. We are thrilled we had that experience so we can share it with our daughters as they get older. We even took pictures together. The overall experience of adopting Grace and Sophia has been wonderful. They truly are the light in our lives. They are both such beautiful, happy, bright little girls that make us laugh and love more every day. Because of them we now are experiencing life to the fullest. We see glimpses of God everyday through them. We have more love than our hearts can hold, a tiny hand to hold, and big hugs and kisses. There's someone to laugh yourself silly with no matter what the boss said or how your stocks performed that day. They are perfect in every way. They are truly gifts from God.

While filling out all the paperwork involved in adoption, I can remember thinking to myself, "What if it never happens for us?" I have made it a priority in my life to let others know, "It CAN and WILL happen through adoption." It isn't about being pregnant; it's about being a mom. And I love every minute of it!

We are hoping, God willing, to be able to adopt again in the future. Yes, three! We will anxiously await the next phone call, the next journey, and to meet the next amazing addition to our family.

Trials And Tribulations

by Linda Miller-Gardner

My name is Linda Miller-Gardner from Allentown, Pennsylvania. Twenty-one years ago, I received the worst and best news of my life: you cannot have children, but here is a child for you to adopt. My life has been enriched with a love that has no boundaries. This poem sums it all up: Heredity or environment which are you the product of? Neither my darling, neither, just two different kinds of love.

Well, it is 21 years to the day and I have the most beautiful, intelligent, honorable daughter anyone has ever laid their eyes on. Of course, all adopted children are so special, so wanted, and each one of us think our child is the best; maybe because we learned appreciation the hard way. Let's recede to the beginning of my personal adoption story.

I was in my early 20's and my brother, at the young age of 28, died of a heart attack. Our family was devastated. In the harshest way, my husband and I discovered life is short and decided we would start a family. We tried to conceive without success, so we turned to infertility testing. I went to the doctor and, test after test, showed nothing. My husband was tested and they found he had a low sperm count. We were both put on the fertility drug Clomid, which caused me to develop ovarian cysts. I was taken off of it but we kept trying. I didn't like how slow this doctor moved. I wanted a baby NOW. I searched until I found a doctor that moved as fast as I wanted. I waited precious months to get an appointment.

When the day came, I traveled an hour and waited hours to see him. It would be worth it if I could conceive. He informed me my uterus was inadequately shaped for harboring a fetus, but it could be corrected with surgery. I was ecstatic knowing it was repairable. Prior to surgery, they injected dye into my fallopian tubes to see if everything was clear. That evening, the doctor called and gave us the devastating news. My uterus could not be fixed. It appeared the DES my mother took during her pregnancy caused me to be infertile. Nothing could be done.

I was utterly heartbroken. How can this be? I am a woman. I was born to reproduce. Why, why, why? Everyone around me was getting pregnant and there were babies everywhere. All my friends were starting their families and I had nothing, not even hope.

I read an article in a magazine about a fertility doctor with a new method. I called and again waited months for an appointment. Once again I traveled an hour to get there. He said my cervical mucus was too thick, and they would mix my husband's sperm with a donor's to give us a higher chance of conceiving. I would have to drink a bottle of Robitussin a day to thin the cervical mucus and start giving myself shots of Pergonal. "Get dressed, go see the nurse, and she will teach you how to give yourself shots," he said. In addition to the shots, I would have to come back for artificial insemination and an ultrasound to see how many eggs I had.

At home, I mixed the dry medicine with the wet and prepared my shots. I sat in the bathroom with sweat beading down my body and punched my leg with the needle. They would tell me, "you have eight eggs" or "you have ten eggs." Months and months went by with no pregnancies. I was willing to cut my leg off to conceive.

Finally, after years of this self-inflicted torture without any success, it was time to stop. My body and my nerves were shot so I had to find another solution.

Our final option was adoption. I put my name into every Jewish, Catholic, or state adoption agency there was. Finally one day, a man called from an agency. He told us we were required to attend a meeting every Sunday no matter what. Adopting a child had to be the most important thing in our life. I obeyed; I was willing to do anything possible to have a child. He made it known the more you did for the agency the quicker you received a child. I volunteered for everything. One night, I drove to Philadelphia International Airport at 1 a.m.

. . . the years of infertility testing and trials and tribulations of trying to adopt had destroyed our marriage . . .

to pick up a woman with a newborn baby. This agency had us care for birthmothers until they delivered. After the babies were born, they were not given to the prospective adoptive parents who cared for them; they were given to other adoptive parents. I attended meeting after meeting at the agency and saw this couple and that couple receiving babies.

What seemed like a lifetime went by without a new baby, but one glorious day, I got the call. I was to be the mother of a baby girl. I was ecstatic! I would name her after my brother so she could carry our family name. When my darling daughter was four days old, my husband went out for diapers and never returned. It seemed the years of infertility testing and trials and tribulations of trying to adopt had destroyed our marriage and my husband had found a girlfriend. I was filled with immense sorrow but I had a baby to take care of. I mourned the loss but rejoiced in the new life I was caring for.

I notified the adoption agency that my marital status had changed but I still wanted to be a mother and raise this beautiful child. I was told, "Then the child is yours." Five months later I received a call to come to the agency and bring my daughter. I knew this wasn't good. They said they had changed their mind and that they didn't want a single parent. I immediately found a lawyer who gave me no false promises. The case dragged on for 18 months. I had to visit a child psychiatrist to see if my daughter had bonded with me, and I had to go to another psychiatrist to prove I was capable of raising a child alone. There were no limits to what I would do to continue being this baby girl's mother. Finally, my lawyer and I decided to go to arbitration and either I would hand my daughter over or they would allow me to adopt.

Since you read the beginning of this story, you know the end. I won, and did I ever! It has been 21 glorious years of joy. I remarried in 1994 and my husband adopted my daughter in 1997. She still uses my maiden name, only now it's hyphenated with her father's last name. She is a senior in college studying to be a research psychologist. I have never, ever been so fulfilled in my entire life. She has brought me happiness beyond compare. I thank God every day for the opportunity to be her mother.

Some say you aren't a real mother unless you birth your child, but I disagree. I couldn't love my angel more even if I gave birth to her. My life with her has been happiness after happiness with her school plays and band concerts. I have taught her that nothing is beyond her reach. I would catch the stars for her. I am a mere 48 years old and should I die today, my life would be totally fulfilled with the joy of raising my daughter. ✍️

Linda's daughter, Rikki Miller-Gardner, has written "My Real Mother," which can be read in Chapter Three.

Two Bundles Of Joy

by Dawn

Who am I? I have a Master's Degree, I have worked at the same company since 1990, I have two dogs and two cats. My husband and I met on the Internet and after two years of being together, we married. More important than all that, I am the mother of adopted twins. Here is how I got the babies/children I've always wanted.

For some, the decision to become a parent happens accidentally when the "stick" turns blue. For some, the decision requires time to get used to the idea. For me, I barely recall a time when I didn't want to be a mom. My husband talked about winning the lottery and what he'd do with the money. If I won, I'd get a huge house and fill it with children. That's how strong my desire to be a parent is and how much I love children.

Who knew such a strong desire could be tested by emotionally-charged challenges like infertility? We, like so many others, have gone through the ups and downs of infertility that included frequent monthly visits to the specialist. After several IUIs I did get pregnant and found myself on bed rest at 12 weeks due to bleeding. At 16 weeks I went into premature labor. While I was still in the hospital, my water broke, causing what doctors considered an early, second-trimester miscarriage, since the fetus wasn't viable. We were devastated. The doctors kept saying, "You got pregnant before, we'll get you pregnant again." After several more attempts at IUI, it didn't happen.

One day, I drove by a sign about adoption. Adoption was always in the back of my mind. After all, we just wanted to be parents. It didn't matter how. Shortly after I saw the sign, my husband brought up adoption. To me, this was a different kind of sign. I am not someone who sits idly by and procrastinates when I have a passion, and when it came to becoming a mom, my passion was very strong. I did some research and found American Adoptions. Their site was well-organized and had lots of information, so I gave them a call. We met the criteria, I filled out the initial application, and our journey began. We continued to go through infertility treatments. We figured, why not have our "eggs" (so to speak) in more than one basket? One way or another, I felt strongly that we were going to be parents soon.

One of the most exciting days of our lives was when we got the call for the match. I work from home. So when did we get the call? Not when I was at home but the one day I was in training at the office. During my lunch break, I called my husband to tell him I wouldn't be getting home until late and that is when he told me. One of the social workers had all of our numbers and was able to reach him. I couldn't concentrate the rest of the day. That night my husband and I were up late talking about names, what colors to do the nursery, etc. We couldn't sleep that whole night because we were so excited. It was amazing. Not only had we been matched in under two months, but the birthmother was 33 weeks pregnant with a boy and a girl. Twins! I couldn't believe it. All this time we wanted a baby and we were getting two of them.

The agency cautions perspective parents about getting too excited ahead of time because birthmothers can change their mind. Though that is true, I had a sense this was going to work out. I spoke with the birthmother and was instantly comfortable. We asked each other questions and she relieved many of my concerns. I found out afterwards I did the same for her. There were so many things that felt right about the match, from the birthparent's nationalities (the same as ours) to the original due date (the day before my birthday). We knew this was it.

Then, at 3 a.m. on March 20, 2003, the call came telling us the birthmother was in labor. Thankfully, we had already packed and were able to get on a flight a few hours later. We met the birthmother and got to see our treasures that same night.

People often ask if it is tough having twins. My answer 99.9% of the time is, "No, not really." After all, I have two arms to hold them both, feed them, and just love, love, love them. Besides, it's all I know so I guess I'm used to it.

As I said, I can hardly remember a time I didn't want to be a mom and the fact that I am is nothing short of a miracle. We were literally three days away from starting IVF when the call came for the match. Thanks to that call, we no longer have to endure the ups and downs and uncertainty of infertility treatments. We have our family. Each day that goes by brings new and exciting wonders from the perspective of little ones. A day doesn't go by where the babies don't amaze me. Every day as I look into their eyes, I know everything happens for a reason and these were the babies God meant us to have.

Our Amazing Journey

by Andrea Wiggins

I am a MOM! My husband Steven and I live in Central Florida, with our son and three cats. Recently, two more children were placed with us for adoption. My husband works in utility maintenance and I am a MOM!

We tried for six months to start our family but with no success. I saw a doctor who advised we try six more months. We tried for six more months but again had no success. We went back to the doctor, and Steve and I were put through a variety of tests. The final diagnosis: I was not ovulating each month. Fertility treatments were recommended. We asked a lot of questions and decided to go through with it, but cautiously. In March 2001, I had a miscarriage. That day was full of every emotion possible. We were pregnant and then all of a sudden we were not pregnant. We just looked at each other and cried because there were no words to comfort one another.

We decided to try one more round of treatment. When I went for my mid-cycle ultrasound we saw there were four follicles that had formed. It was at that moment we decided to stop treatments. We knew my body would never support four babies and we realized families are formed in so many different ways.

For the next 18 months, we talked about everything: fertility, family, goals, parenting, and adoption. Thinking about adoption was never a scary thing for us because we both have family members who were adopted. However, the decision to adopt and acting on that decision are totally separate. We had to overcome so many emotions and feelings before we knew we were ready.

Our journey began in November 2002. After researching several agencies, we chose American Adoptions. A few days later, we received the HUGE packet of papers. This was the most overwhelming part of the whole experience. If that stack of papers were related to anything else, we probably would have cried. But we actually looked forward to diving in. We read and re-read. It seemed as if we signed our names a thousand times.

The most difficult task was writing the letter to the birthparents. We kept putting this off. It is hard to describe why this was difficult. You have to explain what kind of family you want and your parenting values to someone you don't even know. And that person could change your life forever. We finally just stated the facts. We wrote about the real emotions we were having and tried to convey how much respect we had for the birthparents. We decided to think of it as writing a letter to God and pleading our case to Him. We started by thanking the birthparents for reading our letter and looking at our profile. We let them know we respected their decision of adoption. We then described our relationship, how long we had been married, and how supportive our families were of our decision to adopt. We talked about how Steven's father and two of my cousins were adopted and that this gave our child a huge support system. We then talked about how involved our extended families would be in our child's life. We discussed our careers, and that I was going to be a stay-at-home mom. Then, we talked about our involvement with our church. We closed our letter with the following paragraphs:

"Our commitment and love has kept us together. We plan on sharing our values, life, and many happy memories with our child. We promise to provide everything necessary to raise a happy, healthy child.

Thank you for reading our letter. We will always be honest with how your child became ours. We will share with your child the respect we have for the decision you have made. We will always be grateful for the gift you have given us."

Our home study took place in December. The words "home study" sounded so negative. It lasted about two hours and was very relaxing. It wasn't an interrogation or even an interview. It was just a casual conversation. After the social worker left, we knew it was time to wait. By mid-December we received the activation agreement and mailed it back all in the same day.

On January 8, 2003, we received notice that our profile would be complete in about ten days. We knew our baby would be home with us soon, so we started going through bags of hand-me-down clothes. On January 21, we received the notarized copy of our home study report. We immediately turned to the last page and read the last sentence: "It is therefore, without hesitation, recommended that Steven and Andrea be approved as adoptive parents." Smiles all around! We knew the day was getting closer.

We didn't realize how close that day was. Just two days after our profile was posted, the agency contacted us to say we had been matched.

The next day, a social worker called with some details. Our boy was six weeks old and very good-natured. Unfortunately, it was Friday, and we would have to wait until Monday to figure everything out. The social worker overnighted us pictures and the hospital records. This was one time we hated the weekend. We finished setting up the nursery and went shopping. We were afraid we wouldn't have everything we needed when our son came home.

The following Monday we found out we would be parents by the next weekend. That week was full of phone calls, ironing out travel plans, and getting paperwork in order. It was full of every emotion. We were excited to become parents, but scared to death at the same time. After all, we had seven days notice!

February 7, 2003 aka GOTCHA DAY! Jacob Allen arrived home at 10 a.m. We were so nervous that morning. When we finally held him, a calming sense came over us and we felt true peace. All of the fears seemed to vanish. We instantly felt a bond and a love that's indescribable. We quickly settled into a routine and almost instantly forgot what life was like without our son. On June 24, 2003, Jacob's adoption was finalized.

We have had an incredible journey. Our family and friends have been so supportive. They adore Jacob. He is one very loved little boy. Today he is 19 months old and very curious. He is always climbing on all the furniture. He is so full of energy and keeps us moving. He has a vocabulary of about 50 words. He loves to sing, especially "The ABC's" and "Kinkle, kinkle, ittle tar." Our journey from start to finalization was only seven months long. We now have an amazing family already full of lasting memories!

Roads To Adoption

Bumpy But Worth It

"Pray to God, but continue to row toward shore!"

- Russian Proverb

A Reason For Everything

by Barbara James

Once my husband and I were ready to start a family, adoption was the only path we chose to pursue. I can't honestly say why. I spend every day learning something more about adoption. This helps me better understand the issues my children may face. When people tell me my children are lucky to have me, I always correct them, because I'm the lucky one to have them in my life.

In December 1993, my husband Bob asked me what I wanted for Christmas. "A baby," I told him. He agreed a baby would enhance our lives. I mentioned adoption. He agreed again, and so we began that long, strange trip for which no one is ever really prepared.

Unlike many adoptive parents, we had no history of infertility tests and treatments. I had gotten pregnant unexpectedly a few years earlier and miscarried. We kept trying but nothing ever happened, and month after month, we grieved anew and wondered what was wrong. Neither of us believed fertility treatments were right for us. I was not comfortable taking unnecessary drugs, having surgery, or other treatments for which long-term side-effects (on mother or child) were not known.

I started calling all the adoption agencies listed in the Yellow Pages. Most of the people I spoke with were very discouraging and suggested I consider adopting an older child, one with special needs, or a child of color. I contacted attorneys who quoted

We'd jump every time the phone rang! We got lots of calls; many of them crank calls, some from lawyers, some from other agencies, and some from women trying to sell us their children.

exorbitant figures and told me I'd have to "find a birthmother on my own." I called one agency on their toll-free number and was asked if I was a birthmother. "What's that?" I innocently asked. "I want to adopt a baby, can you help?" She told me the toll-free number was for pregnant women who wanted to place their children, and I could darn well call back on their regular number!

I was discouraged, but as luck would have it, the last call of the day proved fruitful. I spoke with a lovely woman at Adoption Services Associates in San Antonio, Texas. She explained that agencies no longer matched babies with parents. Now the birthmothers choose. Not only that, we might have to advertise to find a birthmother, then support her, and she could still change her mind. Undaunted, I decided to request an information kit.

Soon after came the home study. We cleaned, we polished, the house shone, and the social worker could have cared less! She just wanted to make sure we had a room for the baby and working smoke detectors. She was more concerned we wanted to parent for the right reasons and spent time talking with us about potential difficulties.

While waiting for home study approval, we put a portfolio together, wrote a "Dear Birthmother" letter, and tried to get on with our lives. We joined a local support group, Concerned Persons for Adoption, and began attending meetings to learn more about adoptive family life. I heard wonderful things about our agency and began to think we would eventually have a baby in our lives.

Our home study was approved and we were accepted into an adoption program. They began showing our portfolio and we started advertising in newspapers. It was hard at first. We'd jump every time the phone rang! We got lots of calls; many of them crank calls, some from lawyers, some from other agencies, and some from women trying to sell us their children.

The agency sent us portfolios on birthmothers, but none seemed right for us. We had no problem with bi-racial or full Hispanic babies, but there was strong drug usage in just about every case. We declined the cases and hoped it wouldn't be held against us.

Just when we were getting discouraged, we heard from K. She was 21, had a two-and-a-half-year-old son, and said she was five months pregnant. We talked and for the first time we felt positive and hopeful. K went to the agency with the baby's father. He was 17 and had dropped out of high school. He immediately signed relinquishment papers. We received complete medical information on both parents and the baby and decided to proceed. We were going to be parents!

Months passed. Months of mixed emotions, confusion, fear, and unrest. Sometimes K would call us daily, other times we wouldn't hear from her for days. She refused counseling and started missing doctor appointments. She kept telling me she didn't want to be pressured by anyone; she knew what she was doing, felt fine, and couldn't wait for the pregnancy to be over so she could get on with her life and go back to school.

K was so many things to my husband and me: best friend, worst enemy, sister, but most of all, she was an enigma. I respected her wish not to be pressured and told the agency over and over not to bug her about missed appointments. As her due date neared, the calls got more frequent. Sometimes we'd get messages from her during the day, just to say hello! Once she called the house ten

We left Texas heartbroken, devastated, grief-stricken, and unsure of what to do next.

times on our 800 number, which showed on the bill. When I asked her why, she said she liked hearing my voice and proceeded to keep calling us. She called at all hours of the night and would chat away about mundane things such as the pizza she'd had for lunch. Her joke was we had better get used to being up all night anyhow with a new baby!

One day in February, the phone rang, and it was K. She was in labor and on her way to the hospital. And then, we had a daughter! We named her Sara Ann and immediately called family and friends to share the good news.

On Tuesday, we flew down to Texas, even though she hadn't signed relinquishment papers. We were pretty nervous despite all her talk about her commitment to the adoption. When we got off the plane, we learned she had taken the baby home. The agency was as worried as we were. However, that evening she and the baby showed up at the agency and we all went to dinner.

We got along well, she assured us of her plans to sign papers the next day and asked for one last night with the baby. We agreed to meet her for lunch the next day but she never showed up. She wouldn't answer the phone or door at her apartment, even though we knew she was there. Finally, I reached her on the phone and she said she'd overslept. She promised to meet us at the agency the next day. She never came. We left Texas heartbroken, devastated, grief-stricken, and unsure of what to do next. The agency reassured us we would be parents. Skeptically, we decided to let them try again while we went on with our lives. We returned home and had the horrible task of calling people and telling them what happened.

On March 16 my husband said he had a feeling we were going to be struck by lightning, and we would soon be parents. I felt optimistic for the first time. The next evening I came home from work to a blinking answering machine light; it was the agency telling us to call as soon as possible. I nervously dialed and my husband was on the extension. A woman had given birth the previous night and had asked the agency to help place the baby boy. She selected our portfolio and signed relinquishment papers. Were we interested? I wanted to say no, we weren't ready, we wanted a girl, but I didn't. We got the medical reports and took the referral. Two days later we met Eric. I don't remember much, only the tears that splashed on him as I cried. We brought him home a few days later and the most incredible feeling was knowing we'd walked out the front door as a couple and were returning as a family.

During the three weeks between the disruption and the placement, everyone kept telling me the same thing; K changed her mind for a reason. Everyone was right! Even though I wanted to slap the next person who told me, in the back of my mind I agreed. Now I know the reason—our son hadn't been born yet.

There is a family waiting for every child that is born and how the child comes to that family is not important. What's important is adoptive parents need to be patient, strong, and have faith that it is not a matter of if, but a question of when their family will be complete.

I tell everyone thinking of adoption to be prepared, to read books like *The Adoption Resource Book*, by Lois Gilman, and *There Are Babies to Adopt*, by Chris Adamec. Most importantly, join a support group, meet as many adoptive parents as possible, and talk to everyone. It's the only way to learn, and it's the one step I didn't take early enough.

The Internet is also a great place for support and information. If anyone needs on-line resources, I'll be glad to help. Please e-mail me at CybermommyLJA@cs.com.

Not As Planned

by Krissy Lundy

If I had to choose one lesson I've learned during my lifetime it would be families don't necessarily have to be related by blood. God always has a plan for you and those you love. All you have to do is be open and you'll soon see. Sometimes you have to exercise a lot of patience.

We were married in July of 1992, and started trying to conceive about a year later. Five years later we were still trying. We were both tested and told there was no apparent reason we shouldn't be able to get pregnant, but still nothing happened. A couple of years after that, I ended up in intensive care with heart failure. My doctors said getting pregnant would be extremely dangerous, so we stopped trying.

I was devastated until my husband reminded me that I always said I wanted to adopt. At first he wasn't sure about it, but his desire to be a daddy was as strong as my desire to be a mommy. Still, we questioned whether we would be able to love a child who wasn't a part of us. We weren't sure we were actually ready to be parents, but our desire was so strong it could not be ignored.

We soon learned the waiting list for babies from private agencies is about 10 years. What were we going to do? We couldn't wait another 10 years. That's when someone suggested we become foster parents because it's easier to become an adoptive parent through the Department of Family and Children Services (DFACS) if you're a foster parent first. We decided to sign up for training. Now the question was, would we be able to give a child the love so desperately needed while keeping our hearts at a safe distance?

Our first foster child came into our lives a couple of days before Christmas 2000. My grandmother had just passed away so we weren't really in a holiday mood. But this one little eight-month-old boy changed all that. What a miracle! No one can imagine how much joy he brought to our family. All of a sudden, Christmas mattered. As the year went by, it was beginning to look like we were going to be able to adopt him. My husband and I could not believe our luck. We were so convinced he would be ours that we totally and completely gave our hearts to him. There was only one thing that could have brought us down from our cloud of happiness. That occurred in April, 2002, after he had been with us 16 months.

We went to court one morning thinking the case worker would ask to terminate the father's rights. We could not believe our ears when they asked for reunification of the father and child. The judge told us we had about five hours to pack his things and say goodbye. We later learned the father had been doing everything DFACS asked him and was trying his best to straighten his life out. We were never told any of this before.

For the rest of my life, I will never forget his screams as we, the only mommy and daddy he had known, were forced to leave him with a stranger. After almost two years, I still don't think the shock of what happened has worn off. There's not a day I don't relive the events of that day in my head. I still think every time the phone rings it will be someone asking if we want him back. We feel like our first child had been taken from us.

After that day, we were reluctant to deal with DFACS, but we still had one other five-year-old foster child in our home. Not wanting to cause her any more pain, she stayed with us for a few more months until she also went back to her parents. After that we were placed on a list of couples who take only children who are at very little or no risk of being sent back to their parents. This gave us some time to recover and look back over the past couple of years. In retrospect, we realize God gave us that precious little boy to show us we could love a child who wasn't "ours." This insight gave us the courage to go on.

Around mid-December, one of the social workers came to do a re-evaluation of our home. My husband and I talked and decided we would ask about Dede, one of the children who had been with us a few weeks the previous Christmas. Before we could ask, the worker said they were looking for a permanent placement for her, and would we be interested. Dede came to live with us on January first. She is a blonde-haired, blue-eyed cutie who had just turned three years old. She has some abandonment and attachment issues that we are working on. She loves giving hugs and kisses as well as having you kiss all her boo-boo's at least 10 or 20 times each.

According to her caseworker, she should officially become ours by the middle of the summer. We're cautious, but what else can we do? She's stolen our hearts. She loves our whole family immensely and is more than a little attached to her baby brother, Caleb, but that's another story.

Krissy writes about Caleb's adoption in "Can I Call Her Now?" which can be read in Chapter Five.

A Love We'd Never Felt Before

by Carla King

My name is Carla and I am 36 years old. My husband and I tried to have a baby and were unsuccessful. After five years of infertility treatments we decided to adopt. It was a tangible means of fulfilling our dream. Adoption has made us a family.

Dave and I met on a blind date in 1995. We were married in 1998 and dreamed of having a family. After years on the infertility roller coaster we realized being pregnant was no longer important—we just wanted to have a child.

A work colleague had recently adopted a baby. I called his wife and she answered many of our questions regarding the adoption process, the uncertainties of being able to love an adopted child the way you would a biological child, and many more. She assured us once we adopted a baby we would have an overwhelming love for that baby—a love we'd never felt before. The next day I called the agency she had used and asked them to send us an information packet. Dave and I read through the paperwork and decided adoption was what we were looking for. Our desire for a child outweighed the fear of the unknown.

We had our home study in January and all of our paperwork was completed by May. We were told we could wait up to 18 months or more. Six weeks later we got a call saying a birthmother had chosen us and her baby was due in August. I remember all I kept saying in my head was, "Wow! a birthmother chose us—US!!"

The baby was in the state of Maryland and the birthmother had 30 days to change her mind. That was a big risk . . .

Two weeks went by without a word from the birthmother. It was as though she vanished into thin air. We continued to get the nursery ready because we wanted to be as prepared as possible. Then the call came telling us the birthmother went with an attorney in her home state. Our dreams of this baby were gone. My husband and I never even cried. We looked at it as a stepping stone. We knew something wonderful would happen for us in the future.

We were reactivated the next day and began our wait yet again. Just three days later I received a call at work that literally changed our lives forever. The call came around 11 a.m. They said, "We have a baby boy who was born yesterday and want to know if we can show your profile to the birthmother?" The baby was in the state of Maryland and the birthmother had 30 days to change her mind. That was a big risk but something felt right. We gave our permission. An hour-and-a-half later the agency called and said, "The birthmother loved you. Can you be here tomorrow to discharge the baby from the hospital?" Our baby was already born and waiting for us. We had a son! We made all the arrangements: travel, hotel, and someone to watch our cats. We had no clothes, blankets, bottles, diapers, nothing! Dave ran to the store for some things while my neighbors brought over baby clothes, a diaper bag, and anything they felt we would need for our trip. I remember thinking—How could one little person need all this stuff?

We got to the hospital and met the social worker. Finally the nursing staff pushed over a bassinet with this beautiful little boy in it. Let me tell you, there is nothing in this world that could ever prepare you for the overwhelming feelings of that moment. We cried and laughed and thanked God for this living miracle in front of us. It was the end of a five year journey and the beginning of a lifetime one. The 30-day waiting period passed without much thought and then at six months we went to court to finalize our adoption.

We can't believe how fast time has flown and how our lives changed overnight. Adoption is a wonderful thing. Our lives are full and we feel extremely blessed. Our mornings are started with a big smile. Our days are full of laughter and play, and our nights, well they're still interrupted for an early morning feeding but we don't care. Every sleepless night is worth it just to have and hold our precious miracle.

I proudly tell everyone we adopted a baby. It is a wonderful thing and I love to share our story. My friend was so right about the love you feel for your baby. It is overwhelming and different than any love ever felt before. It's truly amazing! I'll never forget the feeling in my heart the first time someone said "Congratulations mom." I was finally a mom!

I remember going through all the infertility treatments and hearing everyone's story about how they got pregnant and wondering how our story would end. I love the ending of our story. All the years and heartache of longing to be a family is erased the second you hold your baby. You no longer look in the past. Instead you look in your arms and see the future.

People In Our Path

by Jessica Ritter

> *My name is Jessica and my husband and I are 26 and 28,*
> *respectively. We adopted our son 15 months ago, at birth. Ours is an*
> *open adoption and we have an ongoing relationship, including*
> *visitation every few months, with our son's birthmom. We did not*
> *go through a typical agency adoption but met through a mutual*
> *friend and completed the adoption with the help of attorneys.*

My husband and I wanted to lead a bible study with young married couples so we started a new group with four couples we didn't know. Little did we know what starting this group would lead to.

The following month we went to our first adoption meeting and decided we were going to move forward. We told our bible study group and our new friend in the group told us of her cousin who was 19, pregnant, and planning to have the baby adopted. We met her right after New Years. She liked us and we liked her, and I went to every single doctor appointment she had for the rest of her pregnancy.

In January we found out the baby was to be a boy and he was due in May. At that time, there was a whole fiasco with the birthfather. He wasn't supportive of the adoption plan and when he found out our names he started calling us. He was very disturbing. I learned his last name and thought it was a coincidence because we had a good family friend with that last name. I started wondering if she might be this guy's aunt and soon found out she was. But I hadn't seen this family friend in years, so I didn't really understand the point of this connection. Anyway, while things

Adoption is not a process for the faint of heart. It is an emotional roller coaster.

were still good with the birthmom we were getting a lot of phone calls from the birthfather which were shaking us up.

I was thinking of starting a scrapbook once our son was born. So I went to a craft store across town, (I am not usually in craft stores) and who do I run into but our old friend, the birthfather's aunt. I tell her what's going on and she is absolutely furious about her nephew. She tells me not to worry because all of his family is supportive of the adoption and no one will support his causing any problems for us. She told me she would talk to him right away. I couldn't even believe it. It was like God had come right down to put my heart at ease.

It ended when my old friend and the birthfather's dad (her brother) had a long conversation with the birthfather and he backed off completely. He signed his relinquishment papers without even requiring an open adoption agreement which he had insisted on for awhile. Oh, I should mention that he is an ex-convict and still on parole, thus, we did not want to pursue an open adoption agreement with him at this time. We didn't believe it was in the best interest of our son, at least until the birthfather became more mature and trustworthy.

So, it ended up that before our son was conceived I had befriended his biological great aunt and had known his biological mom's first cousin in high school. Is it this small a world? God knew about our son before we even knew we were going to pursue adoption, and he put people in our path to make sure our son found us. And we just so happened to want to lead a new bible study of younger married people that we otherwise wouldn't have ever known. It is incredible and I can't believe anything of this magnitude could ever happen again. God is good and we are so blessed.

Adoption is the most challenging and most rewarding thing to happen in our lives thus far. We are actually beginning to pursue another adoption and are hopeful of another "independent designated" adoption. Adoption is not a process for the faint of heart. It is an emotional roller coaster.

One thing I didn't know when I started the process was that when you are matched, it is not all of a sudden, smooth sailing. I thought getting matched would be the hard part, but I was wrong. After you are matched, the wait is grueling. It is so hard because you don't get the perks of having people excited by the end of your pregnancy—you simply have to wait, pray, and hope the birthmom keeps her adoption plan, that everything will work out, and that your baby will be yours soon. Most of your loved ones are far more concerned about the outcome than you are, so seeing their anxiety and doubt is certainly not a comfort.

I didn't realize the wait after the match would be so challenging. I am only thankful for my husband and for the Lord, because without our faith and each other, I don't know how we would have handled those four months of being matched and waiting for our son to be born. But we survived and can only say that adoption is a wonderful way to build a family and we could not be happier.

Dreams Can Come True

by Missy

I was born and raised just outside of Salt Lake City, Utah. I have been blessed with a very close family, two sisters, and one brother. I was also blessed to marry into a close and supportive family. I love being a mommy to my daughter and also to our two dogs. I studied Chemical and Fuels Engineering and enjoy working in the Dietary Supplement Industry.

After years of dealing with infertility, we finally came to terms with the fact that our children were not meant to come to us in the conventional way. So we signed up with foster care and after a year were blessed with our first foster daughter. She was fantastic. We got to be her parents for eight months before she went home to her biological family. After finding out we would not be able to adopt her, we decided we wanted a child we knew would be ours for a lifetime. Even though our foster daughter was going to a family who loved her and would take wonderful care of her, losing her was a heartbreak we still feel.

We signed with our adoption agency after nearly nine years of waiting to be blessed with a child. We looked at several agencies and it took six months of research before we found the one we wanted to pursue adoption with. The first time I spoke to our counselor on the phone I felt comfortable. I went to the agency and was given all the paperwork we needed to begin. If only all parents had to go through the paperwork that adoptive parents go through. We had to do background checks, home studies, have letters of reference, and our finances analyzed. Then we had to write Dear Birthmother letters and come up with a great profile about us that showed a birthmother what kind of parents we would be and what kind of a family they would be sending their child to.

I was so ready to be a mom I had all of the paperwork (other than the profile) completed and returned to the agency in only two days.

Being matched brought on the next stage of emotional torture . . . There is the constant fear the birthmother will change her mind.

After a month our background checks were completed. Our social worker came to our home and did a home study. During the month we waited for our background checks I spent many hours working on our Dear Birthmother letter and on our profile. The profile was the easy part. The Dear Birthmother letter I agonized over. I wanted it to be perfect. After many hours in front of a blank screen and much time doing some research, I was able to write what I felt was a sincere, down-to-earth birthmother letter.

We told our parents we signed with an agency and were waiting to be matched. Once our family understood what we were doing they were excited for us and very supportive. The waiting would have been much harder without the support of our family.

I spent the next month searching the Internet and researching everything there was about adoption, reading the good and the bad. I began conducting a search for a birthmother. Once we were signed with our agency I pretty much went crazy and lived and breathed adoption. I probably know each adoption site on the Internet. I made friends on the adoption forums and found helpful stories and opinions from other waiting adoptive parents, adoptive parents no longer waiting, birthmothers, birthfathers, and adoptees. I also started putting together our nursery and purchased items that could be used for a boy or girl.

We had been signed with our agency for just under two months when we attended a meeting for adoptive parents. We learned of a potential birthmother who was going to be looking at profiles soon. I just knew our profile must get shown to this girl. After the meeting we waited to talk to the social worker. I could not leave until I had stressed to her that our profile must be shown.

I went home that evening, pulled out our profile, and redid the whole look of the thing. I chose nicer paper, improved the overall look of the profile, and dropped it off the following morning.

Two days later I received the phone call that changed our lives. It was from the agency and I nearly stopped breathing when asked if I would like to meet a young lady considering an adoption plan. It was the girl spoken about in the previous meeting. I nearly screamed YES into the phone. We made arrangements to meet at the agency in two days. I hung up, then shrieked, then cried, then called my husband, and then my mom.

I got another call from the social worker later that day to give me more information about our potential birthmother. Everything about her sounded wonderful. I did not know how I was going to sit through the next two days worrying about meeting her.

The day finally came and my husband and I headed to the agency. We arrived early and could barely sit still waiting. I was so afraid the birthmother would change her mind and not show up. I was not prepared for the angel that came through the door. She was a beautiful girl and happened to greatly resemble both of our families. She was smiling when she walked into the room and was very outgoing. She made us feel very comfortable and we really hit it off. She told us, that from reading our profile, she already had a feeling we would be good parents for her child. After meeting us she said she was reaffirmed that her decision was the right one. She said now that she had chosen and met us, she was finally at peace with herself and her decision.

The funniest thing about our being chosen is that my mom was concerned about some of the honesty we used in our profile, such as we have big dogs and motorcycles. Our birthmother chose us for reasons such as these. She said when she looked at other profiles she felt a lot of information seemed falsely written just to sound good. She said our profile stood out because she felt we were honest and down-to-earth about not only our lives but what we wanted and expected out of our adoption experience. We had to call my mom and tease her that we were chosen for our honesty.

Being matched brought on the next stage of emotional torture. These emotions are something the agencies all talk about and try to prepare you for but I do not think there is any way to explain to somebody who has not been there what these emotions are like. There is the constant fear the birthmother will change her mind.

Our birthmother was 28 weeks into her pregnancy when we were matched. She wanted to spend lots of time with me before the delivery so we would get to know each other. We did lunches and dinner and I went with her to all of her doctor appointments. I got to feel our baby move and I got to talk to her. I was excited to be so involved in the pregnancy. She kept telling us this was going to be our daughter and it was our right to be involved. Even though she kept reaffirming that her decision was final and this was going to be our daughter, I lived with an ache inside; the ache of not knowing whether or not the papers would get signed when the time came.

Each minute we spent together I bonded more and more with her as well as with our unborn child. I missed them when we were not together. I was so happy about becoming friends with her. We met each others' families and I felt we all got along very well.

Of course, now that we were matched and knew we were having a girl, I had a heyday with the nursery. I finished everything and had plenty of little girl things to start her out in the world correctly. Having so many girl things only made the not-knowing feeling deep inside worse. What would I do with all these things if she changed her mind? Even though it hurt so much to think about, we had to talk about the fact she could and had every right, to change her mind. Potential adoptive parents must always go through their days knowing this is a very real possibility. Sometimes upon hearing about somebody's failed adoption I would comment that, "Oh, it happens." My husband once got upset with me and said I would be devastated if that happened to us. I knew without a doubt how right he was, which was why I tried to play it off so simply. You have to harden yourself somewhat to prepare for the pain of it, if it were to happen to you.

The day finally came when our baby was going to come into the world. We were with our birthmother throughout her labor and for the delivery. My husband and I spent time alternating between one of us spending time with the baby and the other with our birthmother so she would not be alone. For two days in the hospital we shared our daughter. We both mothered her and took care of her. Though I loved the time the three of us shared and am grateful for it, it was also a time of the greatest fear of my life. I had already bonded to our little girl. I felt she was so meant to be mine. I was scared the relinquishment papers would not get signed. I was afraid the more time our birthmom spent with this beautiful creation the harder it would be for her to give her up. Even though she was still referring to her as our daughter and saying she had not faltered in her decision, the fear was still there. You could almost cut the fear with a knife it was so thick in my mind and heart.

The day our birthmother left our daughter with us in the hospital is a day that will live in my mind forever. I can't even begin to explain the emotions of that day. Though I was gaining a blessing I had dreamed about for years and years, I was devastated watching her leave us behind. She had so much love for the life she brought into the world. Her decision to place was one of pure love and complete unselfishness. I will not say anything more about this day because there is no way to help anybody to know or even try to comprehend what it's like until they have been there.

We have now had our beloved daughter for two months. She is truly a dream come true. We are also blessed to have her birthfamily in our lives. We feel open adoption, as long as it remains comfortable for all parties, is best for our daughter, her birthmother, and us. I sometimes wonder how the birthmother can see our daughter and walk away, because my husband and I have a very difficult time visiting the foster daughter we had. Seeing her hurts, and walking away hurts worse. I guess our feelings for our foster daughter help us understand what the birthmother must be going through.

Women always say the pain of childbirth is forgotten. The nine years of emotional pain I have gone through before bringing home our daughter is not yet forgotten, but I am healing. I have found talking to people who have been through similar situations helps a lot in the healing process. A lot of the emotions I feel today are no longer for me but for those who have not yet arrived at the place in life I am now in. I ache for those trying to conceive and I ache for those adoptive parents still waiting for their dreams to come true. My heart goes out to each and every one out there who is in any of the stages I have been in the past nine years.

I know my story cannot ease anybody's pain, but I hope it can make somebody feel less alone and give them some hope.

Dreams can and do come true.

Patience, Love, And Faith

by Barbara Chewning

Our names are Barbara and Glen. We live in Marengo, Illinois, about 75 miles northwest of Chicago. After years of unexplained infertility and many medical treatments, we decided to pursue adoption. I speak about adoption in local seminars and to the local high school child development classes.

O ur adoption journey started in the fall of 2002 when we chose our agency. One of the main reasons we chose them was that when we called and requested information, we were able to speak with a real human being and not just leave a message. For any couple that has dealt with infertility, you can understand how important it is to speak with a person who has the information you need and is generous with answering your questions and concerns.

Like most couples who have struggled through infertility, the thought of adoption was slightly intimidating (oh no, starting all over again!) but exciting at the same time (a new quest!). A person may ask, "What made you feel intimidated?" Let's start with the state-required home study. You question, "Is my home going to be safe enough, clean enough, roomy enough, for the caseworker?" Once your home study is complete and you start the process of being matched with a birthmother you start thinking "Will the birthmother like us?" (Little do we as adoptive parents know, birthmothers wonder if we will like THEM.) or "How much contact will the birthmother want after the birth and adoption?"

It was disappointing when we were not "matched." Couples—please, please, do not take these disappointments personally!

These are just a few of the issues you need to deal with from the beginning of your adoption journey. My most important piece of advice to adoptive couples is DON'T WORRY! Yes, easier said than done! Focus your energy on preparing yourselves and your home for a baby. Couples need to educate themselves on adoption processes, state laws, etc. You will feel more secure with the decisions you have to make during your adoption journey by being knowledgeable.

We continued preparing for our adoption home study during the holidays by having our home visit, fingerprinting, and CPR class completed. We attended workshops which were great because we met other couples just like us! One very important workshop was listening to two birthmothers. It became evident many of the adoptive couples felt threatened by the idea of further contact with the birthparents. As we continued to listen to the birthmothers, it became clear they only want to know their child is growing up happy and healthy. Think about it from their perspective; how would you feel if you gave the baby you love to another couple and then didn't know if your child was growing up happy and safe? Birthmothers continue to think about their children years later. Eventually, your child will want to know about their birthparents. It is only normal. If your child wants to meet their birthmother, don't you think having a good relationship between you and the birthmother is important? How would your child feel if they got to meet their birthmother and she told your child, "Your adoptive mom wouldn't let me know anything"? Now, not all adoptions situations are the same and you may have a birthmother that does not want contact. More advice: if it is hard for you to correspond, try to do the best you can for your child.

It was late March and our home study was complete, which meant we were activated and our profile was being shown to birthmothers! On two different occasions we received a phone call about an adoption situation. One situation was a one-year-old. The other situation was a baby already born in Florida. It was disappointing when we were not "matched." We continued our lives as normal. Couples—please, please, do not take these disappointments personally!

In July we received a call from Megan, our adoption coordinator, asking if we would be interested in having her show our profile to a Hispanic birthmother named Sabrina. Of course, we told her "Yes!" Megan said she would call us later that day. It was 7 p.m. and I didn't think we would hear back that night but we did and it was a match! A few days later we had a conference call with our birthmother and loved her!

What was even more exciting was Sabrina was to be induced in a week! We made our travel plans and packed our suitcases! Everything was happening so fast we didn't have time to be nervous! We left on a Saturday; it was a seven hour drive. Saturday evening we settled into our room and called our birthmother to let her know we were here. The next day we met Sabrina at her hotel and brought flowers to her room. We talked, showed pictures, then went to the mall, and then out to dinner. It was great being able to spend the day with her and getting to know her. We realized we had a lot of child rearing ideas in common.

The next day was Monday, the day Sabrina was to be induced. We met her at the hospital at 7 a.m. and stayed with her all day.

At 4 p.m. she asked me to get a nurse and when the nurse examined her, we received the news that it was time I asked Sabrina if she wanted me to stay in the delivery room and she said, "Yes." My husband, Glen, waited just outside the delivery room. I felt honored to be a part of David's birth! I even got to cut the umbilical cord! The day after David was born, we visited Sabrina and she signed off her rights. Wednesday came and it was time for David to be released from the hospital and Sabrina wanted desperately to go home to Arizona. We all met one last time to say goodbye and hug. I promised Sabrina she would see her son again. See, just goes to show, if Glen and I had matched with one of the previous babies, I would not have had the opportunity to watch our son be born!

After our long drive, we arrived home to a welcoming committee. (That day was also our wedding anniversary!) In November we traveled back to Kansas to finalize David's adoption. It is hard to believe in a matter of five-and-a-half months we adopted a beautiful baby and had it finalized.

We continue to correspond with Sabrina through pictures and phone calls. One of the greatest experiences was to have Sabrina call me on my first Mother's Day to wish me a "Happy Mother's Day." David definitely has his birthmother's sweet disposition and smile. I must say, I in no way feel threatened by corresponding with David's birthmother. Relationships are what we make of them. One of the most amazing things is that David's birthmother and birthfather are both Hispanic, and Glen and I are both Caucasian. David has blonde hair and blue eyes and strangers tell us he looks just like his dad! We just laugh.

I pray for all adoptive parents that all of their dreams come true. The greatest thing I have learned from this experience is patience, love, and faith. Best wishes to all!

Our Journey To Alex

by Susan Reardon

I reside in Rochester, New York with my husband and daughter and enjoy my new role as mother immensely. Adoption has changed my life forever. Not a single day goes by that I will not think of my daughter's first parents and the sacrifice they made for her.

The room is completely dark, only a sliver of light from the baby monitor shines on the side of her face. As she lay in her crib so sweet, innocent, and pure, I can barely comprehend she is mine. I lean in close to hear and feel the soft pattern of her breathing as she sleeps. I take in the fragrance of her recently shampooed head, something I have waited so long to smell. Her fingers are wrapped tightly around a corner of her blanket, her other hand tucked beneath her chin. Only a few months earlier, this now beautifully-adorned room was cold, bare, and empty; much like my soul. I remember sitting on the dusty hardwood floor wondering if motherhood would ever be mine. I yearned to experience the bond only a mother and her child could have. The moment had come, and my love for her was immeasurable.

I take a step back and look at my beautiful baby. She is perfect in every way. I realize my life will never again be the same. The lump now formed in my throat is followed by a single tear that slides down my cheek. The tear is partly of joy, partly of sorrow. My thoughts travel to a place far away where another woman sits

Was my sole desire to become pregnant? No. My longing was to be a mother, and the method was not important.

alone, just her and her empty womb. I think of the young man alone in his house, wishing there was more he could have done. I imagine the heartache and sense of loss that is sure to be theirs. I pick up my sleeping baby and hold her tight. I surround her with all the warmth and protection I can muster. Does she miss them? Can she remember the smell of her first mother's skin? Does she wonder where they are and what they are doing? I hope that somehow I am able to transfer to her the deep love of her parents, all of her parents.

In August 1997, Shawn and I decided to start our family. From my medical history I assumed it might take awhile to become pregnant but I had no idea of the road that lay ahead. I cannot recall in detail the events of the next several years nor do I wish to. I try hard to bury and forget them as the pain is someplace I never want to return. Emotionally, I hit rock bottom and was falling apart. I did not tolerate the medications well and felt I'd go insane if I stayed on them. Though I wanted a baby so badly, I needed a break. We decided to forgo treatments and concentrate on other things.

By July 2002 I began to think about what I really wanted in life. Was my sole desire to become pregnant? No. My longing was to be a mother, and the method was not important. Until that point, I had never really thought much about adoption. It was a world I knew nothing about. I imagined it would be a difficult and costly road. I studied and thought long and hard and finally decided on domestic adoption. Shawn surprisingly welcomed the idea. We eventually found a wonderful agency which we were very comfortable with, and in October sent off our completed registration form and fee. Several weeks later, we were scheduled to begin our home study classes. We had complete peace that our child would be born to us through adoption.

The following months were filled with adoption classes and home study visits, with hopes we would be chosen by birthparents and fears we would not. By March, we were approved. We received a call in May stating we might be a match for a young woman looking to place her baby. Though it was devastating when another couple was chosen, it was a realization at just how fast life could take this turn. We would think positive and know our baby was out there somewhere and would soon find his or her way to us.

On an ordinary Monday in June, I was about to leave work for the day when my cell phone rang. To my surprise, the display read Adoption STAR (our agency). I got a sick feeling in my stomach. My mind raced with a thousand possibilities and I quickly answered. "Hi Sue, it's Melissa. I'm calling to let you know of a birthmother currently in our office. She is not sure of her due date but guesses it to be within the next three weeks." It was all happening so quickly. I nervously searched for a pen to get all the information. The conversation was brief and she asked if she could show our profile. I told her we would love for her to show it.

After hanging up I was filled with so many emotions. I gathered my things and drove to my sister's to tell her. I tried not to get my hopes up and was quickly sickened by the thought that the next time she called it would be to inform me another couple had been chosen. As I drove, I began sobbing. I knew the disappointment the next few hours might bring. I got angry and frustrated with the roller coaster of emotions I was forced to ride. As I neared my sister's home, I tried to gather my composure half knowing it was a futile attempt. I did my best to put on a happy face. As I looked into the kitchen to find my sister, our eyes met. With my sister's simple, "What's wrong?" I was quickly reduced back to sobs. She was startled and worried and I couldn't compose myself enough to explain. She must have thought something terrible had happened. I gathered myself together to explain that I had just received another call to be profiled. I told her how difficult it was to get these calls and then experience such disappointment. Just then my phone rang. I again saw it was Adoption STAR. I fell to pieces and pushed the phone to my sister. She answered and was told they needed to speak to me. Somehow I was able to get out the word "Hello." I had no idea in the next five seconds my life would change in the most dramatic way. We had been chosen by the birthmother! By then I was crying so hard I didn't even try fighting it. Melissa asked if I was okay and I enthusiastically replied, "I am now!"

Everything was happening so quickly. I listened intently to all the details she was giving. Everything sounded perfect. She said the birthmother was due for a doctor's visit the next day and we would be contacted with the results. I hung up and filled in the blanks for my sister. By then, she and I were crying as we hugged one another knowing life had suddenly changed forever.

I drove to Shawn's work to tell him, not totally believing it myself. Thrilled at the news and the thought of being a father, he told his boss he was leaving for the day and why. I shared the events of the last hour with him and we planned our evening. We would need to reach our parents, grandparents, and his two sisters. Though at that point anything could happen, we were too excited not to tell our families.

The evening was filled with phone calls and visits to friends and family. By the time we got home, we were exhausted. We lay in bed chatting about the turn our lives had suddenly taken. We wondered what the sex of our child might be and tossed around some baby names. Soon, Shawn was sleeping and I lay awake with thousands of things racing through my head. I began to worry about the health of the baby. What if something was wrong?

Would we still adopt him or her? I quickly realized it didn't matter to me. Was I searching for a child with special needs? No, but like a biological child, in my heart this baby was now ours. As of that first phone call, this baby was mine and I loved it regardless. After what seemed like hours, I too, eventually drifted off.

Tuesday seemed to fly by. I was busy at work coordinating time off and tidying up loose ends. I made lists of things to do and lists of things we must buy. I was still in a bit of shock. That night we chose names. Our choice for a boy was Myles David. For a girl, Alexandra Jennifer-Grace; Jennifer after my dear cousin who passed away three months earlier and Grace after my grandmother.

The struggles and injustices of the last six years were suddenly erased. Everything we'd been through over the years was all worth this very moment.

The next day we received word regarding our birthmother's appointment. Lindsay (our birthmother) and the baby were perfectly healthy and they determined it was a girl! We would have our Alexandra. I think that is when it all started to sink in. Once I knew the sex, I felt I could identify with the baby so much more. And all anyone needed to hear was the word girl, and that meant shopping, shopping, shopping.

I was in a meeting at work when I received a call from the agency. They had just admitted Lindsay into the hospital and expected her to deliver the next morning. They would call tomorrow. I gathered up my things and left work.

By the time I got home I was beat. I had hardly slept in days. In bed, I lay thinking about what might be happening 90 miles away. How was Lindsay doing? Had Alex already been born? I prayed for Lindsay and Alexandra. I think I fell asleep praying. I woke up at 5 a.m. and was sure that by now our baby had been born. We would have to wait until the agency called. I arrived at work at around 8 a.m. It killed me to watch the clock. At 9 a.m. Melissa called; our daughter Alexandra was born at 3:35 a.m. She was six pounds, nine ounces, and perfectly healthy. Tears began to flow. I was a mother. I quickly inquired about Lindsay. My heart broke for what she must be going through. I admired her courage and selflessness. Though we wanted so badly to meet our daughter, we realized this time was special for Lindsay and Alex. We would not meet our daughter until Sunday.

Saturday night was like Christmas Eve to a child. I just couldn't wait to get to sleep so in the morning I could meet my baby. Surprisingly, I fell right asleep. It wasn't until 3:30 p.m. we were finally told to come get our daughter. Upon arriving at the agency I expected to be greeted by the long awaited sight of our child, but unfortunately piles of paperwork would need tending to first. After all the papers had been signed, it was time.

Shawn and I were escorted to a nursery and I sat nervously waiting to meet my baby. Moments later I laid eyes on my child for the first time. She was absolutely beautiful. With perfect timing, she woke up and looked into the eyes of her new parents. It was, by far, the greatest moment of our lives. The struggles and injustices of the last six years were suddenly erased. Everything we'd been through over the years was all worth this very moment.

Several months later, a friend called very excited about sharing the video of her recently performed ultrasound. When the short video was over, she looked at me with sorrow. She quickly apologized for being insensitive if the video of her growing baby was hurtful to me in any way. It hadn't even occurred to me. My response to her was, "Yes, it is true. I will probably never know what it is like to be pregnant. I will never experience carrying my own child. I won't know the hardships and delights of pregnancy. But likewise, you will probably never know what it is like to adopt.

You will never feel the exhilaration of getting the call. You will never know the honor of having someone choose YOU to parent their precious child. You will never truly know the pure joy that adoption has brought to me."

So you see, families are created in very different ways; each unique and special in their own right. I wouldn't trade our journey for anything; it was our journey to Alex.

The Extra Kiss
by Susan Reardon

To the birthparents of my beautiful daughter

Sitting here holding this child,
My thoughts, again, travel to you.
The ones who gave us our dream,
And love this sweet child too.

I wonder how you are doing,
Is time really healing your pain?
Still at peace with your decision?
Or are you now going insane?

I wish I could do something,
To help comfort in some way.
To help lead you to your healing,
Or know the words to say.

Instead I will hold her close,
And give her an extra kiss.
From two beautiful people,
For the moments they will miss.

Answered Prayers

by Ilene Stargot

The pursuit of parenthood was the most difficult hurdle to jump in my life. Adoption gave me the ability to be a mother without becoming pregnant. My husband and I are happily married. I am fulfilled, and my children are my greatest joy.

I am also the Founder and President of the National Infertility Network Exchange, (NINE) www.nine-infertility.org a non-profit support and referral organization for infertility and adoption.

We were excited. For the first time in many years, we felt hopeful. After all, you never know who knows someone who knows someone else who, in fact, knows someone else. Interestingly, I noticed that each time we gleefully answered the hated question of, "Do you have any children?" with word of our plans to adopt, it became license for people to tell us every horror story they ever heard regarding adoption. "You're adopting? Well, my friend's friend's brother's wife adopted and the kid turned out horribly!" Or, "Oh, adoption? That takes so long and costs so much, my neighbor did that and spent hundreds of thousands of dollars and never got a baby." I couldn't help wonder why they just couldn't say "Good for you, that's wonderful!"

In all honesty, pursuing adoption was not our first choice. Like most people, we were hoping to bring our best DNA together to create the perfect biological child. As we learned this was no longer an option, we began to explore adoption. The idea of putting our name on an agency list seemed to be too long of a wait. Another option was independent or private adoption. We learned many couples were successful within a year by running advertisements in newspapers. We hired an attorney who specialized in adoption. We were evaluated by a social worker who reported her findings in a home study. Paperwork for the state was filed along with our fingerprints. A separate phone line was installed in our home for the express use of answering prayers. I dreamt of this; she would read our ad looking for a healthy newborn to share our love, life, and everything we have to offer. She would call our toll-free number. We would both be scared but we would talk and find out more about each other. In the end, I would answer her prayers of providing for this child in ways she was unable to do and she would answer the prayers of building our family. Despite the knowledge that independent adoption does work, I just couldn't imagine how anyone could place their child into the arms of another.

And so began the wait; perhaps the hardest part of all. We waited for the phone to ring and placed an immense amount of hope on the idea that the next phone call could be the one to make us parents. I swear my heart stopped each time the phone rang, and my blood pressure would take a massive drop as the voice on the other end solicited me for a newspaper subscription. Until the one day when the voice on the other end shyly asked if I was still looking for a baby.

All the preparations and intelligence in the world does not prepare you for this type of Kodak moment. I compare it to dating. You know what you want, you date a hundred people looking for "the one" but it isn't there. Then you meet that person and nothing is the same. From the moment we exchanged nervousness, I knew she was the one. She would be the birthmother of my child. It was her choice that we didn't meet.

From the time we placed our first advertisement to the moment my daughter was in my arms was four months. I will be the first one to say we were lucky, but the truth is adoption does work. Babies are placed with loving parents by selfless birthmothers trying to make right by their child. Forever families are created. Adoption, while not always your first choice, is not second best.

Feeling empowered by our positive adoption experience, my husband and I decided to test the fates once more by adopting a second child two years later. Having already been through the process didn't seem to change the anxiety with each phone call. In fact, I feared even more that a birthmother would want to give her child to someone who didn't have any children rather than place her child with us.

Thankfully, I was wrong. She was thrilled her child would have a sibling. The door now open, we exchanged information about ourselves and found we had so much in common. We enjoyed our conversations. We couldn't wait to meet. We met at the hospital, in her room. No introductions were necessary for our hearts had met almost two months prior.

My son and my daughter are my greatest accomplishments. They are the proof of where your heart leads you. They are my children. While they do not have a gene pool of my husband and I, they are loved unconditionally, by us, our family, our friends, and the birthmothers who put their children's needs first.

Adoptee Stories

It's Great To Be Wanted

"You didn't give me the gift of life,
But in my heart I know,
The love I feel is deep and real,
As if it had been so."

- Unknown

My Long Amazing Journey

by Sera McManus

At the age of almost ten, my adoption was a miracle. I was so happy to finally go home. Although I didn't know much English, poetry and journal writing helped me express myself. With the encouragement of my family, I still have a passion for writing as well as reading. This passion has helped me have top grades in school and a very bright future.

Life was tough, but I managed. That all changed on August 30, 2000. I will introduce myself first. My full name is Sera Sveta McManus. I was born in Smolensk, Russia, on October 14, 1990. About that time Russia was trying to change from communism.

In Russia, I never had good clothes or food or anything valuable. My house looked very bad. The roof was slanted and almost falling off the house. Inside, the house looked awful too. I did not have heat, water, electricity, a bathroom, tables, couches, stools, or anything. We didn't have any furniture except two beds. One had a hole in the middle and the other one was pretty good.

When I was between four and five years old, I was moved to my granny's. A year later my older brother and I were moved to the orphanage because my granny could not take care of us. My old father was always drunk and stole money from her. My older sister was an adult and was sent to my aunt's apartment. Later my brother went to another orphanage because he was always in trouble.

The orphanage was not great but it was better than being at home. They had inside bathrooms, electricity, a little heat and water. The bathrooms were awful but it was better than having none. Where I lived in the orphanage, there was a bathroom and a wash-up room where you brushed your teeth and washed your hands. The girls had their own little room and the boys had theirs. It was not very clean and it was very old.

The cafeteria was a building that was not connected to the other buildings. The school was huge because it was first through eleventh grade. Our food was not so good. It was like mush or kasha, only worse. We also got fish and always soup. With that we got a piece of bread and a cup of tea that probably had three teaspoons of sugar in it.

One day in second grade Natasha just came up and asked me if I wanted to be adopted. My mouth fell open and I said "Yeah!"

The school is next to the cafeteria. In school about every 20 or 30 minutes we had a break. And once a day we went to lunch. After lunch if it was warm we had more time to play with chalk, jump ropes, hoops, and other stuff. Our school was for three to four hours. After school we played outside and then went back to do homework. After that we had dinner, washed up, and went to bed.

We had warm water to wash ourselves every week or two weeks. We did not have our own clothes. Girls shared clothes with girls and boys with boys. Clothes were not washed for a long time. Our beds were small and we had skinny blankets to cover ourselves. If it was our birthday, we got nothing. Some kids didn't know when their birthday was. Maybe some kids would make a card for you. That would make you happy.

One day in second grade Natasha (she worked at the orphanage) just came up and asked me if I wanted to be adopted. My mouth fell open and I said "Yeah!"

First it all started when Nastia got adopted. Her mom and papa (who are now my mama and papa) came into our room and took pictures of her and me together. Then they left and I was very sad. I remembered the pretty doll they brought for Nastia. I would never have such a doll in my whole entire life. Nobody did. Then two months later I was told Kevin and Jane wanted to adopt me too. My eyeballs almost fell out. The orphanage took a movie of me to send to my new family.

I waited about nine months. Then mama and papa came to see me. They gave me a lot of presents and went away again. Then I waited another month. Then Natasha took me to a courtroom and the judge decided if I could be adopted. It seemed like hours and hours before he said yes. Mama and papa gave me new clothes and I changed into them. Then they gave me a cross necklace. Then we had to go to more buildings. At one of them papa got a second medal. That was because they adopted two kids from Smolensk, Nastia and me. We drove for more than five hours back to the hotel in Moscow. The hotel was huge. We had dinner and went to bed. It was late.

In the morning we walked and went to more offices and a doctor. After waiting six days we were ready to go home. We spent a long time in the airport. For me to go to America, mama and papa had to show lots of papers. Finally we were on the plane. I was so excited I went to the bathroom about ten times every hour.

After ten hours we got off the plane and drove five more hours home. It was about 7 p.m. when we got home. When we got to our house, I thought our house was beautiful and asked, "How many people live there?" Papa went to get Nastia, and I looked at my room. It was very big and had furniture and toys. I liked it a lot. I did not have to share my room with anybody. Then Nastia and I realized we couldn't talk to each other anymore because she couldn't remember Russian and I did not know any English. I thought it was so weird how she was talking. Then we went to bed. I fell asleep in about five seconds.

I spoke a little English after a month. I was speaking very good English after three months. Then I started to forget some Russian. When I came home I started writing in my journal a lot. I still do but I have lots of schoolwork now and not much time. I also like to write poems.

After two-and-a-half months, I went to school. Everybody was so nice to me. They said things like, "Sera, this is where you will sit. This is a math book. We have math at 11:30. That is a clock. It shows time. Do you know what time means?" I hated that.

In our family we have three dogs, Toby, Abbey, and Quinn. Toby is a Welsh Terrier and Abbey and Quinn are Fox Terriers. There is mama and papa, and I have two younger sisters. They are Alia and Nastia. Nastia is ten and Alia is five.

Before I go any further, I forgot to tell you how my house looks. My favorite parts are the kitchen, family room, playroom, my bedroom, and the sunroom.

Well I guess I wrote enough. I hope you learned more about me. I wrote everything about me and how my life was. I hope it goes on as good as it has been.

Sera's mom, Jane, has written "Where Did I Come From,"
which can be read in Chapter Six.

On Being Adopted

by *Richard Lockwood*

I am a single dad in my early thirties living in Mounds View, Minnesota. When I'm not writing, singing, or acting, I keep busy camping in the forests of the upper midwest. I have a Liberal Arts Degree in Theatre from the University of Minnesota, Morris.

I have a mom and a dad. I have had them for as far as my memories can recall. Where memory stops, I have photographic proof that shows me with the two people I KNOW to be my mom and dad. Since I was six weeks old, my mom and dad have watched over me, cared for me——loved me.

I am adopted.

I'm often asked, "Do you know who your parents are?"

"Of course," I always reply, "My dad is the one who taught me how to fish, how to stack a pile of wood, how to throw a ball. He taught me to be caring and engaging with children. He taught me to lead groups of people by example and responsibility; not by demanding respect, but by earning the respect of others. My mom's the one who taught me how to care about and for other people. She taught me compassion and sensitivity, in addition to cooking, baking, and cleaning up after myself. She instilled in me the value of family, both immediate and extended. She showed me it is better to allow your conscience to be your guide to ensure you live life as a good person. My mom's name is Shirley. My dad's name is Bill."

"No. Not them. I mean your REAL mom and dad."

"They are my real mom and dad," is the only response I'd give.

Now, this conversation would go around in circles until the inquiring person would either give up or I'd grow bored with repeating my little game.

I'd always smile about these exchanges. After people would realize I had a sister, they would press me if she was my REAL sister. What do you say to that? Aside from, "No she's my imaginary sister that rides a winged pony and lives in the magical land of Sisteria." I would usually resign by saying, "No, we were adopted separately."

I have always known I was adopted. If I didn't when I was little, the whole "birds and bees" talk would've really been confusing as I distinctly remember going to "get" my sister when I was almost four years old.

I have always been curious about my biological background. It's always nagged at the back of my mind.

I was taught (by my REAL mother) that I was a gift; that my biological mother was responsible enough and caring enough to make the difficult decision she made so many years ago. I was told she loved me so much she wanted me to have a good life because she was too young to provide one for me.

I was never taught scorn. I never felt out of place. It never occurred to me to feel slighted by the whole affair. I felt I was special. I was a blessing to a couple who was unable to conceive a child of their own. I was taught that this family, the only one I'd ever known, was my own. I was taught right!

As I grew older, I started to appreciate the similarities between my family and me. I also learned to appreciate the differences. Similar or different, my mom and dad always supported me. They didn't force me to be the person they or their relatives were. They encouraged me to be who I am. They celebrated my talents and gifts and proudly stood by me as I made good decisions and stupid, teenage mistakes.

In truth, to those that have always asked but never got a straight answer, I have always been curious about my biological background. It's always nagged at the back of my mind. Who do I look like? Are there other actors/singers/writers I might be related to or am I truly an anomaly? I had been close to initiating an adoption search so many times throughout adulthood, but never took that final leap. I never NEEDED to know.

I wanted to figure out first who I was. I needed to establish myself, become whatever it was I was going to be when I grew up. In my mind, if I ever made contact, I wanted to be able to show how well I had done for myself. I wanted to show I was successful. I wanted to go into it without any pretense I wanted anything from my biological mother. I didn't want a handout. I didn't want to seem like I was after anything more than an opportunity to say "thank you."

Then it happened. In my late twenties, my son was born. Suddenly, thoughts began to form. For the first time in my life, I was looking into the eyes of the only biological relative known to me. My family tree, which started with me, grew a branch.

I have always imagined what I would say to my biological mother if I ever had the chance to meet her. So many times I have run the words through my mind. What do you say to someone so close to you that you have never met?

How would I reassure her I meant no harm?

How does one convey that, despite the potential emptiness and resentment and anger that so many people report feeling as an adult adoptee, that she need not fear a confrontation?

How was I to tell her I was raised right, with the lessons of love and appreciation for my lot in life?

How do I think about any of this without the overpowering fear of rejection? What would it be to hope and wonder and search your entire life, track down this person, only to be told they didn't want to make any manner of contact? Would it be worth the risk?

To me it would be well worth it. What is life, but a series of adventures? Take what you're given and live to the fullest. If I never fill this portion of my life, so be it! If I never see her face, look into her eyes and show her the appreciation I have held in my heart, I would hope she and all of the other women that chose to give their child a better life through adoption would hear my words:

> Thank you!
> From the bottom of my heart, thank you!
> Thank you for the gift of life.
> Thank you for having the strength to make the right decision.
> Thank you for giving me and others like me a good life.
> I hold no resentment toward you.
> I was raised by a family that taught me you were (and are) a good person, a person that cared.
> I don't want to intrude upon your life.
> I don't want a hand out.
> I don't want to make your life difficult.
> I just want to meet you and thank you.

If I ever have the grand opportunity of meeting you in person, of seeing your face, of holding you in a warm embrace, I promise to whisper into your ear: Thank you, I love you for who you are and what you have been through. Hopefully, together, we can get on with our lives, whether together or apart, but with the closure we both need.

FOR MY MOM AND DAD

I am not pursuing this search to find my "real" parents. That is what makes this easier for me. I have a mom. I have a dad. I have a sister. They are my family. They are grandma, grandpa, and aunt to my son. They are the ones that give me love, attention, companionship, frustration, nagging, birthday presents, unsolicited advice, leftovers, and coupons. My "real" parents are the ones that, when I hit "Mom and Dad" on my speed dial, I expect to answer. I appreciate them. I love them. I would never dream of trying to replace them.

My Real Mother

by Rikki Miller-Gardner

My name is Rikki Miller and I am a 21-year-old senior Psychology/Neuroscience major at the University of Pittsburgh. Even though my mom lives across the state, I talk to her all the time. She is my dearest friend and I love her more than anything. The message I want people to take with them when they read my story is even though my birthmother gave me up, there was a woman out there willing to give me all the support, strength, and love that would last a lifetime. There is no greater gift you can give a child than unconditional love, and being adopted by a woman who provided that for me is the greatest thing I could have ever asked for.

It's interesting when my peers ask if I feel abandoned being an adopted child. They inquire about my "real" mother and are confused when I tell them I am proud to be adopted. It seems there is a stigma for adopted children that says being adopted means you weren't wanted and that you should be ashamed because you were given away. I laugh at these thoughts because the people who formed them probably have never met an adopted child and certainly are not adopted themselves, so who are they to set the record on how being adopted feels?

Personally, being adopted has made me who I am. It is the foundation of my values, and it is the mold for my perspective of the future. I, of course, cannot speak for all adopted children, but I don't think being given away by your birthmother to a man or a woman who would do anything to have a child and do anything for that child can be considered abandonment. In fact, I think I'm luckier than all of my non-adopted friends, because I know how desperately I was wanted. Just read my mother's heartbreaking story of the years she tried to conceive and her wait to adopt. She dragged herself through hell and back just to get to me. In her eyes, I am a gift from God, a prize for the years she endured fertility drugs, testing, injections, and the loss of a husband. How many children can say that about their moms? My mom is the strongest woman I have ever met, and I pray I have half of her drive and determination. She is compassionate, loving, and supportive in everything I do. No matter how bad I fail, she is always there to pick up the pieces and tell me she loves me. Her love for me, as mine for her, is unconditional and that is more comforting and more important than knowing I came from her womb.

People ask me if I'm mad at my birthmother or if I want to meet her, which is a fair and reasonable question. If anything, I am grateful to my birthmother. Regardless of her reasons for giving me up for adoption, in the end I was given the opportunity for a better life, to be given to people who could love me and care for me better than she could. I think if I had stayed with her, I would not be in college, and I would not have a loving family to come home to. I used to want to meet her when I was younger because I just wanted to see what she looked like. But when I got a little older, and even now, I have no interest or curiosity in meeting either of my birthparents. To me, they created me, but my real mom took care of me when I was sick, came to all of my school functions, gave me a roof over my head and food on the table, and loved me more than I could have ever imagined a mother could love. I am incredibly fulfilled and as far as I'm concerned, I would be no better off, and there is no void in my heart that would be filled in my meeting my birthparents. They were my beginning, but after my mom adopted me she was the one who placed me on my path to self-confidence, a successful future, and a loving life.

My mom is not the only one who thanks God every day that she has the opportunity to be my mother. By being given up for adoption, I was given the opportunity to lead a better life, and I have. I love my mom more than words can say, and because of her, I am a confident, strong, compassionate person who can also see the good things in bad situations, laugh at myself, and appreciate every single day. My mom went through hell to receive me, now all I want to do is make her proud by changing the world with her knowing she is my every inspiration, my guardian angel, and my real mother.

Rikki's mother, Linda Miller-Gardner, has written "Trials And Tribulations," which can be read in Chapter One.

My Search

by Maxine Chalker-Mollick

As an adult adoptee, I decided to put my life circumstance to my best advantage and open an adoption agency. After completing my own search, I founded Adoptions From The Heart, which is now one of the first U.S. agencies to do open adoption and one of the largest infant placing agencies on the East Coast.

My life began being born to one woman and then immediately being placed in the arms of my "parents." I was lucky enough to have these life circumstances turn out positive, and I am grateful for that. My parents always told me I was adopted, and at one point I said I was going to stop eating and become smaller and smaller so I could grow in my adoptive mother's belly.

After growing to adulthood, getting married, having a child, getting divorced, and then deciding to pursue a career in social work, I was offered employment as a social worker in a child welfare agency. I was told there were several openings and that the one in the adoption department would not afford me the opportunity to climb up the career ladder of this civil service job. Needless to say, the adoption job was of more interest to me and I chose that position. Part of my job involved helping adoptees and birthparents do searches. I was successful in a few cases, and they were always very emotional experiences. It was through these experiences I realized I had unfinished business I needed to complete.

This began my decision to do a search for my own birthfamily. Up until then I denied any interest in doing this and, in fact, I think I did feel that way on some level. I had sent for my original birth certificate many years prior, and it said my birthmother was born in Greece. Whenever I ate in a Greek restaurant or attended a Greek fair at a local church I would look at people and see if I resembled any of them. I made an appointment

She immediately called me and said "your search is over." She was my birthmother

to see the judge that handled my adoption (can you believe he was still working?). I told him I knew my birthmother was from Greece. He told me that actually she was from Albania. I asked him if he would tell me my grandfather's name and he did. From there I wrote letters to all the orthodox churches in the Philadelphia area and found a priest that said the family did, in fact, belong to his church. I asked if I could come in and see him, and it was arranged. Amazingly, he did not ask me why I was asking about the family and told me all about them. It turned out my birthmother's name was listed as Mary on the birth certificate, and Mary had died the previous year. There was one other female child in the family who I will refer to as E to protect her identity. I then told the priest why I was there, and he was fascinated. He agreed to contact E and see if he could find out whether she or her deceased sister was my birthmother.

Unfortunately, when he later contacted me he said E had denied being my birthmother and knew nothing about me. I decided to write to her stating she was either my mother or my aunt and that I did not want to interrupt her life but I would like some medical information. She immediately called me and said "Your search is over." She was my birthmother. We met and it was a very tearful, joyous reunion. After I was born E had gotten married and had three more children. One girl died in a house fire as a teenager, but there was a remaining girl and boy. The girl was five years younger than I, divorced and living in Virginia Beach, Virginia. The boy was living at home and was considerably younger.

E decided to tell her daughter about me when she was visiting but only said she had something to talk to her about. She was told there was a special friend she wanted her to meet. When the truth came out, she was shocked. As she was growing up, her mother was constantly warning her not to get pregnant, and she wondered why she was dwelling on this so much. Now everything became clear. Since her sister had died, the incoming of a new sister was welcome to her, and she was glad to have the chance to get to know me.

My half-sister and I got to know each other gradually and found we had a lot in common. We had the same taste in clothing and shoes and we both loved to dance. We were also both divorced and dated foreign men. She had two sons, and I had a daughter. We began vacationing together and had the time of our lives. We spent holidays together, and our children grew up together.

Personally, my relationship with my birthmother and her husband deteriorated, and we do not remain in touch. My relationship with my half-sister remains strong. Presently she is living with my current husband, his son and me. My half-sister's two sons are both married, and one has two children. We all remain in close touch even though my birthmother is not involved in any of our lives.

Interview With An Adoptee

by Courtney and Karen Ledbetter

My adoptive family has corresponded with my birthfamily all my life. When I was eight years old, I asked to call my birthfamily on the phone. Both families agreed. Shortly after that first phone conversation, I shared the experience and my thoughts with BellaOnline's adoption host.

Courtney's (adoptive) family and birthfamily have always corresponded with one another. Courtney's families recently began telephone contact. I sat down with Courtney and discussed her thoughts on adoption and telephone contact.

BELLA: Who did you talk to on the phone today?
COURTNEY: My birthmother, birthsister, and birthbrothers.

BELLA: Who asked to have telephone conversations?
COURTNEY: I asked my mom if we could call. She asked my birthmom if it was okay. About the same time, my older birthbrother asked his mom (my birthmom) if he could call me. My birthmom sent her phone number to my mom and we called her.

BELLA: What was that first phone call like?

COURTNEY: I was nervous and excited. I called all afternoon and there was no answer. Finally, my birthmom answered. When I told her who I was, she started crying. We both laughed and cried at the same time. My birthmom talked to my adoptive mom, and they cried and laughed at the same time. My sister cried too. I almost cried. I didn't get to talk to my older brother that day, because he wasn't at home. When I did get to talk to him a few days later, he cried too. My younger brother didn't want to talk.

BELLA: Do you like talking with your birthfamily on the phone?

COURTNEY: Yes, I like talking to my birthmom and my older brother best.

BELLA: How does talking with your birthfamily on the phone make you feel?

COURTNEY: Now they seem more real to me. I have voices to go with pictures.

BELLA: Do you call them, or do they call you?

COURTNEY: Both. If I have a question or need to tell them something, I call. They call me sometimes too. When we lost electricity during an ice storm, my birthmom called to check on us. That made me feel really good. I know she cares about me and my mom and dad.

BELLA: What do you talk about?

COURTNEY: My older brother and I talk about bikes, our birthmom, our brother and sister, our pets, school, and sports. My sister and I talk about gymnastics and her favorite things. My birthmom and I talk about lots of stuff like their home and pets.

She answers my questions, and I answer her questions. We always end our conversations with "I love you." My birthmom always tells me to tell my mom and dad that she loves them too.

BELLA: What have you learned about your birthfamily from telephone conversations?

COURTNEY: That their family has rules just like my family and my brothers and sister sometimes get grounded or lose privileges when they don't listen to their mom. I used to think my brothers and sister never got time-out.

BELLA: Do you hope to meet your birthfamily in person?

COURTNEY: Yes. My mom says if we ever travel to their state, we'll meet them, if they want to. My mom reminds me that we have to consider my birthfamily's feelings too.

BELLA: What do you think you'll do when you meet them?

COURTNEY: I'll hug them all. I'll probably cry too.

BELLA: Do you think having contact with your birthfamily is a good thing?

COURTNEY: For us it is. If my mom doesn't know the answer to a question about my adoption or birthfamily, then we can call my birthmom and ask her. I don't have any brothers or sisters in my adoptive family, so it's good to be able to talk to my (birth) brothers and sister on the phone. I'm glad I asked to call them, and I'm glad both my moms said it was okay.

Courtney's mother, Karen Ledbetter, has written the pieces Questions To Ask A Potential Birthmother and To Tell Or Not To Tell (The School) That Is The Question, which can be read in Chapter Ten.

About Me

by Caitlin Chun

I live in Mililani, Hawaii, and am a junior at the local high school. I'm the sports editor for the school newspaper, "The Trojan Times." I love to write and enjoy sharing my personal experiences through my writing.

My name is Caitlin Chun. I'm 15, have an older brother, and I'm a die-hard fan of Josh Hartnett. But who cares about that nonsense. The real me is more complex than a list of random facts. I'm probably the most complicated person you will ever encounter. Most people talk to me and mid-way through the conversation slowly wonder how they stumbled across such an exhausting girl.

Maybe my complexity comes from my background; I have gone through a whirlwind of adjustments. No matter how far I traveled, I eventually came back to where I started. My mother gave me up for adoption when I was four. I was placed in an orphanage in my hometown in Vietnam. A year passed and my mother never visited, so I eventually gave up hope of someone to hold onto for love. It was a lonely kind of forced independence.

Then out of the blue, I was told a family wanted to adopt me. I didn't know what was happening at that time so I wasn't the nicest person. If I had known they were going to be the greatest gift I would ever receive, I would have been most zealous. I was escorted to Hawaii and began my life a second time.

I had trouble learning to trust and love others. I gradually matured and learned about genuine love. My adoptive parents taught me everything. They are the greatest people in the world. They took me as I was and provided me with unconditional love and support. They showed me love and how to embrace it instead of pushing it away. The greatest lesson of all was when I learned to love myself. When I finally accepted myself, I was a new person. I wasn't as insecure, didn't seek attention from everyone, and loved others around me.

When I was ready, our family took a trip to Vietnam. While there, I was offered the opportunity to meet my birthmother. I was scared, extremely nervous, and excited at the same time. I had fantasized about meeting her for eight years. I had many questions to ask so I could move on knowing the truth about my other life.

When I met my birthmom, she was beautiful, petite, and had an obvious mental disability. I immediately dropped all my grudges against her and forgave her. The realization of why she gave me up hit me like a ton of rocks. Meeting her was like a weight being lifted off me. It opened me up to different emotions such as forgiveness, understanding, and compassion.

I really needed the trip back to Vietnam. It offered closure to a part of my life and gave the opportunity for a new one to begin. Vietnam is no longer a place of my past, but a place of the present. I am not afraid of my homeland anymore because I know there's nothing but love there.

All these experiences influence the person I am today. Through all these changes I have grown and discovered who I truly am. I have so many other lessons to learn and journeys to take in the future, and I can't wait for them to come!

A Bed With No Wheels

by Linda Sylvester

My name is Linda Sylvester. The story I have written was the beginning of a new life. Being adopted by a wonderful family gave me a life and love I never knew existed. I hope my story will inspire other adoptees as well as families who are interested in adopting. Special thanks to my parents Jennifer and Torrey, my brother Steve, and sister Sue. And in loving memory to my brother Sam, who always encouraged me to believe in myself. He was not only my brother but mentor and friend. Sam, I will always love and miss you.

When I first laid eyes on Jennifer and Torrey Sylvester I was seated at a table eating peanut butter and jelly sandwiches with another foster child. I was living in my third and what would be my last foster home. During my first six years, I had met many people, most who came and went like a rainstorm passing through—people who eventually became a blur. The day Jennifer and Torrey came through the door was a day that would change my life, although I had no way of knowing this at the time. I remember noticing that both were tall and had large smiles. I took in how curly Jennifer's hair was and how black Torrey's mustache was. They seemed nice and happy to meet me. After what seemed like a few minutes the

Sylvesters left. I never had a thought about it. I couldn't have known they would play a very important role in my life as mom and dad.

Soon arrangements were made for me to leave the foster home and go to live with the Sylvesters. I was thinking temporary—after a children's home and three foster homes, I was used to moving from place to place. I remember meeting my siblings Steven, Sam, and Sue at a hotel and how excited they were to see me. I was feeling very overwhelmed, a bit scared, but happy to see other kids. I was given my first present, a Sylvester the Cat, exactly like the one on TV. It was a cuddly stuffed animal, and I enjoyed holding it. It was my special gift from everyone, and it was a security blanket for me. I still didn't understand that this was the end of one journey and another was yet to begin. I didn't really grasp that Sylvester the Cat was my family's way of saying, "Welcome. You're here to stay. We are your new family."

On the ride to Maine I threw up in the station wagon—nerves I guess. I remember feeling scared. Where was I going? It was one thing to visit and play for awhile but now I was in a car and going on a long trip, and I wasn't sure what was going to happen and where I would end up.

Walking into their big blue house was a complete shock for me. I felt so small and the ceilings were so high. They never seemed to end. There was light blue carpeting, and it was clean and smelled nice. A place like this I was never familiar with. My first thought was what if I get lost? I shared a room with my sister, Sue, and I slept in a rollaway bed that was used when guests came—A Bed with Wheels, I called it. It was comfortable and I got used to sleeping on it. I could have extra pillows and blankets (a luxury for me). One afternoon when Sue and I were sitting in our bedroom playing with Barbie dolls, I remember feeling warmed by the sun that shone through the window and lit up the spot on the floor where I was sitting. Everything was peaceful until I told her that I was going to pack up now because it was time for me to go to another home. "What do you mean?" she asked me. "You are home." "No," I told her, "this isn't my home. I have to go to a new one." Sue became extremely upset because she couldn't get through to me that I was here to stay. She called mom in and by that time I had a little suitcase

I've battled with identity for years, even up until recently when I found an adult adoptee support group. . . It really helped.

filled with my things. Mom was quite teary-eyed as she realized this was the only way of life I had known. She explained to me that this was my home and I don't remember everything she said. I just remember listening intently to every word and trying to understand the words "forever family."

I had been with the Sylvesters a little over a year when my adoption was finalized January 4, 1979. I was seven years old. The judge spoke to me for a few minutes, and I nodded my head yes— I understood what my being there meant—I was going to stay with my family. Afterwards we all went to the furniture store where I picked out my own bed—it was beautiful! No more moving from place to place. This bed was going to be put in one place, a place called home and it didn't have wheels!

Once I became used to living in one place, getting adjusted to being part of the family was a challenge on both ends. I've said to my parents throughout the years—How did you do it? How did you find the strength? I knew nothing really of how a family worked. But the patience everyone had paid off, and for me, I felt like a good deal of my childhood was salvaged. I began to come out of my shell and participate in things. We had family outings and took family trips. The biggest one was in 1980 to Saskatoon,

Canada to meet my mother's mom, my nanny, cousins, aunts, and uncles. We were a family unit and to this day we are all close.

As an adoptee—no matter what age we were when adopted— we all go through the "What am I supposed to be?" and "Who am I?" phase. I've battled with identity for years, even up until recently when I found an adult adoptee support group and was able to join in and listen to other adoptees who had unique stories and dealt with some of the same issues. It really helped. Connecting with my two biological brothers helped put closure to the gaps that had been in my past allowing me to forgive my biological parents for their wrongdoings and find the person within that I choose to be today.

I've had the privilege of traveling to many beautiful places, have met interesting people, have made close friendships, and been a teacher. I am currently working as a caregiver for two children in a private home and am changing careers to move into the Esthetics field. I feel I've done well, and I'm here today because of "family."

Birthmother Stories

A Loving Decision

*"What we have once deeply loved—we can never lose in our hearts.
For all that we love deeply forever becomes a part of us"*

- Helen Keller

Advice From A Birthmother

by *Melanie Beth Mosberg*

My name is Melanie and I am 32 years old. Although I planned to have children someday, circumstances prevented me from going about it in the conventional manner. Thus, seeking open adoption became my ultimate path.

I found out I was six weeks pregnant in October 2003. The birthfather and I had a very brief and casual encounter and were no longer on speaking terms. When I contacted him about my pregnancy he was not very supportive, to say the least. I told him abortion was out of the question, and that I honestly wanted to carry the baby and have her adopted in an open adoption. He didn't think I would be able to go through with it once the baby started to grow inside me. Boy was he wrong!

The hardest thing was telling my mother. Even though we have a great relationship, I felt she would not be very supportive so I did not tell her. I called my brother and asked him to do it for me. It was a few weeks before my mother and I spoke about my pregnancy and my decision to start my adoption journey. She, too, wanted me to have an abortion and continued to talk about it until my fifth month. I think she got the picture when I was still pregnant and still searching for adoptive parents.

I did not know where to begin, so I started searching on the Internet and found tons of agencies. Another good place to start is to check your local area for a pregnancy crisis center; most cities and towns have them. You really have to do your homework and make sure you take your time. Do not rush into anything. You are in the driver's seat. Make a running list of questions to ask both the agency and prospective parents.

Here are my suggestions of questions and thoughts to keep in mind when searching for prospective parents:

1- Figure out what type of family you are looking for. Is it a nuclear two parent family, gay couples, or single parents?

2 - How many siblings do you/they want?

3 - To what extent will the adoption be open?

4 - What are the expectations on both sides? For example, visits, pictures, emails, phone calls, videos.

5 - In what religion will your child be raised?

There are so many questions to ask. However, each situation is different from the next. Keeping these questions in mind is a huge help and makes all the difference in finding the right match.

I found a local pregnancy care center and asked if they had anyone on staff experienced in adoption. They referred me to a volunteer who specialized in birthmother support. I am very grateful to her for being there for me unconditionally throughout my pregnancy as well as at the hospital when my daughter was born. She continues to be a huge support in my life and I am eternally grateful for that.

Back in the fall of 2003 I started looking on the Internet for adoption agencies. I knew I wanted an open adoption, because I wanted to be a part of my child's life forever. Some agencies were not very supportive or birthmother friendly. I did find a few couples on my own which did not pan out. I desperately needed financial support to survive, because I had no source of income. I had no medical insurance, and the bills were mounting. I found a couple on-line who were located in Connecticut. The

Birthmothers too, have horror stories about the journey in the adoption process.

first time we spoke I thought I finally found the match. They had twin boys who were two years old and adopted. Unfortunately, this couple was with an agency out of Texas and were not able to assist me with my finances as there were too many legal restrictions. Each state has different laws in covering birthmother expenses as well as the overall adoption process. Please EDUCATE YOURSELF.

In March, I found an attorney who specialized in adoption. She was located in California and found a few couples for me who truly matched my needs. I finally felt there was light at the end of the tunnel. I had talked to so many couples and had so many empty promises. Birthmothers too, have horror stories about the journey in the adoption process.

At the same time, I contacted a local agency, which had a couple that met my criteria. This couple just happened to live only ten minutes from my home. I met with the agency and spoke with the adoptive mom for the first time. We had dinner and spent about four hours together. I knew this was finally the MATCH.

A few days later I met with both adoptive parents and pretty much sealed the deal. This was the right couple to raise my daughter and I knew in my heart God had matched me with a good family. They have a six-year-old biological son as well as a dog, which were on the list of things I was looking for in an adoptive family.

I had just started my seventh month when the adoptive mother started going to my doctor appointments with me. My last few months of pregnancy were a bit difficult as I had very bad edema (swelling of feet and hands). I had only gained 23 pounds my first seven-and-a-half months.

I had my daughter in May, at 37 weeks. Sarah Grace weighed nine pounds, three ounces. We had some time together in the hospital, which was wonderful. I recently saw Sarah for her one month birthday. It was a great night for the both of us.

The next year will be very challenging for both the adoptive parents and me as our new relationship evolves. I am very grateful to them for adopting Sarah and giving her a stable, loving, and caring home. I know in my heart Sarah has a great life ahead of her.

In the beginning, becoming pregnant was very scary but I can honestly say it was the best thing that ever happened to me. Yes, I was 31 years old and this was my first pregnancy, but I knew from day one this was the right decision. Thankfully, during those nine months I discovered a lot about myself. I was able to define goals in my life and truly lay out a plan for the future. I have Sarah to thank for that and her parents for allowing me to carry out my dreams, and to them I am eternally grateful.

A few things I ask all women to do are educate, educate, and educate themselves. I cannot stress that enough. Make sure you have an advocate. That is something I lacked and probably will always regret. The agency I filed with should have had a birthmother representative and did not. Do not be afraid to speak your mind because you might regret it later. The Internet has been a wonderful tool for research and information.

Thank you for reading my story.

Doubly Blessed

by Nicole Strickland

My name is Nicole Strickland, known as Coley to most. I am birthmom to Charlie, who I placed in an open adoption right after his birth in September 2001. I enjoy pictures, phone calls, and visits with Charlie, his big sister, and his parents. I am also super-mom to Noah and wife to Jason. Since Charlie's birth I have become active in the adoption community, writing articles, hosting forums, and, most importantly, being the co-founder of BirthMom Buds, a large website and organization for birthmoms and pregnant women who are considering adoption. For more information please visit us at www.birthmombuds.com or call 1-877-790-4174.

When I was in high school, there was a girl who had a baby and placed the baby for adoption. I remember thinking she did the right thing for her baby, but that it must have been incredibly hard at the same time. Little did I know then that, years down the road, I would have so much in common with her. I am a birthmother, and this is my story.

I had just left the health department and felt like a failure for the second time in my life, because I was single and pregnant. When I was 19 years old, I became pregnant and forced myself into a loveless marriage, because I thought it would be the best thing for my child to have two parents living together. Noah was born in 1996. He had a lot of complications at birth and was diagnosed with cerebral palsy and epilepsy. His father and I had married for all the wrong reasons, trying to do what we thought was best for our child, but the difficulty of parenting a child with special needs was more strain than our marriage could handle, so we split up.

I had been dating and was seeing someone on and off for a few months but we realized we did not want the same things out of life and moved on. We had been intimate, though, and I thought I had nothing to worry about since I was on the depo-provera shot. It was practically foolproof. Boy, was I surprised when I took a routine pregnancy test before getting my shot. The test was POSITIVE! I immediately made an appointment with an ob-gyn to find out how far along I was. I stared in disbelief at the screen as the ultrasound tech told me I was nearly five months pregnant. "How could this be?" I wondered in dismay. I was automatically considered a high-risk pregnancy because of all my complications with Noah's birth. I was overwhelmed and afraid. I knew immediately it was the guy from months before and we had gone our separate ways.

I had since moved on and became involved with Jason, someone I sensed would be a part of my life forever. When I first found out I was pregnant I tried to break up with him. It is hard enough for a man to love a single mom of a kid with special needs without adding a baby to the scenario. But Jason surprised me and said he would support whatever choice I made. I contacted the biological dad and he pushed for abortion even though I was five months along. I suggested adoption, and he did not like that option saying, "I don't want junior showing up on my doorstep 18 years from now." I was taking things one day at a time trying to let the fact that I was pregnant sink in. I was in denial and I knew I had to accept reality and begin making plans for my unborn child.

Just a few days after the ultrasound appointment, I was at the Tex Mex restaurant where I had been waitressing for quite a while. One of my regulars, Angee, came in for lunch on a slow day and for some reason I mentioned to her I was pregnant. She and her husband, Scott, congratulated me and I explained to them it was very unplanned and I was thinking of adoption. Saying that was so out of the blue. Although the thought had crossed my mind, I had never spoken the word aloud. Scott and Angee told me how their daughter, Natalie, who I had always assumed was their biological daughter, was adopted in an open adoption arrangement. She briefly explained open adoption and said they were planning to adopt again. She mentioned the lawyer they had worked with before, and said if I wanted more information about them or wanted to contact their lawyer to look at other couples, they would be happy to help. Angee gave me her phone number, probably thinking I would never call and wished me luck.

Knowing I would be bringing this baby into the world, but then handing him over to another family, was extremely hard.

I called her that night. We talked on the phone and got to know each other a little. She told me about her, Scott, and Natalie. I told her about me, Jason, and Noah. Angee and Scott came to the restaurant over the weekend and brought Natalie with them. Angee explained to me how Natalie had always known she was adopted and knew she grew in another lady's tummy. We set up a dinner meeting for Jason to meet them, and he liked them as much as I did.

And so our adoption agreement was beginning. Angee and Jason started going to all my doctor appointments with me. We all spent a lot of time together. Natalie and Noah would play together and Natalie would amaze me, because it never fazed her that he could not walk or talk. She would get on the floor and crawl with him. God was working in all our lives.

That doesn't mean this was not hard. Knowing I would be bringing this baby into the world, but then handing him over to another family, was extremely hard. I tried to think of him as Angee's baby and not mine as a defense mechanism, so when I went home without a baby maybe it would not hurt so much. I am a strong person and was trying so hard to be brave and follow through with my adoption plan.

Our son, Charles Kelby (fondly known as Charlie), entered this world four weeks early on September 20, 2001. He was healthy yet small, and very loved by both his birthfamily and adoptive family. I spent time with him in the hospital and Angee was right there, too. We cared for him together those three days. Many of Scott and Angee's family came to visit in the hospital and I got a chance to meet Charlie's extended family. All throughout my pregnancy, Jason and I had talked about how Charlie would be doubly blessed—having a birthfamily and an adoptive family that both loved him dearly.

Since we had planned an open adoption, I had held onto the fact I would be doubly blessed as well; that I was doing the right thing and would get to see my son grow up over the years. I still struggled emotionally after his birth. I was grieving for the child I lost—the child I willingly gave a better life to. I felt as if no one else in the world understood what I was feeling. I was desperate for someone who could understand.

About a week after his relinquishment, when I was sleepless, I saw an "Is anyone out there?" post on www.adoption.com. As I read the post I noticed this was from another birthmother, Lani. I instantly replied and we began chatting via e-mail. The similarities were amazing. Lani lived in the next state and the same city as my grandmother. Her baby was born on my birthday, just four days before Charlie's birth, and placed in an open adoption similar to mine. I never imagined when I responded to her post we would end up becoming as close as we are. Without our babies' births we never would have met each other. At first all we talked about was adoption. She understood what I was thinking before I could even get the words out of my mouth. Now, though, our friendship is about so much more than adoption.

As we began to watch our children grow from a distance, our emotional pain began to subside. We both knew that without each other our post-partum grief would have been so much more difficult, and we didn't want others in the same situation to have to search for a friend that understood. Together, we started a non-profit organization called BirthMom Buds and a website for birthmothers and pregnant women considering adoption. We started in February 2003, with ourselves as the founding members. A year later, we have over 200 members, a substantial mentoring program for pregnant and potential placing birthmothers, and a toll-free help line.

I still maintain contact with Charlie and his adoptive family. I have seen him at Christmas, been at his birthday parties, and his mom was even a bridesmaid in my wedding. My good days outweigh the bad, although I have now learned the pain will never totally subside, but I have allowed myself to move forward.

I still believe that Charlie is doubly blessed, but I believe my life is doubly blessed as well. I have had the privilege and pleasure of meeting and getting to know many birthmothers as a result of BirthMom Buds that I never would have had the opportunity to meet had I not chosen adoption.

To visit Coley's website, go to www.birthmombuds.com.

An Amazing Life

by Caryn Leslie

I am a 21-year-old female living in Wisconsin with my significant other who is the birthfather of the baby girl we placed for adoption two years ago. I work in customer service full time and live paycheck to paycheck, struggling to pay bills. I'm hoping my story will assist other birthparents in making a decision about adoption.

I was away from home and lonely in a moldy motel room in Colorado. Trapped in a small, stuffy, smelly room with only a bed and a toilet, my only companions were my guitars and the mountains. I was 1,300 miles away from my friends, my family, and everything I loved.

Throwing pebbles off the top of a mountain, staring into the big beautiful blue sky, a tear fell from my cheek and landed on the dry rock beneath me. "Why did I leave?" I wondered to myself. "Why did I leave everything behind?" Eighteen years old. I was on top of the world. I knew everything, just like every eighteen-year-old. I thought I could make it on my own.

With no money to buy food or pay for my moldy hut, I was faced with a horrible fear. A fear only a few could imagine. To survive the next few weeks, I had to sacrifice one of the only things that kept me sane: my guitars. I had to sell them for money.

Just as I thought everything would be all right with the money I had received from the pawnshop, and the job I got hired for (although I wouldn't be able to start for another month), I started getting sick and losing a lot of weight. I got concerned. Not knowing why or how this sickness came about, I tried to suck it up and live with this sickness for a whole week.

Sitting in a rusted bathroom, nauseated, I began to cry. I realized I was pregnant. There was a life growing inside my frail body. At that time, I couldn't take care of myself. How would I take care of a baby? All I could think about in the dirty motel room in Colorado was to go home to Wisconsin to be with my friends, my family, and everything I loved.

My wonderful, understanding parents sent me money to buy a bus ticket home. I packed only what I could carry from bus to bus; everything else I left behind. After two days and two nights cramped on a bus, having to run to the bathroom every few minutes to either throw-up or urinate, I finally reached Milwaukee.

I tried so hard not to doze off in the Milwaukee bus station while waiting for my ride to pick me up. Being alone and everything my eyes would open and close periodically. Opening my eyes, I jumped up really fast. There he was, my knight in shining armor, coming to rescue me. We ran to each other and I wrapped my arms around him. The only way I would have let go is if he had ripped my arms off.

My significant other and I found a quiet place to talk. There was no way we would let this life die, but there was no way we could raise or financially support this amazing life. Neither of us had a job. No place would hire me because they thought I would take maternity leave right away. My significant other was hired for a liquor store position, but didn't make enough money to even pay his rent. We chose to place the baby for adoption.

I moved back home to live with my parents and my brother. I can't express how much my parents helped me through this tough time. Mom and dad gave me money for clothes, food, hospital co-payments, anything and everything I needed. Bless their hearts with love; I owe them so much.

I looked up adoption in the phone book. There were so many places to choose from. I went with the one closest to my parent's house. This adoption agency mostly deals with international adoption, although they respected my decision and helped my significant other and I find parents for the baby.

I knocked on the hollow door of a fancy hotel room where the adoption agency was located. Behind this door were four envelopes sitting on a coffee table waiting to be read. I picked up one envelope and my significant other picked up another. There was silence as we read about four different couples who all wanted to adopt a child. After we read about the couples, we discussed what we liked and disliked about them. We chose one couple we both really liked and wanted to meet.

Thinking that we will never see this life again is heartbreaking. It tears you apart into tiny pieces.

When placing a child for adoption, you have to give up your rights in court, therefore, I had a lawyer. The lawyer was to set up meetings with the couple we chose, assist with any questions I had on legal rights, handle the court procedures, and legally set up the adoption procedures. The lawyer was also there to go over the questions I would be asked in court.

The lawyer suggested we meet the couple in a quiet restaurant close to my parent's house. Before the lawyer arrived at the restaurant, it was just us and the prospective adoptive parents. At first there was silence as we all looked at the menu, then the couple started talking about themselves. My significant other and I were very interested in what they had to say. The lawyer arrived and was happy to see all of us comfortable and talking with each other.

After the meeting the lawyer asked what we thought of the couple. We went home and discussed how we felt about a different couple raising the baby my significant other and I created. It is so difficult to think about adoption. So difficult that no one would ever be able to feel the emotion you feel, unless you've placed a baby yourself. Thinking that we would never see this life again was heartbreaking. It tore us apart into tiny pieces. Even though we knew we were doing the right thing, we still had a feeling of loss.

The next eight months were spent going over paperwork, appearing at court dates, and signing documents. My significant other and I chose the first couple we met to be the parents of the baby. We asked the adoption agency if they would ask the adoptive parents to be at the hospital for the birth of their child. The adoptive parents were so excited to hear the news, and happily accepted our invitation.

The baby didn't quite want to come out on the due date, so a week passed and my doctor suggested I be induced. After hours of horrible contractions that felt like someone was literally grabbing my insides and squeezing really hard, I couldn't handle the excruciating pain anymore. An anesthesiologist came to the rescue and relieved the disturbing pain. After a while the nurse came in the room to check up on how I was doing and noticed it was time to deliver the baby.

The adoptive parents came in the room. The adoptive dad kept his distance and stayed by the door. I don't think he had a very strong stomach for labor. The adoptive mom was helping hold one of my legs, and my significant other was helping hold the other leg. Before I started pushing I asked if the adoptive mom and my significant other would like to cut the umbilical cord. They agreed they would cut the cord together. After two hours of pushing, a beautiful baby girl arrived into this world with eyes wide open. It was time to cut the umbilical cord. At the last second my significant other gave the scissors to the adoptive mom and said, "Here, you can cut it."

So much was going on at this point! The nurses were getting the table ready for the baby, I was just exhausted from pushing for two hours, and the adoptive dad was waiting eagerly to see the baby. The adoptive mom was so excited that she started to faint. The doctor yelled at the nurses, "She's going down! Help!" My significant other caught the adoptive mom before she fell to the floor, and as he was placing her gently in a chair, the doctor had already grabbed the scissors and cut the cord himself.

While I was getting stitched up, everyone was by the baby table. The adoptive dad was taking pictures of the baby girl and all the nurses were admiring how gorgeous the baby's eyes were. So many laughs and smiles—even I was smiling and I was getting stitches. My significant other and I were so happy to see the look on the adoptive parent's faces. Everyone witnessed a miracle; the adoptive parents had received a miracle.

To this day, my significant other and I can request pictures from the adoption agency twice a year. With pictures, we also get notes telling us the progress of the baby. We have chosen such wonderful parents, and we know this from the smiles in the pictures we receive. I thank the adoptive parents for everything. I know this baby girl would not have a wonderful life without them. Until the baby is a grown adult, my significant other and I will always wonder if she will ever want to meet us. If she chooses to locate us, we will be waiting with love and open arms.

An Amazing Life
by Caryn Leslie

An amazing life was growing inside,
From a couple that wouldn't let it just die.

An amazing life was on a couple's mind,
Where to go and who to find?

An amazing life was picked for another,
Who already had their life together.

An amazing life was born December 3, 2002,
From a couple who knew the right thing to do.

An amazing life from a couple that will never
*   forget her,*
An amazing life where so many miracles
*   could occur.*

The couple waits for the amazing life to grow,
They will always wonder if this life chooses to
*   ever show.*

A Birthmother's Dilemma

by Heather Valentine

As a young 20-year-old woman, my experience was astounding and like no other. Having a baby is bound to turn anyone's life around, but it especially affected me. I was able to bring a baby into the world, and I was able to give another family the gift of a baby. I think of my daughter everyday and will never forget her no matter how often or not I see her.

The day I found out I was pregnant was a long-dreaded day, since I had many suspicions I was pregnant. As soon as I got my proven confirmation I drove to my friend Jessica and showed her the test. The rest of the night was like a blur; I don't remember much.

I was scared and dumbfounded. I almost didn't think it could happen to me. I called the baby's father, who was my boyfriend at the time, and let him know the news. He sat on the phone with me for a little while and tried to figure out what to do. I had so much going on inside. No matter what anyone suggested, I would have gone along with it. That's why when the word abortion came out of his mouth I said "Okay" while my heart was saying, "NO NO NO!" For about two weeks, until my abortion date, I went back and forth trying to figure out what I really wanted to do. I hadn't told anyone but my boyfriend and one other friend. It came time for ME to go to the doctor's office and get the abortion. The father went with me so he could pay for it.

It's illegal in my state to do an abortion in the office past 13 ½ weeks of gestational age, and I just happened to be 14 weeks along. My heart was screaming for joy, but the baby's father was mad things didn't go his way. I really wanted to keep my baby but I knew I could neither afford to or give the baby the life it truly deserved. Time went by. I started telling more and more of my friends. When I was around six months it was beginning to get pretty difficult to hide it from my family. They were suspicious. By this time the baby's father had already broken up with me.

I decided to write my mom a letter because I could not bear to tell her to her face. I gave her the letter right before she went to work and told her not to read it until she got there. I knew she had finally opened it and had read it when I got the crying phone call. Later that night we talked it through, and I shared my feelings about telling her. She wasn't mad; she loved me.

My mom suggested adoption. I really wanted to make her happy after all of the disappointment I had given her, but in my heart I wished I could keep my baby. Through someone she worked with she found a family who already had one child they adopted and wanted another.

My mom e-mailed them back and forth and we decided to meet at their home, just 30 minutes away. As we entered their home, shook hands, and sat down, I was shaking with fear. We learned a lot about adoption by listening to the prospective adoptive parents, since they had already been through the process. They seemed like nice people who really had their stuff together.

I hadn't looked at or talked to anyone else but I knew they would be really good parents and a really good family for my baby. They were very lovely, caring, and had tons of support from their entire family. After the first meeting we saw each other here and there, met for dinner, e-mailed, and just got to know each other a little bit. By the time I was eight months I was counting down the days until I got to see the baby inside of me. I was almost regretting every moment because the baby wouldn't be mine to keep. I still didn't know the baby's sex, so names were up in the air, but I still helped with, and had input on, the baby's name. After many doctor's visits, it was finally decided I would be induced.

> *The day I got back home from the hospital I broke down in tears, missing my little girl so much and not knowing what to do.*

On a Monday morning I arrived at the hospital at 6:30 a.m. I called the prospective adoptive parents and told them they could come down to the hospital. After 22 hours of labor, 30 minutes of pushing, and one epidural, my daughter, Jane Madison Kay was born. I couldn't help but cry at the sight of her on top of my tummy. I thought it was a miracle. I had given birth!

I lay in bed as I watched her adoptive mom and dad marvel at her with tears in their eyes. For the rest of the time in the delivery room it was mostly silent. I was finally transferred to my room. Everyone was tired from a restless night, so they decided to go home, get showers, then come back to see me. I was sort of grateful because I knew this would be my first alone time with my new daughter, and I was excited to be able to sit there and stare at her with no one in the room.

There wasn't much of anything on my mind; I was just soaking up my newfound reality that I had just brought a baby girl into this world. I fed her, changed her, and I kissed her. I just loved her entire being. I knew it wouldn't be long until she was leaving in their arms and not mine. At the end of the next day it was time for the both of us to go to our separate homes, her to hers without me, and me to mine without her.

It was sad, but at the same time it was happy. Even though I was losing a daughter, two other people, and two separate families were gaining her. We waited for the nurse to come escort us to the nursery to get her security tag taken off. During that time her new adoptive mother and father presented me with a skinny white box. I knew it was going to be something entirely special.

I opened it with tear-filled eyes and I saw it was a silver locket. I opened the locket and inside was a picture of Janie on the left, which they had taken just after she was born, and a picture of me on the right. I was trying to keep it together as best I could, not letting a tear fall for anyone to see. It was a much sadder moment than I had realized. At this point I still didn't know what my true feelings about adoption were, but I soon began to find out.

The day I got back home from the hospital I broke down in tears, missing my little girl so much and not knowing what to do. I just cried. There were so many feelings I was hit with all at once. After much thought and conversation with my mom, I decided I wanted her back. I would call her new parents the next morning to tell them so. It was so hard to pick up the phone and tell someone that I cared about so much I was going to take their new daughter away from them, but I just couldn't bear the hurt I felt. I was completely overwhelmed.

As soon as I finished the phone call I went out and bought all the necessities in preparation for my daughter coming home. The drive to pick her up was a silent one, with lots of feelings running through my head. When I picked her up, the adoptive parents were just as sad as I had been when I had left her. They were hardly able to keep the tears back. In fact, everyone was crying.

All I could think about was I wasn't going to hurt anymore because I had my baby with me. The late night and middle of the night feedings came easy to me, as well as the diaper and outfit changes. My maternal instinct was totally in tune. I loved having her home. However, the day after I got her home I started thinking about her future, and about how there was no way I would be able to provide for her the way a proper family could.

It wasn't fair to her. If I kept her I would have to live dollar-by-dollar. With her prospective adoptive family she would be able to have everything she needed and much more. It wasn't fair to keep her from what she truly deserved. So yet again I changed my mind and decided to talk to them to see if they would consider going through with the adoption. After some talk I found out even though

Because of everything I had been going through, I decided to talk to a counselor to help me better understand my situation.

they were angry, they still loved Janie and still loved me and still wanted her in their family. So about two hours after I made the phone call they drove over to my house to pick her up.

It was a hard goodbye, yet again, but it still didn't feel final or complete. The day after she was gone was okay, and the day after that was all right too. But on the night of the second day, I broke down and almost couldn't stop myself from crying because I was so enwrapped in the sadness of my baby being gone. My heart hurting—I mean literally hurting—was unbearable. I needed her back. So, for what I thought was the last time, I contacted them and, lots of words later, both painful and truthful, I told them I wanted her back. At this point they were both very angry and when I went to pick her up the next day it was in total silence. Not many words were spoken as I gathered her stuff and put it in the car. This was the most confusing time that I had ever felt in my entire life.

I didn't know what to do. I kept going with what my heart felt, and I had no one to talk to. The entire time what mattered most was what was best for her. In my head I didn't know what was best: I just wanted her to have the world. Because of everything I had been going through, I decided to talk to a counselor to help me better understand my situation. Immediately after I got her back I had thoughts again of sadness and confusion. I contacted a local adoption agency that had social workers and counselors available. Even though I loved her more than life itself I knew she wouldn't have the best life with me. During my meeting with the counselor we concluded I should try to contact the prospective adoptive parents and ask them how they felt about Janie and the adoption.

After many words, thoughts, questions, and feelings, it was determined I was going to keep Janie until we went to court. Then I would bring her to court and when I signed my papers they would take her home. The morning of court was peaceful and I knew this would be the last time I would be getting her dressed, changed, and fed. The entire time I had felt so horrible about switching her back and forth. It just wasn't right. By the time we got to the courthouse, I truly believed I was ready to hand my child over to someone else because I knew this wasn't the end of my involvement. I knew the way our adoption was designed I would be able to continue being an integral part of her life, even though she would be calling someone else mommy.

I love her more than life itself, and I love them for giving her a life I couldn't. Even though she's two months old, I still receive counseling every week. I talk to birthmothers learning more and more everyday about how I can grieve the loss of my child, because that's really how it is. I do need to grieve for her. I heard a birthmother once say, "I will ALWAYS be her mother but they ARE her parents." I don't regret my decision, because I chose something wonderful for her, and I know she will be loved.

My view of the world, of myself, and of other people is completely different now. I'm not the same person I was before Janie was born, and the world just doesn't seem the same. It's brighter, I'm brighter! I now have a daughter. Even though she is not with me she is in my heart and in my life, forever. I can now separate what is important and worth my time from what is not. I cherish everyday I'm alive knowing I have a daughter out there I need to make proud and do good by. I just live my life loving her and it will always stay that way.

A letter to my Janie:

> I can't begin to explain to you how the birth of you made me feel. Confused, happy, joyful, sad, overwhelmed with love, those are just a few choice words. I could not provide for you the way you deserved, so I chose a better life for you. Two loving parents, mother and father, a big brother, and an enormously loving extended family. What more could you ask for? There is one thing I could ask for, it's that I wish I could have kept you, that I could have raised you, but it wasn't possible, and you only deserve the best. There is no doubt in my mind you will be the most loved baby girl ever, by both me and your new family. I'm still here, and I'll never leave. I love you, and I think of you everyday!

> Love Always and Forever...
> Your Birthmother,
> Heather

The Choices We Make

by Michelle Wellwood

My name is Michelle Wellwood and I am a birthmom who recently began working for American Adoptions. I placed my son in February 1998 and am truly grateful to all the people who helped me with my adoption plan. I really love sharing my story and being able to impact all of the wonderful people who are dedicated to making the lives of birthparents, adoptive families, and the child as successful and happy as possible.

First of all, I want to say I am very confident in my decision to place my son with his adoptive family and have had an unbelievably positive experience.

I met my baby's birthfather, Shawn, when I was a sophomore in high school. He would always sit right next to me. We dated less than a year. There were many times throughout our relationship when I really thought we were meant for each other. Things were working out perfectly and I thought I was in a relationship that would never end. However, things aren't always that easy. We began fighting constantly and our relationship soon changed to a very unhealthy and unstable situation. We continued dating but after many rough nights of arguing and jealousy, Shawn decided he did not want to be with me anymore.

In September, I realized something was seriously wrong. I walked up the stairs to go to my room and get ready for bed and noticed I was short of breath and swollen underneath my ribs. When I showed my parents they immediately rushed me to the emergency room thinking I had a tumor. The idea that I could be pregnant never crossed anyone's mind. But after an examination in the emergency room I was forced to face reality. I was a 17-year-old varsity volleyball and basketball player and three months pregnant. I thought to myself, "How could this be happening to me?" Every night I would just go home and cry wondering how I could have been so stupid.

I couldn't provide him with everything so I found a family that could give him everything I wished I could have given.

Due to the difficulties I was having with the choices I was faced with, my family pursued a counseling service. After attending two sessions my self-esteem increased greatly and I could think clearly and not be so frightened of my mistake. I want to clarify that my little boy is not a mistake, but the decision to have sex was a mistake.

I gathered my thoughts and knew what I had to do. Adoption was the only option for me. I love little kids, but I knew I was not financially or mentally prepared to raise a child on my own.

My mom mentioned she had a close friend who had adopted a little girl about a year ago. Coincidently, she had called my mom the week before and asked if my mom knew of anyone who was pregnant and thinking about adoption, because they wanted to adopt again. They didn't want their little girl to be an only child. I called the family and immediately they were thrilled. I actually think the husband was crying. In his eyes I had made his dream come true. That was the best feeling. I couldn't believe I was making a couple so happy, while at the same time my pregnancy seemed like such a bad situation.

The decision was made. The adoptive parents were chosen. I knew how they raised their child and how they would raise my little boy. Our families had similar lifestyles and he would have the same opportunities growing up I had, and more than likely, more than I had. They were Catholic just as I was and had similar beliefs and values. This was something that was very important to me.

I met with the adoptive parents to discuss the situation and also to reassure them my mind had been made up and I was going to go through with the adoption. I told Shawn about my decision. He agreed with me that it was the best thing to do. He was not ready to help me raise a child and therefore it just reinforced the fact that if I were to keep the baby he would not have a father figure in his life. My parents volunteered to help raise my child, but it was my fault I was pregnant, not theirs. I was willing to do what I had to in order to do what was right for my child and make the best out of the situation I had placed myself in. The life and future of my child was important to me and he deserved the best. I couldn't provide him with everything, so I found a family that could give him everything I wished I could have given.

I began growing very quickly and in my fifth month had to begin wearing stretch pants. My monthly check-ups continued to be positive and the doctor said, "Even though you haven't gained that much weight the baby seems very healthy." It was also in the fifth month when I began the meetings to get the papers arranged and the legalities figured out for the adoption. It was amazing to me how much paperwork goes along with the adoption process. However, I was prepared to follow through with my decision no matter what it took.

My due date was March 18, 1998, and the closer the date came the more nervous I was. I have a journal that I wrote in throughout my pregnancy, from the first day I learned my little boy was inside of me until the present time. This is something I would definitely recommend to any birthmom to help with the healing process. It is something I like to reflect on and add new entries to when new things happen in my life. I want my little boy to know what I was doing when he was growing up.

Another surprise came on the evening of February 23, 1998. As I sat in classes all day long these sharp pains filled my entire body. As the day went on they occurred more often, but obviously since I did not know what contractions felt like I did not assume I was going into labor. After all, the baby was not due for another three weeks. When I arrived home I knew something was happening. I told my mom when she got home I had been having pains all day and she said, "Well it might be time." So my mom, my dad, and I went to the hospital. I was definitely ready. However, I was also very nervous because I was supposed to have three weeks left. I knew he would be a premature baby and just wanted him to be healthy. I was praying everything would go well.

When we arrived at the hospital I was put in a room, where eight hours later I would deliver my beautiful baby boy. Bradley Tyson was born February 24, 1998, at 2:50 a.m. When they first handed Bradley to me all I could do was cry knowing the next 48 hours would be the last I would get to spend with him before he would leave with his new family. The next two days our room was filled with friends and family. Shawn was there and we spent all the time we could with Bradley. Within the next few hours the adoptive parents arrived. They lived in another state so they had to drive some distance to meet us at the hospital and meet their adoptive son.

They were so excited yet tears just filled my eyes. They were tears of joy and also of pain. I was upset because here I had this little child inside of me for eight months, we had bonded and I had grown to love him more than I had loved anything in the entire world, and I knew I was going to have to say goodbye. I had to face reality. It was a decision I made knowing it would be the most difficult thing I was ever going to have to do, yet it was the best thing for Bradley. He would grow up having everything I only wish I could have given him. Although we could have given him love, there would have been no stability. Shawn and I had no future together besides our love for Bradley, and with the adoptive parents he would be able to grow up playing all the sports and doing everything little boys love to do.

Finally the time had come to leave the hospital and go home. Sometimes arrangements can be made for the birthparents to stay with the baby for a week or so, but in our situation it would have been too difficult. I was already attached to my little boy and did not want the process to be any harder than it was already going to be. The attorney arrived shortly after. As soon as the legal papers were signed, stating Shawn and I relinquished our rights to the adoptive parents, they were called and came over to pick up their new little baby boy. They chose to change his name to Ryan, which was okay with Shawn and me. After all, it would be the name he would have and that they would call him for the rest of his life.

It was most helpful to me when I had someone to talk to who would just listen to me without making any judgments or conclusions about who I was as a person.

I was very confident with the adoptive parents I had chosen for my son and therefore it was comforting to have them by my side. It was also difficult at the same time because I knew my life would never be the same again. I couldn't believe everything was over. I handed my 5 pound, 15 ounce little boy to the adoptive mom and we all cried and hugged. They thanked Shawn and me continuously and promised to always keep in touch and send pictures and letters as often as possible. It was the hardest thing I ever had to do, but at the same time I knew it was the right thing for me to do. In my heart he will always be my little boy and my son, even if someone else is raising him. I never knew it was possible to love someone so much. As they walked out the door I just stood motionless and watched as they drove out of sight. All I could do was whisper, "Goodbye, I will always love you."

The next few months and years have all gone by so fast and Bradley, now known as Ryan, is always with me in my heart. I have kept in touch with the family and they have kept their promise to send pictures and letters with updates of all the activities he is involved in. He is six years old now, going to first grade this year, and is involved in many different activities. He plays basketball, baseball, soccer, and even has tried wrestling. He also had the opportunity to go on a jet ski and on the boat at his parent's lake house. He has all these opportunities because of adoption. If I were to have made the decision to try and raise him he would not be able to have all the wonderful opportunities he has been able to experience.

It has been a very successful adoption and even though I do miss him a lot, I have all the support I could possibly ask for. Seeing his smiling face in the pictures makes all my fears and doubts go away. I want to encourage people to always do what is right for them and understand that adoption is a positive alternative. I was very fortunate to have my son's adoption go through so smoothly, but I believe it was because of the people that I encountered along the way and all the support I received through my counselor, school, friends, and family. It is because of them I am able to talk to others about adoption and share my story with so many wonderful people in the adoption community. I am confident I will one day get to meet Ryan again. I continue to write in my journal so when that day comes, he will know every moment we were apart I loved him and was waiting for the moment when we would be together again! The adoptive family and I have a wonderful relationship. I am grateful to them every day for giving their son and my little boy everything in life I had always dreamed of giving to him.

It was most helpful to me when I had someone to talk to who would just listen to me without making any judgments or conclusions about who I was as a person. Adoption is about what is in the best interest of the child, and without adoption many children would not have the wonderful lives they have today. I encourage anyone out there who is facing the challenge of an unplanned pregnancy and does not know what to do to consider adoption—after all, it is the best gift you can give your child when you are not capable of parenting at that time. I wish all birthmothers luck along their journey and hope they always realize there are other birthmothers, like myself, out there who have been in their shoes. Remember: you are not alone!

I dedicate this story and the opportunity to share my story to my little boy Ryan. He has been such an inspiration to me and I would not be where I am today without him by my side. He motivates me to be a better person and always strive for more. Ryan, I will love you always and forever!

The Power Of Choice

by Lynn Skogs

I grew up in a small town in the Midwest. I became aware of adoption when I found out I was pregnant at age 17. After placing my birthdaughter in an open adoption, I went to the College of St. Benedict in St. Joseph, Minnesota, majored in Social Work, and planned on working in the adoption field. I am currently living near Fairbanks, Alaska, and continue to educate people about openness in adoption. My birthdaughter, her family, and I have built a strong relationship and see each other as often as we can.

I'm sitting on the floor of my tiny one room cabin, sort of in the living room, but sort of in the kitchen. I kind of have to go to the bathroom, but don't really feel like going to the outhouse. I know most people wouldn't want to live like this, but I'm rather fond of my choice. I love my cute little cabin nestled in the woods.

The phone rings. (Yeah, I know what you're thinking; a phone, but no running water!) I answer. There is a short pause, and then an excited nine-year-old voice squeals, "I get to come visit you at your house in Alaska! My mom and dad bought me a plane ticket for my birthday!" As we talked about her birthday party and the other gifts she got, it occurred to me this was the first time I had spoken to Cora on her birthday since the day I gave birth to her.

I was 17 when I got pregnant. It was the summer before my senior year. I expected to spend my last year in high school playing basketball, being a TA for the photo/video class, and visiting colleges. Instead, I was focusing on rethinking my entire future, getting notes from my mom to go to prenatal doctor appointments, and dodging small town, high-school gossip. While my carefree classmates were skipping school to go to the Dairy Queen, I gravitated toward the parenting section of my school library. Somehow, I stumbled upon a book on adoption and read a bit about "the new trend toward openness." With that one line as a scrap of hope to hold onto, I decided if I could know where my baby was and how she was doing, adoption might be right for me.

It was hard to see her and know that I missed her first smile, her first steps, and the first time she said "Mama."

As the weeks passed, I figured out exactly what I wanted for my adoption plan, but didn't tell anyone. At seven months along, only my family knew I was pregnant and only I knew I was considering adoption. Then, at one of my prenatal appointments, a social worker asked whether I was planning on breastfeeding or bottle feeding. I looked at her blankly and said, "I don't think I'm going to feed my baby." Her face went white, her jaw dropped and I realized what I had just said. I stammered a little as I clarified, I was thinking of placing my babyfor adoption.

A few weeks later, my boyfriend and I were anxiously awaiting the arrival of the prospective adoptive parents we were going to interview. We spent two-and-a-half hours together and I knew that these people were meant to raise my baby. They were everything I was looking for: open-minded, talented, interesting, stable, and ready for children. Plus, the immediate connection we had was just amazing. They were exactly who I was hoping to find.

During the weeks before the baby was born, we met a few more times to talk about how much openness we wanted. We decided to go for it all. We exchanged full names, addresses, and phone numbers and then just did what felt right. Even though I was heartbroken even thinking about leaving the hospital without my tiny, perfect, beautiful baby, seeing how happy her parents were and knowing I would see her in less than a month gave me peace.

And so, that's how it went. It was tough, especially that first year. But I started college, became really involved with a couple of volunteer programs, and started to really like my life again. Every once in a while I would get some pictures in the mail or a phone call or I would go for a weekend visit. People would ask why I went to see her and then say they thought seeing her would make it much harder. It was hard to see her and know that I missed her first smile, her first steps, and the first time she said "Mama." At the same time, it was pretty amazing for me the first time she smiled at me, the first time she climbed onto my lap and the first time she called me "birt-mudder."

While she was accomplishing all of these firsts, I was doing some growing of my own. I was a successful college student and earned my degree when Cora was four years old. I spent the year she was five doing volunteer work. When she was six, I moved to Alaska and swore I would find a way to see her no less than once a year, even though I would be 3,000 miles away. So now I'm racking up the frequent-flier miles and joke with her parents that we spend more time together now than when I lived only 100 miles away.

Just last year we had our longest separation—the eleven months I was living abroad. The first thing Cora said when I got there was, "You were gone too long. I missed you too much." I agreed, and reassured her our next visit was only three months away.

So that brings me to today. I flew back to Alaska a couple of weeks ago. I've been settling back into cabin life, reconnecting with friends, and reacquainting myself with my town. Now, though, I'm looking around with the eyes of a nine-year-old. What should my birthdaughter and I do when she visits me in my neck of the woods? Although I have been able to see the life I chose for the little tiny baby I brought into the world, this will be the first chance she will have to see the life I have chosen for me.

A Pregnant Teen's Choice

by Lisa Scheen

My name is Lisa and my childhood dream wasn't to become a pregnant teenage statistic, though that is exactly what happened. I was faced with a choice: do I keep my child and raise him in a one-parent home, possibly aided by state assistance programs and working in low end jobs because I hadn't graduated high school— or do I put aside my own wants and needs, put my child first, and choose a future for him which I was unable to provide? I chose the latter and my mistake became God's miracle.

Where do I start? At 17, I thought I knew everything. I was indestructible and had the world under my feet. I also wanted to fit in with the friends I was hanging out with.

Though I was raised in church my entire life and taught right from wrong and knew for every action there was a consequence, I rebelled against all I knew. I was young and wanted to get out and live it up for a while. And I did, for three whole months. I wanted so desperately to fit in, I began doing things I knew nothing about.

That's when I met the birthfather, while I was out there living it up. You've heard the old saying, "It just happened." Well that's what happened. One time. That's all. I ended up pregnant.

Suddenly, my world was jerked out from under my feet and I hit the world of reality hard and fast. Not only did I lose my self-respect, but all my "friends" disappeared into the night.

I didn't tell my mom. I didn't get the chance before my aunt (who I had told) called to see how she was taking the news. My mom was waiting on the front porch. I remember her not yelling at me, only talking softly and saying that together we would work this out. I think she might have been in shock. My dad, on the other hand, simply didn't talk for two weeks. Then one day he just acted like nothing had ever happened. My family stood beside me through it all. I could not have had a better support group.

I did a lot of thinking and praying about what to do during the first two months of my pregnancy. Of course, what else is there to do when you're so sick you can't get out of bed? The birthfather wanted nothing to do with me or the pregnancy, so he joined the army and told no one where he was stationed. Not surprising.

The more I thought about it, the more I knew I wanted to choose adoption. Now, my only choice was where would I go? Would I stay at home? Would I go stay somewhere? I wanted out of that town. So we looked and called and searched until I found The Gladney Center here in Texas. I still needed and wanted to be close to my family. So, I moved to Fort Worth. I was almost three months pregnant when I arrived there in October.

For the first time, I met others who were in the same situation I was in and I knew I wasn't going to be judged. Each of us was facing the same life changing decisions and we were able to lean on each other during the hard times. I worked on getting my GED (general equivalency diploma) while I was there. Having gone to private Christian schools for so long getting my GED was easier for me than going to public school. I also worked for and earned my CNA (certified nurse's aide) license.

We had to go through many difficult procedures in order to

find the father. Since he had gone into the army and didn't tell me, it was hard to find him. All the papers sent to him were returned by his family unsigned. The legal team sent those papers straight to the army and within two weeks they were sent back signed, sealed, and notarized. That army doesn't mess around.

The doctors were sure I was having a girl. And you know, they're never wrong! My mom asked if she could pick out a name for her first granddaughter. She named her Kaydawn Marie. Kay is my mom's middle name, Dawn is my middle name, and Marie is my grandmother's middle name. I knew the adoptive parents wouldn't keep it but we wanted something special for her.

When I had less than eight weeks left in my pregnancy, I started to look for adoptive parents for my little girl. I was able to choose things like religion and other things I wanted the parents to have. The Gladney Center found three families for me to choose from and all had pictures with their letters. One of the pictures accidentally fell on the floor. With that quick glimpse, I knew they were the ones I wanted but I couldn't just choose them based on a picture alone. In fact, I really wasn't supposed to see the pictures until after I had chosen. I read all the letters and asked if I could think about it. Later, after much prayer, I chose the couple I wanted. I saw the pictures and it was them! In my heart, I knew they were the ones.

On Good Friday, the 17th, my mom drove up to be with me, hoping I would have the baby while she was there, as I was due on April 18. The 18th came and went and no baby. My mom was going to have to leave on Sunday. But as luck would have it, I went into labor at about 1:30 in the morning. I was so sick and at 1:55 p.m. on Easter Sunday, I had my baby. I was sure surprised when the doctor asked if I wanted to hold my SON. A boy! Not a girl like we had thought. I guess they were wrong after all!

I won't ever forget the day he was born. Nor will I forget when the doctor laid him in my arms. He was beautiful. They even let my mom in, though they weren't supposed to. He was the most precious thing I had ever held. I couldn't believe he was part of me. As I lay there holding him, I remember telling my mom that while his parents were eating Easter dinner I was having their baby. I knew they would be happy to know they had an Easter bunny. It's strange the things you think and say at a time like that.

I told him how special he was, not only because he was born on Easter but because he was the luckiest little baby in the world. He was going to his new home very soon and he would love it. I told him he was going to have a big brother to teach him to play football, and a daddy to take him fishing and a mommy—a very special mommy, who would love him and care for him and wipe away the tears and who would pick him up when he fell.

Today's society often tries to make birthmothers look bad . . . What they don't understand is that it's because we loved them so much that we let them go.

I had one week to spend with him. One week to sit and think about the choice I had to make that would forever be with me. One week to last me a lifetime. It was a bittersweet seven days. The last day was the hardest. After I signed the papers, my parents and I were able to see him one last time. I didn't spend long there that day. You would think I would have but I couldn't. I told him how much I loved him and how I would always be a part of him but that his new parents needed him. I think he knew we were saying goodbye. I kissed him then handed him to the nurse and he began to cry. And so did I. I left that room with a piece of my heart missing. I left a part of myself there that day, yet I knew I was doing the right thing. I had no questions, just a shattered heart.

I know that in a lot of people's eyes I was just a statistic, just another teenage pregnancy, but to my son's parents I am what made their family complete. I made a family whole. Without me and my love for my son, they could not have the wonderful family they have.

I have received some pictures through the years and four letters from his mom. The one I liked the most was the one in which she told me she knew one day the two pieces of the necklace would come together and be made one. (I bought a necklace for us to share. I kept one half and I gave the other to him.) I love him with my whole being and I know one day the necklace will be put together.

I was very lucky in that I had a family who supported me and let me make my own choices. So many girls out there don't and I think it's very unfair to them. Yes, at 17, I made choices that had serious consequences, but I learned from them and grew from them. I definitely was not the same girl going home that I was when I left.

Today's society often tries to make birthmothers look bad as if we were being selfish and didn't love our children enough to care for them and raise them. What they don't understand is that it's because we loved them so much that we let them go. I loved my son enough that I knew I had to let him go.

There used to be a commercial on TV that said, "Life. What a beautiful choice." Yes, it is.

It's now 12 years later, I am married to a wonderful man who knew all about my son from the moment we met, and has been supportive of me ever since. God has blessed us with three daughters. Kaydawn (I did say my mom could name the first granddaughter!) and my double blessings, Kaelyn and Kylie.

Open Adoption

No Whispering Needed

"I believe it is better to tell the truth than a lie.
I believe it is better to be free than a slave.
And I believe it is better to know than to be ignorant."

- H.L. Mencken

No Secrets, No Lies

by Stacy Christie-Cook

I am a proud mom and wife living in suburban Atlanta, Georgia. Besides working full-time, going to school part-time, "mom"-ing and "wife"-ing, I enjoy reading, movies, knitting, blogging, and painting. We are in a fully open adoption with our daughter's birthfamily and wouldn't have it any other way.

I am my daughter's mom, but I am not her only mother. I am an adoptive mother. My daughter, Molly, is only two now, so she doesn't understand there was another mother before me—her birthmother, Helaine.

Our adoption is what's known as a private, identified adoption. When Helaine and Douglas, Molly's birthparents, made their decision, they contacted my cousin, who is an adoptive mother in a fully open adoption. They asked for the name of her attorney, who was in another state. She not only gave them an attorney, she gave them adoptive parents! She immediately thought of my husband and me and called us that night.

We met Helaine and Douglas in November 2001. I liked them. I liked their sons. I couldn't help but stare at the boys, wondering if this baby would look like them, if she or he would have that one's smile or the other one's eyes.

Helaine and I share a family connection of the most complicated kind. My step-grandmother's great-nephew's second wife is Helaine's mother. Helaine was 19 when we met. She and Douglas, the baby's father, were already parenting two little boys. They knew they couldn't parent another child. By the time we met, their decision was made. I asked Helaine many times if she was sure about this; in fact, I asked her so many times she asked me if I had changed my mind. When I said "no," she told me to quit asking her. So I did.

At first Helaine and Douglas thought they wanted a closed adoption. By definition, since we all knew each other's last names, it was already too late for that. But they thought they wouldn't want to spend a lot of time with the baby in the hospital and they would only want letters and pictures once a year. Surprisingly, I was the one who wanted more.

Before Molly's placement, I didn't know what open adoption would really entail. Sure, I'd read Jana Wolffe's *Secret Thoughts of an Adoptive Mother*. I'd had long conversations with my cousin. I thought I was ready for it. I had written in the calendar every three months "send pictures to Helaine." I thought maybe we'd get together for friendly trips to Disney World every other year. I thought I'd handle this like a business transaction, friendly yet appropriately distant.

> *When we did speak, I never knew what to say. What do you say to the person who has forever altered your life?*

Nobody told me, though, what it would be like to spend a week with Molly's birthfamily before her birth. Nobody could have explained I'd start to fall in love with Helaine's boys, Molly's brothers, or that I'd feel a pull in my heart to see one's crooked smile, to get a hug from the other.

Nobody told me what it would be like to see my daughter enter the world. The nurse who was supposed to hold Helaine's leg was mysteriously absent when it came time for her to push, so I stepped in. I wanted to run away. Her pain was too much, the responsibility was too big, and my shoulders were too small. Nobody told me that four seconds after Molly was born, Helaine would turn to me and say "Congratulations," and I would cry into her hair with gratitude, awe, and grief. I had no idea that moment would bond Helaine and I in a way I can't describe to anyone else.

Nobody told me that no matter how many diapers you've changed in your life, when you change your child's first diaper with the nurse and the baby's birthmother looking on, you will look like you're trying to perform brain surgery with salad tongs.

Nobody told me watching Helaine and Douglas and their sons leave the hospital would have me sobbing on Helaine's unmade hospital bed while holding Molly in my arms. I couldn't have imagined the feelings of sadness I would experience at what was supposed to be one of the happiest moments of my life. I didn't know the hot, bitter tears that were streaming down my face were changing everything in my heart. I couldn't have anticipated the grief I would feel on Helaine's behalf.

I was shocked to find that mere days after we returned home, baby in arms, I wanted to talk to Helaine. I wanted to tell her I stared at Molly for hours on end. I wanted her to know Molly developed colic. As it turns out, I was just like every other first-time mom, completely obsessed with every sigh and burp this alarmingly beautiful creature could produce. I knew there was only one other person in the world who would listen patiently as I recounted every breath she'd drawn.

When we did speak, I never knew what to say. What do you say to the person who has forever altered your life? What do you say to the person who has just given you part of her soul? "Thanks.

You're a peach!" All I could say was, "We love her. We love her. We love her so much."

Nobody told me how I would struggle with the other people in our lives. I had no idea there would only be one person who could support the openness in our adoption—my cousin, who's been there and done that. I found myself defending my parenting choices over and over, trying to explain to people what I knew to be true in my heart: we were doing the right thing. While other new parents have to explain to strangers why their child's shoes weren't on, or why they'd chosen to give the bottle over the breast, I was defending to the people nearest and dearest to me my right to send e-mail photos and plan visits.

I couldn't have imagined the people I counted on most in the world would devastate me, phone call after phone call, with their disapproving silences and snide comments when I would excitedly recount my latest conversation with Helaine. I couldn't have imagined I would have to defend her, over and over. I thought we, as a society, were beyond having to cast someone as the saint and someone as the sinner. I was wrong.

We had our first visit not long after Molly's first birthday. We had the anticipated trip to Disney World, which, in retrospect, was a rookie parent mistake. Going to Disney World on a hot day with a three, two, and one-year-old was disastrous. As it turns out, we had a better time just sitting on my brother's couch, watching the kids interact.

Nobody told me how it would feel to watch my reserved, almost shy daughter blossom when she was with her brothers. As nerve-wracking as that first visit was, I loved seeing Helaine's face when Molly laughed. And I really wished somebody could have mentioned that the visits would get easier. That I would look forward to them like I look forward to visits from my favorite far-away relatives.

Nobody told me how complicated my emotions would be. I didn't know there would be raw jealousy at the knowledge that no matter how great a mom I am, I will never be able to claim this child came from me. I didn't know I would worry about Molly's brothers, and miss them when I couldn't see them.

Finally, I never knew I would love Helaine. You see, I bought into the movie-of-the-week mentality that says birthmothers are dangerous, drug-addicted psychos. Until I adopted Molly, I had no idea what it might feel like to not know your heritage, to not know where you get your eyes, or your talents, or your temperament. Now that I'm her mom, I don't ever want her to have those questions. I want her to see she has her father's eyes, her brother's dimples, and her mother's stubbornness and quirky sense of humor. Now that I've been her mom for two years, I know nothing can take that title from me. Her birthfamily is her roots, and she must know where she came from if she's ever to know where she's going.

But if they are her roots, we are her wings. It is our responsibility to do the very best job we can in raising her, to love her passionately, to teach her all the most important lessons in life. In the end, that is what Helaine and Douglas charged us with; parenting Molly to the best of our ability when they could not. And it is the best way I can think of to honor their decision.

A New Friend

by Julie Branigan

> *My husband, Steve, and I have been married for seven years and live in Missouri. We both work for the state government. We have three dogs, and a cat named KC. After trying to start a family of our own for two years and after one miscarriage, we decided to start our family through adoption.*

Steve and I have been married six years. We began trying to start a family in the summer of 1999. At the end of July 1999, I was pregnant. Steve couldn't quite believe it. He too got teary eyed and was very excited. I was filled with wonderful daydreams of being a mommy and seeing my baby in just nine months. We immediately decorated a room for the baby. I sent out an e-mail to all my co-workers, friends, and family members announcing the joyous news. Three days later I had a miscarriage. I was devastated. Steve put on a brave face for me even though all he wanted to do was cry. For months afterwards, every time someone at work announced their pregnancy I would cry. I'd watch a TV commercial for some baby product and cry. Every time I would go into the decorated baby room, I was reminded of the miscarriage. The hope that each month would be the month I would be pregnant took a tremendous toll on me. The disappointment was made worse after seeking fertility treatments. All it did was heighten my anxieties and feelings of inadequacies since we had no further success at getting pregnant.

I was at my wit's end. It affected my job performance, my friendships, and my relationship with Steve. By December 2001, our options were to take the next step in fertility treatments such as in vitro fertilization (IVF) or investigate adoption. Adoption was a relatively easy decision for us because one of Steve's brothers and other extended family members were adopted. In addition, several co-workers shared with us their own adoption experiences. What helped the most with deciding to adopt was the birth of my niece, Alexis. I had so much love for her, I knew I could just take her home with me and love her as much as I would love my own daughter. Since my sister wouldn't give me her daughter (smile), I knew adoption was a good choice for me. Steve felt the same way.

After researching various adoption agencies, we chose ours, American Adoptions, because we liked the fact that they have an Internet website where birthmothers could research parent profiles. In addition, we liked how they provided 24 hour counseling to birthmothers. We turned in our paperwork in August. In late September, our home study was completed.

Several months went by with no call from the agency. During this wait, I created adoption flyers and mailed them to our local churches, colleges, and various doctor's offices throughout the state. This wait was not as bad as the month to month disappointment trying to get pregnant. But it was nerve wracking in the sense every time the phone rang we would think, "Is this THE call?" The one in which we're told there's a baby for us?

We also read several books on all aspects of adoption. One suggested keeping a journal to help deal with the emotions of adoption and to document the adoption journey. So I started writing down my thoughts, experiences, and feelings. Soon the journal became one long letter to my future baby letting him/her know how much he/she was wanted and anticipated. The journal also became a tool to help me vent my emotions and anxieties. Every now and then I like to read what I was thinking and feeling. I think it will be a nice gift to give to my child.

One night while watching the Hallmark Channel's "Adoption" television series, we learned about a website called adoption.com (www.parentprofiles.com). The birthmother selected the adoptive parents through this website. We decided to post our parent profile there and by the end of the month we had three birthmothers contact us via e-mail. We told all three birthmothers to contact our agency for further information. We were worried about being scammed by people whose only intent was to get money from us and not follow through. So by contacting the agency, we felt this would legitimize the birthmother's intent to place her child. Our parent profile listed my cell phone number. Only one birthmother, Jenee', took the initiative to call. We talked for 45 minutes. The whole time my heart was in my throat as I was afraid I would say something to dissuade her from further considering us as parents of her child.

A few days later, American Adoptions contacted us indicating we had to make a decision as to which birthmother we wanted to exclusively work with. All three had contacted them indicating their interest in us as adoptive parents. Of all the birthmothers, I felt an instant connection with Jenee'. We seemed to have a lot in common: we devoted our whole heart into everything we did, we valued honesty in relationships, and we tried to make those around us feel appreciated, loved, and cared for. My impression of Jenee' was that she was a very self-confident and creative individual, very friendly, spontaneous, and a happy person. Steve also liked Jenee' because she wrote such a thoughtful, well-written introduction e-mail and the fact that she was going to college and had goals. I was looking forward to communicating with Jenee' and beginning our adoption journey together.

We arranged to meet with Jenee'. She lived and attended college in Warrensburg, Missouri. We met her and her best friend, Deanna, at a restaurant there. When we arrived, Jenee' immediately walked up to greet and hug us. Her friendly personality and warm greeting broke the ice and lessened our nervousness. After our meal, we went outside and took pictures. The whole trip home we were excited but worried Jenee' would change her mind. When we arrived home, I immediately e-mailed Jenee'. The following is an excerpt from the e-mail I sent her:

> We really enjoyed meeting you and Deanna. I was worried our meeting might be awkward but instead it seemed like old friends catching up on news. I hope you felt the same way and that our meeting reassured you of our sincerity. I hope you don't have any doubts about us. I can assure you your baby will be loved and cherished wholeheartedly.
>
> Meeting you calmed some of our own anxieties. I can imagine how scary it is to make such an important decision as basically turning your child over to strangers. In turn, for us it is scary to take a leap of faith that you are 100% dedicated to the decision. You hear heartbreaking stories of adoptions not carried out. Getting to know you has made me start thinking about and dreaming about being a mother to your child, a child I haven't even met. Yet I love the baby so much already. It's hard to type when you're crying. Steve's hugging me trying to give me comfort. Becoming a mother means so very much to me.

Jenee' responded:

> . . . I am 100 % sure this is the right thing to do. I am also 100% sure there is neither a better couple nor family on the face of this earth to raise my child than you. Meeting you today was just absolutely amazing. I knew today would just seal the deal. I so enjoyed meeting you and cannot wait to see you again. I feel in my heart I have made the best decision and I know that is right.
>
> Julie, I know I am putting my child in a wonderful, loving, caring home, as well as making great new friends and learning along the way.
>
> I called and woke my parents to let them know about your very sincere e-mail. It brings happy tears to my eyes knowing I have two people like you to support me on this journey.

Since that first meeting we continued an almost daily e-mail correspondence and we met in person several more times. We even attended Lamaze classes together!

One of our most treasured moments together was Jenee's ultrasound appointment when we found out she was expecting a little girl. We all agreed on the name Nikayla Marie. Jenee's middle name is Marie.

Jenee' admitted to me how distressing this situation was for her. She expressed how much she loves kids but knows love isn't enough to provide the best life for her child. She just broke down and cried. Yet, even in her sorrow, she wanted to assure us we had nothing to worry about—she was firm with her decision.

As we got closer to Jenee's due date I increasingly realized I was having conflicting and various emotions. I was overjoyed at the thought of becoming a mother—but, at the same time, I felt guilty about how my joy might cause Jenee' grief. I was grateful and appreciative of our friendship, yet insecure and anxious I would do something to lose it. I was ecstatic Jenee' chose us, but felt unworthy. I was excited about the future and raising baby Nikayla, yet terrified I would fail Jenee's expectations on how she would want us to raise her daughter. I shared my insecurities and thoughts with Jenee' and she lovingly responded:

> Knowing how much we are alike I understand how you might be feeling guilty, however, I want you to be overjoyed. I am happy to give this gift of life to you. I am very grateful we have had the opportunity to get to know each other. Julie, our relationship is what is helping this experience be such a positive experience for me. There is no possible way you are unworthy. I chose you for a reason and that is because I know you are the best couple to raise our little girl. I know you guys will do a wonderful job and she will have a happy life. The reason I am so okay is because I know and feel we have created a relationship that will last a lifetime. One thing that helps this go so smoothly is we are so much alike and I love that.

On March 24, 2003, Jenee' was scheduled to have her labor induced. After 22 hours of labor, a lot of tears, exhaustion, and pain, Jenee' gave birth to a healthy, beautiful baby girl. Steve helped throughout the delivery, holding Jenee's leg up, counting, and cutting the umbilical cord. I got to take pictures and offer words of encouragement. While after-birth care procedures were being performed on Jenee', I held Nikayla and fed her the first bottle. My heart felt like it was going to burst from excitement, anxiety, love, awe, etc. We were so grateful Jenee' wanted us to experience every aspect of her pregnancy including the delivery of our daughter.

A few days later, we went to court to obtain temporary custody of Nikayla. The whole time my heart was caught in my throat as I worried about this part of the adoption process. The court experience was frightening because it felt like we were being interrogated and often had to reiterate that, "Yes! We understood what we were undertaking in the adoption of this baby." I was afraid the judge would see something in our home study that would have him decide to stop the adoption. All my worries were for naught. The judge happily gave us temporary custody. In Missouri, adoptions are not finalized until after six months of adoption post-placement visits and, at present, we have about five months to go. All the way home, Steve and I were in stunned disbelief. We must have called each other mommy and daddy 1,000 times that first day home. It's still sinking in we're parents, but there's no doubt in our hearts we love this little girl immeasurably.

The first month with our new daughter was such a surreal time for us. Steve and I felt like we were babysitting more than taking care of our own daughter. Jenee's birthday was April 22 and we invited her to have dinner with us. Almost a full month had passed since we had last seen each other. It would give her an opportunity to see her daughter again. I really wasn't sure what it would be like to have Jenee' see her. All I knew was I was excited to show her how well Nikayla was doing. This meeting went fine, like friends who hadn't seen each other for a while getting together. Jenee' told me what was new with her and I got to share stories of what it was like taking care of Nikayla. It was during this meeting I truly felt like a regular mom sharing stories of my daughter with a close friend.

Jenee' made me feel I had every right to consider myself Nikayla's mom. She would hold Nikayla but then say something like, "Well Nikaya, I better hand you over to your mom," meaning ME! It meant a lot to me to hear Jenee' refer to me as Nikayla's mom. I e-mailed Jenee' that evening asking her how she felt and telling her my thoughts. She, too, said she felt like a friend visiting her friend and new baby. She said she was excited to see us and enjoyed seeing how much we loved being parents. She felt good about being the person responsible for creating this new family. Ever since this visit, I no longer felt like I was just babysitting but that I was—am—Nikayla's mom.

Jenee' and I keep in touch via e-mail and the occasional phone call. I like writing and letting her know what is going on in our lives as much as I like hearing from her about how she is doing. There are times I want to be selfish and try to ignore the fact Nikayla isn't my biological daughter—ignore I'm not her only mother. But then I think of what a selfless act of giving Jenee' did in placing her daughter in my care. She opened her heart to us, gave us her trust, and gave us the greatest gift of all. The very least I can do is share our lives with her and show her throughout the years what a joy Nikayla is to us. It's our turn to be selfless not only in the care of Nikayla but in being caring towards Jenee'. By opening our hearts to Jenee' we've discovered a unique friendship.

For us, the adoption of Nikayla will not end our journey with Jenee' but will just be a new path we will all take together in one form or another. We don't know where this new path will take us; but with compassion, understanding, and love, we'll all end up with a beautiful expedition along the way.

You can read Jenee's story, "An Amazing Couple For My Baby," later in this chapter.

An Amazing Couple For My Baby

by Jenee' Zapatka

Unexpectedly becoming pregnant was a shock. I was a senior in college and was preparing for my future. I felt alone, confused, and ashamed. Julie and Steve made my adoption experience easier. They supported me, were open, and cared about me just as much as our baby. I was able to go through with my decision because I picked such a wonderful couple. I love them as if they were family.

I recently went through an amazing adoption experience. Adoption is a difficult decision. It goes much smoother when there is honesty and communication.

I chose an amazing couple, Julie and Steve, to raise my baby girl. After our first meeting we decided to make this a fully open adoption and to share everything. This turned out perfectly for all of us and I think if it is possible, an open adoption is the best way to go. I felt so much more comfortable in our open relationship.

Our adoption journey was filled with tons of e-mails, phone calls, and visits. We e-mailed each other at least five times per week. This helped me focus on my decision and encouraged me to stay strong for our baby. I knew I could share my concerns and feelings with them and they knew they could do the same with me. We respected each other and talked out everything on our minds.

We started our relationship asking one another what our fears, feelings, and expectations were for this adoption. We made a lot of our decisions together pending our baby's arrival. Julie and Steve are absolutely wonderful! They included me in the decision of our little girl's name. We went shopping together to choose outfits and necessities for our baby.

They wanted to get to know me as much as possible. They traveled to my town and met my sorority sisters, helped me with homework, met my family, and invited me to their family functions. I felt like I was truly a part of their lives and not just giving them a baby. Our visits were exciting and created very strong bonds between us. Our relationship was filled with lots of happy tears, laughter, and great conversation.

I wanted Julie and Steve to be as much a part of the pregnancy as possible because this was their baby. I invited them to all doctor appointments and Lamaze classes. They were in the delivery room when our little princess was born. They allowed me to see our little girl the entire weekend following her birth before heading home. They came back to town a month after our little girl was born to share my graduation as I received a Bachelor of Science in Photography. Following graduation, we took family portraits of the four of us and the three of them together.

We have discussed our future relationship. I receive monthly pictures of our little princess. She will know who I am and I will meet her when she is older. Julie and Steve keep me updated on how much she is growing and the new things she does almost weekly. I look forward to experiencing our relationship as the future unfolds.

You can read Julie and Steve's story "A New Friend," earlier in this chapter.

Our Two Open Adoptions

by Patricia Younce

We are a family blessed with five beautiful children. Matt and I were so lucky to have no trouble having our first two children naturally. Our boys are Christopher, 15; and Benjamin, 11. With my third pregnancy there were complications; however, the result was our lovely daughter, Mary Katherine, now nine.

Most families would be satisfied to stop at three children but there was a serious stirring in my heart I could not ignore. When I was single I wanted to adopt. I looked at adopting older children of school age because that could accommodate my schedule as a teacher.

God had a different plan. I met Matt and our family began quickly. My desire to adopt never went away and after the complications of my third pregnancy our family embraced adoption through the Independent Adoption Center (IAC).

I looked at many different ways to adopt and open adoption made the best sense. Matt wanted an infant and I knew adopting an infant who could always know his or her birthparents would be the easiest way for our child to grow up. I feel so strongly about its benefit for these children that I find myself talking about our two adopted children with many different people.

Rachel Nakia was born into our arms on the 10th of July 2001. Matt and I were with her at that moment, gave her a first bath, fed her, and I stayed in the hospital with Adriane, Rachel's birthmom. We were lucky to have IAC because the interstate adoption process was complicated. Due to the wonderful professional counseling we had, everything went very smoothly.

Adriane and her seven-year-old son traveled to Ohio with us and she terminated parental rights in our home state while staying at our house. We are proud to have an open, honest relationship with Adriane. Now that Rachel is three, we still talk to Adriane on the phone, write, send photos, and visit when we can.

Erik Mathhew came into our lives at three days old, born on the 28th of October 2002. He was a bit small but healthy. We were able to meet his birthparents at the hospital when we picked him up. It was a quick drive for us because the hospital was in our state.

I sent photos to Erik's birthfamily for several months before receiving a letter from them. They had been undecided about continuing contact and we understood every adoption is different. Fortunately, they wanted to see Erik and us again when he was nearly one-year-old. We drove to the birthfamily's hometown and showed him off to a large extended birthfamily. Every member welcomed all of us and made us feel special and loved.

More than anything, this contact validates the birthparents original decision. No one should be afraid of positive, unconditional love. We are now lucky to have occasional contact with Erik's birthparents and to see them when we can. In both adoptions, I can say both birthmoms (and in Erik's case, a birthdad) have become like special aunts (and uncle) to all of our children. Our older children love getting together with them, and when they call sometimes they all get to talk.

I believe there are many myths about open adoption that linger in our society. Many people tell me it sounds like it would be too confusing to a child to have "two moms." Language needs to be clarified. There is a difference between a mom and a birthmom. Everyone has a birthmom. Privileged children have a mom!!

It is a serious commitment to become a mom. I hope every woman, no matter what her age, would give it a lot of thought and understand the time, energy, and resources it takes. Obviously, a birthmother is intelligent enough to know that commitment.

I find it a sad illusion when people think the birthmother does not love her baby. Nothing could be farther from the truth! Often her love tears her apart inside. That is why connecting with the right counselor is so important. A birthmother will never stop loving her baby. By selecting an open arrangement she has said, "It is okay my baby grows up knowing me. I am not ashamed of my decision!"

There could be some confusion if a child is given a birth story with too many details too early. Rachel is just beginning to talk to Adriane on the phone. Maybe in a few years she will want to know who Adriane is. We already tell her how special Adriane is and how much we all love her. At the right time, in language that Rachel can comprehend, she will be given more details. The same will be true for Erik.

Whether the child you adopt is white, black, Asian, Hispanic or a mix of races, I think keeping the relationship with birthparents and adoptive parents open is the best way for the child to grow up. However, if things change and contact with birthparents decreases, you will always have that initial contact and bond to share with your child. Your child will always know he or she came into their families' hearts out of complete love and concern for their welfare. The open adoption relationship is about love, honesty, and respect for choices we are lucky to be able to make in our lives.

Two Hearts Joined Together
by Chad and Kitty Stockslager

Hi, we are Chad and Kitty Stockslager. This is our story of open adoption. The journey was and still is full of laughter and tears. We hope you enjoy reading the story and may it also bring hope and joy to your lives.

After being married for several years we decided it was time to have a family. We started trying to get pregnant but only found years of infertility ahead. We started looking into adoption and thought that instead of spending money on doctors and treatments why not put our money toward what we wanted: a child. Biology didn't matter, we wanted a child to give our unconditional love to.

In May 1997, while looking through the phone book, we came across the Independent Adoption Center advertisement. We called and I had a really good feeling. Within a few days we had our information packet and soon we were off to our weekend workshop.

After that weekend we knew we wanted to proceed with open adoption. Of course there were some questions as far as how open adoption worked, such as: Are we going to have to share the baby? Do we have to visit? Is she going to be bothering us all the time? Although a lot of different things ran through our minds, we were very excited to get started. Once we returned home, we shared the news with our family and friends.

We finished our paperwork and within a few weeks had our home study scheduled with a local agency. In the meantime we started working on our Dear Birthmother letter. This was a little harder than we anticipated. We knew what we wanted to say but found it challenging putting it in letter format. In between writing our letter we had pictures taken. I think we took about ten rolls of film before we had a picture we really liked. We finished our letter and sent it and the pictures to the agency for approval.

Months went by without any phone calls. We were about to give up. Then in December 1998, we got our first call from a birthmother. We couldn't believe it; after 14 months, finally a call. We talked with her for a couple of weeks and some red flags popped up. She and the father of the baby were still together. She was buying the baby things and talked about having it home with her for a few weeks. We felt a little nervous but still decided to set up a match meeting. The match meeting didn't happen. She was too unsure of her decision on adoption. Our hearts were broken but we also knew in our hearts it just wasn't meant to be.

On May 7, 1997, we got the call we had been waiting for. It was from our birthmother, Amy. She was 21 years old and had two small children at home, a two-and-a-half-year-old and a five-month-old. She knew adoption was the best decision for the child she was carrying. We instantly felt a connection and talked for hours about anything and everything. In our conversation I asked how she chose our letter. She said she received about 65 letters and when she came across ours, our front picture stood out.

I kept telling her how thankful we were, how much we loved her, and that we promised to take good care of the baby.

We looked very happy and loving. By the end of our first conversation we decided I would call the agency and set up a match meeting.

I set up our meeting but it wasn't going to be for a few weeks. Amy wanted to know if we would like to meet before our agency appointment. We thought it was a great idea. In the meantime we continued to talk on the phone. Chad couldn't believe how long we could talk to each other. The connection we had was so amazing.

On the day of the meeting, we arrived excited but nervous. As we were walking up the steps to her apartment, we could hear her little girl say, "Mommy they're here." That made us feel good. I knocked on the door and when she opened it we instantly hugged. We walked in, sat down, and started talking. We had taken along a photo album of our family and friends. She enjoyed looking through it and hearing about them. Before we knew it, it was late and we needed to go. The drive home went by really fast. We were very excited to get home and share the news with everyone.

Our match meeting at the agency went smoothly. It worked out well that we had met prior. It made all of us a lot more comfortable when discussing our adoption plan. We left the meeting knowing we were one step closer to being parents. We were finally officially matched. Yeah!

Throughout the months of waiting for our baby to be born we continued to visit Amy and talked to her on the phone. Our relationship together kept getting stronger. We also met some members of her family who would soon be a part of our family. It was nice seeing her family and friends supportive of her decision.

On October 31, 1999, Amy called telling us she was in labor. We grabbed our bags and hurried to the hospital. It was a long night; Amy was in labor 12 hours. I had the honor of being her coach. Chad came in and out of the room to see how things were going. At 7:33 a.m. November 1, 1999, our beautiful daughter

Miranda was born. Chad immediately followed the nurse to the nursery to be with the baby. I stayed with Amy. I kept telling her

She told her she loved her, then gave her a kiss. It was a very emotional time for all of us.

how thankful we were, how much we loved her, and that we promised to take good care of the baby. She said, "Go be with your daughter, you need to be with her." I couldn't bring myself to leave Amy until I knew she was taken care of. Finally she said to me, "I'm okay, now please go be with your daughter." I walked down the hallway and saw Chad looking into the nursery window. There she was, a perfect, beautiful baby girl. I was still in disbelief we were finally mommy and daddy.

The first time I took our daughter to Amy's room I was nervous. She told me how cute she was and said it was nice to see how happy we were. At one point Amy came to our room and handed me a gift. It was a birthstone charm of a little girl. I started to cry. I put it in a safe place so someday I could give it to our daughter.

The next day the ladies from the agency came to take care of the paperwork. We were nervous because she still could change her mind, even though she told us she wouldn't. Not long after, they told us everything was taken care of. The tears fell pretty heavily.

After the hospital told Amy she could go home, she came to our room to say goodbye to the baby. She told her she was going to have the best mommy and daddy in the world, she was going to have a great life, and this was the best thing she could do for her. She told her she loved her, then gave her a kiss. It was a very emotional time for all of us.

It was a very sad time taking Amy home from the hospital. We wondered if this would be the last time we would ever see or talk to her. That was something we did not want. We had become so close we could not imagine our life without her in it.

We drove Amy home and walked her to her apartment. We had bought her a necklace that had two hearts connecting each other and gave it to her. We told her we got it for her to remember us and it was our heart and her heart joining together, sharing a special bond and friendship with lots of love. She loved it. We hugged and cried for a long time as we said our goodbyes. We told her our daughter would always know about her and the love she had for her. As we were leaving, we told her to call or write us anytime. When Chad and I got to the car, we just hugged and cried. A lot of it was happy tears but some were sad also. We prayed this wouldn't be the last time we would see or hear from Amy.

On November 3 we were discharged from the hospital. We couldn't go home yet because we had to wait for the interstate paperwork to be done. We drove to a hotel as close to the state line as possible so our family and friends could come visit. During our first night together I think we woke up a dozen times in between the two hour feedings, just to check she was still in her bassinet and this really was real. We were in the hotel seven days.

In the passing months we were very busy with the things that come along with having a newborn. In the beginning, Amy called us a few times. It made me nervous when I answered the phone and she was on the other end. I feared she was going to change her mind, but all she wanted was to see how things were going.

On July 31, 2000, our adoption was finalized. The wait was really over. This was one of the happiest days of our lives.

The agency has an annual picnic. In June 2001 we invited Amy to go with us. It was the first time we had seen her since Miranda was born. We took a lot of pictures and had a great day.

On September 18, 2001, I received a call from Amy. It started off as a normal conversation and then I couldn't believe what I heard. She said, "I have some really big news. I'm pregnant and I want to ask you and Chad to adopt this baby, too!"

I couldn't wait for Chad to get home. I greeted him at the door with, "How would you like to be a daddy again?" He gave me a very puzzled look until I explained everything to him. In the past we had talked about what we would do if something like this happened. We thought it would be a wonderful situation.

I called Amy and told her we would love to have another child. Amy was glad because she didn't know what she would do if we said no. She said she couldn't imagine going through an adoption with anyone other than us.

Amy and the birthfather, John, were together. In the beginning we were a little concerned about this. With Miranda the birthfather was not involved. I asked Amy how John felt and she reassured me there wouldn't be any problems. Although she reassured me, I was still worried.

On January 15, 2002, Amy called and said her water broke and we should come to the hospital. Thankfully we already had arrangements made. I called Chad at work and told him to get home. We took Miranda to grandma and grandpa's and told her she would have a baby brother or sister soon.

When we arrived at the hospital we told the nurses our situation and they let us be with Amy and John. Soon it was time. John and I stood next to Amy helping her as much as we could. At 9:58 p.m. our beautiful daughter was born. I continued to stand next to Amy to make sure she was okay. After I knew she was fine I walked over to be with John. He was standing next to the baby watching the nurses take care of her. I put my arms around him and told him how thankful we were. He said he already knew. I also promised we would stay in touch as long as he wanted and the

I don't think a lot of us take into consideration what birthparents go through. They truly are very special people.

baby would know the love he and Amy had for her. He gave me a kiss on the cheek. He asked, "Have you picked a name?" I told him Jenna and he said that sounded beautiful. We stood next to Jenna until they had her ready. They handed her to me and I held her for a little while. Then I handed her to John. He held her, holding back his tears. He handed her to Amy. She held her for a few minutes and said, "I'm going to give you back to your mommy and daddy now." I started to cry. It was finally time for her daddy to hold her. It was late. We went to our hotel to get some sleep and to call everyone to let them know the good news.

When we woke the next morning, we couldn't get to the hospital fast enough. Chad's parents came later that day with Miranda. She was so excited to meet her new baby sister. She wanted to hold her and kiss her right away.

When the agency came to do the paperwork I was in Amy's room visiting. She asked if I could be there while she signed her papers. They said it was okay. I sat there listening and I couldn't believe the way they worded everything. It was straight to the point, which it has to be. It made me feel very thankful to have a birthmother sure of her decision. After sitting with her I understood how a birthmother could get confused and change her mind at the last minute. After they were done, John went to Amy's room to do his part. I remember being nervous, praying everything would be okay. When he was done, he stepped into our room and said, "I'm leaving," and out he walked. I was scared. I thought he didn't sign the papers. But soon the ladies from the agency came in and said everything was taken care of. I don't think a lot of us take into consideration what birthparents go through. They truly are very special people.

Amy came back to our room and said John was fine. He just wanted to be left alone. Before Amy left, she said goodbye to Jenna, gave her a kiss, and told her she loved her.

We were discharged late that evening. Again, we weren't allowed to go home because of the interstate paperwork. About ten days later, we went home. It was nice to finally be in our own home as a family. Miranda loved having a baby sister. To our surprise she was very good with her and loved singing to her.

We continued to keep in touch with Amy and John. Amy went with us to the agency picnic in June 2002. We shared our story with the other couples. It was nice hearing Amy tell everyone how she felt and how much we meant to her. After the picnic we went back to her apartment and visited with John. He was excited to see us and Jenna. We had a good visit and took pictures. When we all get together I always make sure we take pictures for the girls' scrapbook. I think it will mean a lot to them in the years to come.

On July 29, 2002, Jenna's adoption was finalized. This was another very exciting day for our family.

We still remain in contact with Amy and John, and they are still together. We visit several times throughout the year; Christmas is a must. We will always cherish the times we spend with them and they will always hold a special place in our hearts. We truly consider them our extended family and love them very dearly.

We have always been open with our daughters about their adoption. At this point I don't think they understand very much, but it is important to us they know how they came into our lives. We tell them how special they are to have two families that love them very much. It's comforting knowing down the road, when the children have questions we might not be able to answer, we can turn to Amy and John to help us answer them. Open adoption has worked out perfectly for us and our children.

An Open Adoption: Birthmom's Story

by Wendy Pittman

I am 29 years old and very happy in my second marriage. I am raising my 11-year-old son and two nieces, ages five and eight, and also my nephew, age seven. I am a home daycare provider and generally have a house full of children. My sweet birthson lives around the corner from me and is in class with my oldest niece. His mother and I are very close friends.

My adoption story began 11 years ago, when I became pregnant with my first child while in high school. A woman that worked with pregnant teens at our school took me to an open adoption support group after I expressed interest in placing my child. This was my first exposure to what open adoption could really be and I was impressed. The woman in charge of the support group had adopted a child and was dear friends with her child's birthmother. I knew if I decided to place, I would need openness, but I wasn't sure to what degree.

I stayed in contact with the support group leader for a short time, but in the end, I decided to parent my first child. I also parented my second child, but lost her to SIDS when she was four months old. After I became pregnant a third time, I became separated from my children's father. I was 20 years old, with no driver's license and no job. I was on welfare trying to support my son. I knew I couldn't provide a good life for my baby in those conditions.

The hand of God was at work during all this, because all the contacts I had made and all the research I had done during my first pregnancy now came into play. I had stayed in touch with the woman from the school over the years and I called her to let her know what I was doing. She encouraged me to work with a state agency and I actually placed the call and made an appointment. As soon as I hung up I received a call from the support group leader, who I had not spoken to since our first meeting. She remembered me and asked me to consider going private with the placement.

I spent one night tormented by doubts and fears about placing my child with people I had just met.

The support group leader knew of parents looking to adopt and compiled some profiles for me to look at. I was in the last trimester of my pregnancy and nervous about finding the right people in time. I prayed for guidance throughout the process. The third profile I read moved me to tears with the rightness of it and I knew God had directed me to this family.

We met at their home and discussed our wants and needs. I felt so comforted by the laid-back attitude of this couple. They put no pressure on me and wanted to know what I wanted and even asked me about names for the child. They had three older children, and a young daughter from an open adoption. They were also foster parents. I left there with a great sense of peace.

There were a few minor setbacks. I spent one night tormented by doubts and fears about placing my child with people I had just met and barely knew. I prayed through it and again found peace with my decision. Then some shocking news came. The prospective adoptive father called and said they had changed their minds and they just couldn't adopt at this time. There were phone calls made between the support group leader, the prospective adoptive mother (who still wanted the adoption), and myself. I was three weeks from delivery and had no time to really get to know another couple. I was just reeling from this blow because I had felt so sure this was who God wanted to adopt my child. God surely works in mysterious ways. The husband had a change of heart and they decided to adopt my child after all.

I spent the last few weeks making phone calls to the prospective adoptive parents and we agreed the mom would be in the delivery room with the child's father and me. She filmed the birth as well. After the delivery of our healthy baby boy the parents gave me space. I knew I could change my mind and they would be fine with it. I spent my days in the hospital, spending time with my baby and saying goodbye. I started a journal for him about how I was feeling at that moment and planned to fill it in over the years.

On our release from the hospital, my aunt and I drove my birthson over to the adoptive parents' house. We spent some time there and then I went home. Again, I battled my nagging doubts and my family was putting pressure on me to reconsider and offered to help me raise my child. I hadn't signed any papers yet and still had several days until my court date to do so. I called the adoptive mother and asked her to bring him back. She totally understood and had assured me the entire time I could take as

I could not have placed my son if it would have meant spending the rest of my life looking at every child on the street, wondering if that was my son.

much time as I needed to decide. She offered to foster him for a while if I needed that in order to parent him. She brought him home to me and I gave it a shot.

I knew as soon as I held him in my arms again this baby did not belong to me. I felt in every fiber of my being this was their child and God had plans for him in their family. I called the adoptive mother and let her know I knew for sure I wanted to place with them. She agreed to it, but asked me to keep him with me until I had signed papers in case I had any doubts.

I signed the papers three days after she brought him to my home. I was so sure of my decision that day, and I still am eight years later. The beginning of our relationship was a little awkward because we didn't know each other that well, but we agreed on how things would be and both of us have respected those terms. These wonderful, loving parents made me feel like family. I was able to call when I wanted to talk, and see my birthson when I wanted to do so. We celebrated Christmas together and spent more and more time on the phone. She sent letters and pictures to me of him growing and changing. She talked to him about his birthfather and me from the beginning. He has always known who we are and to him it is the most natural thing in the world because that is how it was presented to him. In his home, birthfamilies are openly talked about and seen on a regular basis.

His mother and I have become friends over the years, not just polite acquaintances that get together for the sake of my birthson. No, we share everything and I count her among my closest friends. I still see my birthson and, in fact, we recently moved around the corner from them and my kids attend school with her kids. Our relationship has only grown stronger with each passing year and I thank God that He brought these people into my life.

I am a firm believer in open adoption. I could not have placed my son if it would have meant spending the rest of my life looking at every child on the street, wondering if that was my son. I couldn't live without knowing where he was, who he was with, if he had a good life, and what he looked like as he grew. I also feel that his path has been made easier, as well. He will never have that empty hole in his life that I have heard so many adoptees mention. He will never have to search for me and worry about betraying or hurting his parents in the process. He will never have questions that go unanswered about his identity or his roots. He will never have to wonder who he is and where he came from or who he resembles, because we are right here, in his life right from the beginning and for always.

The Other Side Of The Story

by Janet McMillan

I am married to John and mother to Nigel, Anna, Kathryn and Andrew. I have lived in Brisbane, Australia, for seven years and enjoy the delights of being mother and grandmother to our 11 grandchildren. I also have 15 of what I call adopted grandchildren, children who have no grandparents locally, so all call me Grandma and I love them all to bits.

Having been through the process of adopting a baby and knowing how much I had always wondered about the birthparents and grandparents, who they were and did they know how much we loved this baby, I now have the other side of the story.

Seven years ago our youngest son came to us and told us his girlfriend was pregnant but that they did not want to keep the baby. Knowing we had adopted our daughter, Anna, they wanted to have their baby adopted. They did not want to go through the public system, so their doctor said he would find parents for them.

They were given folders with the details of two couples who wanted to adopt and they could make the choice. They chose an older couple who both had good jobs and lived in the North Island of New Zealand. They met with the couple and got to know one another.

In the meantime we moved to Australia to live and, in some ways. I was pleased about that, as the thought of losing a grandchild was so sad to me.

When the time came for the baby's birth, the adoptive parents came down to Christchurch and saw their birthson Jacob as soon as he was born. Andrew's girlfriend went home and Pip, the adoptive mother, moved into the hospital and took over the care of Jacob.

Contact has continued to this day. We have photos sent regularly. Andrew and his girlfriend married, but sadly, they parted company less than two years later.

At the time of Jacob's birth I grieved so badly and was grateful I was living over here, as the distance seemed to make it a little easier. I exchanged letters and photos with the family as the birthmother did not want contact and Andrew wanted us to be his point of contact for his son. When Jacob was about 18 months old I was able to visit him and meet this precious grandson for the first time. How my heart broke. Here was the only grandchild who looked like one of our children and he was the image of his father at the same age. But Pip and her husband were so gracious and generous allowing us to visit and to visit with us when they came over on holiday.

I do know that Jacob is going to have the best life ever, with all the opportunities he might never have had, just as our daughter Anna had. Still, I saw the heartbreak that Andrew's wife went through losing her baby to another couple.

I wrote Jacob a letter the day he was born and gave it to his adopted parents to give to him when he is older. I know we will see more of him as he grows up. I am so grateful the system has changed and allows this. Yet for me I could not have handled Anna's adoption if we had the open contact that is now in place. Because of that I only write at Christmas and birthday times to Jacob and his family. Let them enjoy bringing their son up.

Last Christmas Jacob met for the first time with his two half-sisters, Andrew's daughters. That natural bond was there and they all got on so very well.

Adoption is a very big thing and as we learn more about the emotional ramifications of this procedure we need to be so aware of what deep emotional changes are happening in the life of the birthmother. I will always be eternally grateful to the beautiful woman who gave us the joy of our lovely daughter. I hurt with the mother of my grandson for the deep hurt and pain she suffers and rejoice with the woman who adopted our grandson for the love and security she is giving him.

Janet's daughter, Kate Dani, has written "My Adopted Sister," which can be read in Chapter Eight.

How Our Family Extended The Circle

by Martha Poller

My name is Martha Poller and I'm a 54-year-old adoptive mom. My husband George and I married later in life, I was 37, he was 40, and although we tried for almost three years, we weren't able to get pregnant. Our thoughts quickly turned to adoption, and with the help of Adoptions From The Heart in suburban Philadelphia, we were matched with a young couple, Jon and Jen, who felt they weren't ready to start a family. But, in fact, they started ours by bringing Rebecca, who turned 14 in June 2004, into our lives. The open relationship our family has shared with Jon and Jen's over the years has been remarkable and something I know Rebecca will treasure forever.

Our daughter Rebecca was dearly loved and wanted even before she was born. Jon and Jen chose us specifically to adopt their baby, and we met with them before Rebecca's birth. She arrived a few weeks early, and we were invited to share in her earliest hours at the hospital, a gift we'll always treasure. Early on, we agreed to stay in touch with her birthparents, keep them appraised of Rebecca's growth and milestones, send photos, etc.

In turn, we've always been open with our daughter about her adoption, and have given her information about her birthparents. But as Rebecca grew older, it became clear to us she needed more than that. The turning point came when Rebecca was about eight years old and learned that Jen had given birth to her third child, a baby girl, and that she now had a sister, in addition to two brothers. We owed it to Rebecca to extend our family to include Jon and Jen's. That took a leap of faith on our part that was scary, but has been repaid to us a hundredfold.

I had many emotions when making this decision. I was worried about a lot of things. Would she be able to handle this? Would it hurt her in any way? But I found the more secure we felt in our feelings, the more we were willing to share Rebecca with her birthfamily. Nothing could ever change the fact Rebecca is our child. Nothing in the universe could change the feelings we have for her or she has for us. Once I really understood that, we were ready to move forward.

We all met at the zoo, with Rebecca really recognizing this family as her birthfamily, and relating to her siblings as siblings for the first time. It was the beginning of an extended family for Rebecca, who she sees regularly, including over holidays and during the summer. It has truly been a positive experience for us all.

"Realizing I have a whole other family out there makes me feel special," Rebecca told me. "In the beginning, I felt a little confused, but then I realized I wasn't all that different from my friends. Everybody has extended family. I just happen to have an extra set of parents and grandparents, along with brothers, sisters, and cousins. It's all one huge family. I call my birthparents Jon and Jen because I only have one mom and dad. But because my mom and dad have been so open with me, I feel really comfortable with who I am, and I understand why my birthparents made the choices they did."

What makes open adoption work for our family is that everybody respects everybody else's rights. There's never a question of who Rebecca's parents are, and who sets limits for her. For us, extending our family to include Rebecca's birthparents and relatives has brought us all closer together. This choice wouldn't work in every situation, but for parents considering adoption, I would strongly advise them to consider this choice. I never have to worry about Rebecca going off on a quest to find her birthparents. She knows everything there is to know about her past, and I think it makes her present and her future that much better.

"I know for sure that when I get older and want to have children, I'm going to adopt," Rebecca relayed to me. "And I'll try to introduce my child to his or her birthparents early on. One of my friends in our adoption support group didn't meet her birthmother in time; her birthmom died in a car accident before she could meet her. I think she may be mad at her parents for that. So I think the earlier you share information, the better for everybody."

Can I Call Her Now?

by Krissy Lundy

Krissy has also written "Not As Planned," which can be read in Chapter One.

M y phone rang one day, and a friend said, "Are you interested in talking to a young woman who wants to put her baby up for adoption with a good Christian family?" My first thought was sarcastic. "Naa. We've only been trying for about 10 years; what's a few more." What came out was, "Are you kidding?! Can I call her now?!" Naturally being the slacker I am, I waited a whole 10 seconds before dialing the attorney's number she gave me. The physical description the attorney gave of the mother could just as easily have been a description of me. Less than a week later, my husband and I were sitting in front of her, dying from anticipation. Would she like us? Would we say the right things? So many questions were going through our minds.

The mother we met with decided to let us adopt her baby and our adopted foster daughter, Dede, has a little brother! Now our family is complete: daddy, mommy, sister, and brother. Caleb was born almost a year ago to a room full of grown-ups praising God and crying like babies. I went to doctor appointments, was able to be in the delivery room when he was born, and my husband got to cut the cord. I got all the joys without all the pain! He's a brown-hair, blue-eyed angel. Nothing can make you forget a horrible day quicker than his smile. He thinks a smile and a wave can get him out of anything, and at this age, he gets into a lot. I don't think I've ever seen a baby who smiles and laughs as much as Caleb, and I feel like it's because we chose a different path than most adoptive parents do.

When we signed the adoption papers, we all agreed we wanted contact with the birthfamily. In fact, the birthmother and her mom were there when we signed the papers! Caleb's birthfamily is like part of our family now.

People who have not been blessed by adoption cannot understand how we can trust them. We are constantly warned to not let them babysit or even see him because they are going to change their mind and want him back one day. As I see it, they have the best of both worlds, so why would they want to mess it all up by demanding him back? They see him whenever they want to, but they don't have to worry about getting up in the night or all the expenses like, clothes, food, insurance, and all the other little things that pop up. Once he gets a little older, I hope they will see him even more than they do now. We invite them to most of our family functions and vice-versa. Caleb's biological grandparents said they want Dede to call them grammy and papa just like all their other grandchildren, and they are wonderful to her. We couldn't have picked a better family if we had interviewed a hundred looking for the perfect ones. It has all been a blessing from God from the beginning.

Maybe we look at it a little differently than most people would. You see, I'm adopted. I have two sisters and a brother. My brother is adopted and one of my cousins is adopted. My cousin and brother actually share the same biological mother so they are birth half-brothers and adoptive cousins, or "cousers," as they call it. None of us can remember an exact time our parents sat us down and said, "We need to talk to you about something." All three of us have grown up with the knowledge we were adopted. Before I even knew what being adopted meant, I knew I was adopted. My dad has a sister who didn't know she was adopted until one of her cousins told her at age fourteen. She's a grown woman with children and grandchildren now, and she still hasn't recovered. I don't want my children to go through that. Just as my parents did, I will always tell my children they are adopted and how special it is to be adopted. There are some differences between my brother, cousin, and me, though. They know their birthmom because she is a family member. I don't know mine. When I was born, the way of thinking was that it was in the best interest of the child to have no contact with the biological family. If they find out they have a medical condition that requires treatment, my brother and cousin can simply look to their family for answers. It seems much better to maintain some kind of relationship in case there comes a day you need answers. When I go to the doctor and am asked family history, I have to say, "I don't know. I'm adopted." No matter how hard I try to forget, it all comes flooding back with that one question.

I guess maybe I look at things a little differently than other people because I have experienced the knowing and the not knowing. I can't imagine what my parents must have gone through wondering if my birthmother would one day knock on their door and want to see me. I hope they would have asked me and not made that decision for me. That's what I hope I am able to do should Dede's biological parents ever knock on my door. I don't feel like it's my decision to make. Of course, she may not be old enough to make the decision on her own, but I feel sure she would give us some kind of clue as to whether she wants to have a relationship. I think that is the only way to handle the situation, should it arise. All I feel I have the right to do is pray it will work out for the best for Dede, and she won't be hurt again. This is probably why I was so eager for Caleb to have contact with his birthfamily. I don't have to worry about him being hurt because his biological family is here reassuring him he is loved by them as much as he is by his adoptive family.

On the wall beside my bed, I have pictures of my mom and me, my sister and me, a special little poem written by my mom when I was little, and a poem my mom cross-stitched for me years ago. I read this poem every day and thank God for my family and for giving me to them before I had to spend any time in foster care, and especially for giving my birthmother the strength to go ahead with her pregnancy and not take an easier way out. This cross-stitched poem says:

> *Not flesh of my flesh*
> *Nor bone of my bone*
> *Yet still*
> *Miraculously my own.*
>
> *Never forget for a single minute*
> *You didn't grow*
> *Under my heart*
> *But in it.*

Life Circumstance—Life Career

by Maxine Chalker-Mollick

Maxine has also written "My Search," which can be read in Chapter Three.

My adoptive sister is my "real" sister and my adopted parents are my "real" parents and I love them dearly. They had a difficult time raising me as I was very headstrong and rebellious. I was average in school, married young, and had a child. I divorced my husband when my daughter was an infant and raised her on my own. After she was born, I saw the light and went to college. I received an award as a Presidential Scholar and graduated summa cum laude, which allowed me to enter a one-year Master of Social Work program. I then got a job at the public child welfare agency in the adoption department.

After working there seven years, I knew most of the ins and outs of adoption and felt there was a better way to do adoptions than what was being done. I was very disillusioned with the public child welfare system, foster care, and seeing children returned over and over to dysfunctional parents. Although I did find adoptive families for many of these children, I knew the years of suffering in the hands of their birthparents and then moving from foster family to home and then back had done damage that these children may never completely recover from. I decided adoption should be done in a more humane manner and began investigating open adoption, which was not widely known in 1984. I decided this was the way to go and applied for a license to operate a non-profit adoption agency. My daughter and I struggled to find a name for the agency and finally called it The Adoption Agency.

Our agency began in the basement of my small twin home. I did a little public relations and advertising and soon a few pregnant women contacted me. Of course, so did a few brave families who were willing to come to my home and attempt the little known adventure. One of the neighbors complained I that I was running a business in my home, so I was forced to rent an office. This was the best thing that happened as it forced The Adoption Agency to become a real social service agency.

My daughter became the secretary while she was in school and two social workers (including one who was my best friend and still works with me) joined the agency. More and more pregnant women started calling. Some of them had no place to live and their parents either didn't know about their pregnancy or had thrown them out. Some were living on their own and had no place to stay. My daughter and I started housing them with us. We had a very small three-bedroom house but there was always room for one more. We managed and the agency grew and grew in reputation and size. Soon we were opening offices in Lancaster, PA, Wilmington, DE and Cherry Hill, NJ. Smaller office space became too crowded and larger accommodations were found. My business was a success. Then an agency in another part of the country ran into some trouble and the news constantly referred to them as "the adoption agency." The confusion over the names caused us to change our name to Adoptions From The Heart.

Today, Adoptions From The Heart is one of the largest adoption agencies on the East Coast with licenses in seven states—

placing over 500 children in 2003, 120 of those by domestic open adoption. The adoptions have become more and more open with families staying in touch with each other and visiting. At our annual picnic it is so heartwarming to see these birth and adoptive families together.

Because of my experience as an adoptee and assisting many birthparents and adoptees complete searches for one another, I realized open adoption was an important practice. Open adoption benefits the birthmother by giving her control over the choices for her baby and being able to keep in touch with the family that assumed parenthood for the child. She, of course, also maintains a relationship with her child as a friend or extended family member. The adoptive parents benefit because they are given permission by the birthparents to raise their child. They know it was a difficult decision and was made out of love. They can raise their child with that information, even if the birthparents do not stay in touch. It benefits the child because they get to know the true story of why they were placed for adoption, have access to medical and social information about their background and can form their identity based on facts rather than fantasy.

It is often said adoptees are not a party to the adoption agreement between their birth and adoptive parents. This is so true and I have been fortunate to have been raised by loving and caring parents and to have been able to turn a life circumstance into a career that is all consuming and important. In addition, I have been able to assist thousands of families in changing their life circumstances into beautiful families.

International Adoption

A World Of Love Waiting For You

*"An invisible red thread connects those who are destined to meet,
regardless of time, place, or circumstance.
The thread may stretch or tangle, but it will never break."*

- *An ancient Chinese belief*

But Why Not A Baby?

by Courtney Rathke

I am a mom twice over: once through the miracle of birth, once through the miracle of international adoption. Our Guatemalan son is a blessing to our entire family and our memories of his homeland will always be treasured. I have made so many amazing friends and learned so much about myself and our world as a result of the adoption process.

Adopting a toddler from another country has an entirely different set of challenges. Toddlers are starting to learn to communicate verbally and need to change gears, as it were, in midstream. They are more aware of their surroundings and they have been removed from everything they've known. Even the food and milk taste different.

But the rewards of adopting a toddler are immense as well. The interaction and learning are fascinating to watch and to participate in as a parent. It is such a joyous thing to offer a child a new experience and to see how the child absorbs it.

Aaron was 32 months old when we brought him home from Guatemala in January 2003. We had specifically entered into the adoption process searching for a toddler boy because we had a seven-year-old son at home. We wanted to reduce any age

So often during those first few weeks, what appeared to be a small issue such as taking a nap or finishing his milk would rapidly escalate into near hysteria . . .

difference as much as possible. In addition, we felt our household was set up for boys, and my husband and I enjoyed parenting more once our older son became a toddler. The give and take and ability to communicate made each day an adventure and more enjoyable for both of us.

Since Aaron's birthmother spoke no Spanish, only a Mayan dialect, English became his third language in less than a six-month time frame. But children that age are such little sponges. Within six weeks of arriving home, he seemed to understand 90% of what we said, and within six months he was reasonably fluent in English. It was enough to make himself understood.

People ask what we did to ease the language transition, and we have finally decided we utilized the total immersion method, purely because we spoke no *Qui'che* and very little Spanish. Someone suggested we try sign language but we chose not to. We felt adding a fourth method of communication, along with all the other changes in his little life, would be an uphill battle.

At first, he mixed all three languages together and we picked up some of the dialect he spoke purely through trial and error. Some of the sentences were awfully cute: "*Lo ti* (I want??) *agua*, please." The couple of phrases we did figure out and used when we spoke to him seemed to utterly delight him; however now if we try to use them, Aaron appears to have selective deafness. He wants English.

Our biological son, Nick, was seven years old at the time Aaron came home. We involved him in the entire adoption process from the day we signed our agency contract. Nick took Aaron's referral picture to school for show and tell, and when it came time to send a gift bag to the *hogar* (orphanage), Nick helped choose the items we put into our bag. We also took the time to explain to him, as most parents do with any new baby, how things would change when Aaron came home. We truly felt that, by being included in the process, Nick would feel more connected to Aaron even before he came home.

Interestingly, Aaron seemed to bond with Nick more quickly than he did with either my husband or me. Perhaps being children the two are more easily kindred spirits. Aaron follows his "Natch" (his nickname for Nick) around the house without ceasing and, for the most part, "Natch" has been a good sport. They seem to revel in their relationship on a level separate from my husband and me.

There was one watershed incident about six weeks after Aaron came home. Children that age, shocked and frightened by the changes in their lives over which they have no control, grieve. The grief can take many different forms and take months to surface. So often during those first few weeks, what appeared to be a small issue such as taking a nap or finishing his milk would rapidly escalate into near hysteria and frequent hiding behind chairs. Sometimes he would stand with his back pressed to a wall and refuse to make eye contact with me.

One afternoon, as he was leaning back against our dining room wall, head turned away, he began sobbing, "Mama! Mama! Mama!" Shocked, I sat down a few feet away from him, and said, "Honey, mama is right here." When he finally looked at me, with a surprised, hurt expression on his face, I realized that to him, I wasn't mama, and that furthermore he had always called me mommy. Eventually, I coaxed him into my lap and we both cried while I told him that his mama loved him and missed him, and I knew he missed her, too. Then I told him that mommy loved Aaron, daddy loved Aaron, and "Natch" loved Aaron, and that we would all take good care of him and be with him forever. I really don't know how much sank in. After all, he wasn't yet three years old and barely understood English. But I think he understood the tears, the rocking, the kisses, and what I wanted to convey.

After that point, it was as if he had made a conscious decision or come to a realization that this was forever; this was his family— this was where he belonged. He could show us who he was when he was at his worst and we would still love and accept him. The first four months were challenging and rewarding as we all learned our roles and our places in our newly created family of four. Aaron learned to ride a tricycle and discovered that plastic Elmo dolls do not go in the microwave. He learned to love yogurt, and that a time-out is no fun. He became so accustomed to hearing "Whoa! Whoa! Whoa!" whenever he wanted to explore something particularly interesting (like the electric can opener) that his first full sentence in English was, "Mommy no-no whoa, whoa, whoa!" By mid-summer, I realized he was calling me "mama" and had been for some time. It happened so gradually I don't think Aaron or I realized when he made the change.

People ask my husband and I if we would ever adopt again, and I honestly don't think we would. However, that has everything to do with the dynamics of our household and that we think two children completes our family, and nothing to do with our experiences in adopting Aaron. If we were ever in a position to adopt again, we would definitely choose a toddler adoption without hesitation. There are more challenges, but the rewards are so much greater.

Unsolicited Comments

by Leceta Chisholm Guibault

I am mother to Kahleah (adopted from Guatemala, 1991) and Tristan (adopted from Colombia, 1994). Our family lives in Joliette, Quebec, near Montreal. I serve as a board member of the Adoption Council of Canada and the Federation of Quebec Adoptive Parents, and moderator of the e-mail list Canadians-Adopting.

When my husband and I became first-time parents in 1991 of our then five-month-old Guatemalan-born daughter, I felt that after the adoption process I was prepared for anything.

On our second day home with our baby, I was extremely proud to be able to tour our neighborhood with her in her stroller. Mother and daughter at long last. We barely made it around the corner when two ladies ran from their homes to meet Kahleah and expressed their amazement, that "from a distance you look like you could be her mother!" I politely told them I was her mother. They said, "You know what we mean. HER REAL MOTHER!" Ouch. That hurt.

Then came the questions. "Where are her parents?" "Are her parents dead?" "How much did she cost?" "Why didn't her real parents want her?" "Can her real parents take her back?" "Will her skin get much darker?" "Why didn't you adopt a white baby?" "How old was her real mother?" "Does she have brothers and sisters?" "Will she ever learn to speak English?" "Will you tell her she is adopted?" "Does she have any diseases?" "How tall will she be?" "Whose fault is it you couldn't get pregnant?" "Did you try IVF?" "Do you suppose now that you have adopted you will finally have one of your OWN?" I wanted to scream, "IT'S NONE OF YOUR BUSINESS!!!!!"

Then came the statements. "That's one lucky little girl you have there! Just imagine the kind of life you saved her from." "There is a special place in heaven for people like you." "It takes a special person to parent a child like that." "I never would have guessed you were not her parents. Why, you treat her just like she was your own kid!" "I would NEVER adopt! You never know what you are getting." "Adoption is a good cure for infertility! Now maybe you will be blessed with a child of your own!" "I hope you know what you are getting yourself into!"

Six years ago I found myself speechless and hurt so many times. I was bewildered and frustrated. What gives people the right to single out my family, in very public situations, and expect responses to very intrusive personal matters? I just don't understand it. Why is it we seem to know enough NOT to ask people how much they paid for their house or car or what their salary is? I would never ask someone how many months they had "tried" before they conceived a child! But others feel they can put me on the spot and ask me these questions.

Now that my daughter Kahleah is six years old and the proud sister to three-year-old Colombian-born Tristan, she is an innocent witness to this invasion. She is extremely proud of her little brother and sees him for exactly what he is: HER BROTHER.

Recently, a man in a shopping center took a long look at me, and then at my children, then back at me. With Kahleah standing beside me, listening intently, he asked, "Are they yours?" "Yes," I replied. "Are they brother and sister?" My Kahleah put a protective hand on her brother's shoulder and replied, "Yes, he is my baby brother." The man looked to me and said, "They don't look alike; they can't be REAL brother and sister!" I glanced at Kahleah and then firmly, yet calmly stated, "They ARE brother and sister." He seemed puzzled and continued with, "But they're not BLOOD brother and sister, right?"

Realizing at this point that what was truly important was what my children were getting from the conversation, I saw it was time to end the interrogation. Smiling at my children we proceeded to walk away. I ended the conversation with, "Sir, trust me. They are REAL brother and sister. Please remember that when you engage me in these conversations, I am an adult. I know what you are trying to say. My children, however, are young and are listening. The hurt in their eyes is much worse than the pain of skinning their knees or falling off a bike. It is much harder to put a Band-Aid on their hearts or self-esteem."

So many times someone comes up to my precious children to inform them how lucky they are. I am quick to jump in with, "No, their father and I are lucky to be blessed with them!" Not everyone we meet is malicious, but I must be on guard. I loved when my daughter was a baby and people would stop and exclaim, "What beautiful black eyes she has! Look at that straight black hair! Nice brown skin!" Although I thought these were positive comments, by the age of four, my daughter had had enough. One day in our community, after numerous people made these same observations over and over again, Kahleah buried her face in my stomach, overwhelmed. She said she was tired of people always pointing out the same things: her hair, eyes and skin. I realized they were pointing out her racial differences, and her differences from me, her mother. She was reading between the lines on her own. Maybe this was just her perception, but she was feeling it.

I ask you, what child deserves to be made to feel differently, simply because of race? Or to intimate, in their presence, that their parents are doing an act of charity by adopting them? My children's birth histories belong to them, and only to them. Why can't people accept us as a family, built with love and a lifelong commitment? Is this so very hard to understand?

Alison's Journey-Home Journal

by Nicole Sandler

After spending 25 years as a personality and program director at radio stations in New York, Los Angeles, South Florida, and Boston, my daughter was ready to start kindergarten, so it was time to settle down. I applied my creative background and talents to form Legacy Video Productions, where I produce custom videos for people from their old photos, slides, home movies, and memorabilia specializing in Family Tree Videos and Adoption Stories. To find out more you can contact me at www.legacyvideoproductions.com.

11-4-2000

Today is my 41st birthday. And I'm finally about to become a mother! It has been a long, difficult "pregnancy." When my daughter arrives, she'll be 18 months old. She's currently living in an orphanage in Kazakhstan and I leave Los Angeles to bring her home November 18! This is going to be a very long two weeks.

I began this adoption journey 18 months ago. I decided I was no longer going to wait for the right man to come along to have a child. So I got on the Internet and began researching international adoption. I dismissed the idea of domestic adoption as I didn't think a birthmother would choose a single, 40-year-old woman as the mother for her child.

My heritage is Russian, so I began researching the plight of orphans in the former Soviet Union. I found two great resources on the Internet for adopting a child from Eastern Europe: Families for Russian and Ukrainian Adoption, at www.frua.org, and The Eastern European Adoption Coalition at www.eeadopt.org.

The first thing I needed to deal with was the Immigration and Naturalization Service (INS) to submit the I600A (Application for Advance Processing of Orphan Petition) to get the all-important I-171H. This process can take four to six months, so it's the logical first step. The second step is the home study.

I filed the I600A, got fingerprinted by the FBI, started the home study and decided which adoption agency to use. I must have sent for packages from 30 various agencies, and joined a bunch of Internet mailing lists to get as much information as I could.

I finally decided to use a small agency based in Wyoming called Focus on Children because they were run by people who are in it for the kids. I requested a baby girl less than 12 months old and was told the wait would be four to six months for a referral after submitting my completed dossier. So, the paper chase began!

11-13-2000

The process of putting together my dossier took three months. It included sending away to New York for three official, certified copies of my birth certificate. The other elements were:

> *Twelve photos of my home, family, child's bedroom, community, school, etc.
> *The home study, plus copies of the home study agency license and the social worker's individual license.
> *Letter of medical approval from my doctor, plus a copy of his license!

*Copy of my most recent tax return.

*Local police statement showing I have no criminal record.

*Copy of my passport.

*Power of attorney for my agency's staff in Russia.

*Declaration (a form required by the Russian government).

*Copy of the INS form I171-H (favorable determination letter).

*Letter from employer stating salary, length of employment, and a work habit comment on company letterhead.

All items in the dossier must be notarized. Then each document needs an apostille seal. I know, you're thinking, "a WHAT seal?" An apostille is a state seal, recognized by foreign countries that basically authenticates the notary's signature.

I got it all done and sent my completed dossier to the agency. I had been given a four to six month referral timeline so I thought for sure I'd be a mom before the summer. In early November I got a note from my agency saying I could plan on traveling in February!

Months passed and no referral. Then in March, Russia elected a new president and adoptions ground to a halt.

More months went by. In October, a year after I sent in my first dossier, I got a call from my agency asking if I would consider a girl in Kazakhstan. She was 17 months old and seemed pretty healthy, though definitely in need of some good nourishment and TLC. They would send me her picture, a videotape, and what little medical information they had. I agreed to see the information.

When I got to the office the next morning, a Fed Ex package with very sketchy medical information was waiting. At 15 months she weighed 14 pounds, was anemic, and had some other typical Russian diagnoses (if you're interested in reading about referral medical reports, you can check out www.russianadoption.org/topten.htm). I went by myself into an office and watched the three-and-a-half minute video which showed a beautiful little girl, obviously a little scared, but following every move very intently. During the last minute she smiled, giggled and completely won me over!

Since I had 18 months to prepare for this moment, I knew I had to think with my head and not my heart. I made a copy of the video and overnighted it to a doctor who specializes in evaluating international adoption referrals. She watched the video and talked to the orphanage doctor in Kazakhstan. She told me the baby looked pretty good—severely malnourished, definitely had rickets, but didn't see anything that "lots of Vitamin M—mommy—wouldn't take care of!" I was also told the little girl would need a lot of work—physical therapy, occupational therapy, and a lot of one on one attention, but the doctor thought she would do fine. I accepted her referral.

11-21-2000

Wow, this has been an amazing few days! I flew to Germany, had a two-and-a-half-hour layover followed by another six-hour flight to Almaty, Kazakhstan. I arrived around 3 a.m. and was met at the airport by the most wonderful woman, Galiya, who works for my agency and is handling the adoption details in Kazakhstan.

She brought me to the apartment that will be my home for the next three weeks or so. For $30 a night, I have a two-bedroom apartment with a full bathroom, kitchen, and living/dining room. I remained there until I was picked up at 11 a.m. and, after driving 90 minutes to a little village called Karakastek, arrived at the orphanage where my daughter is living.

Words can't describe the feeling as the beautiful little girl, who will soon depend on me for everything, was walked into the visiting room! For the past month I'd had two pictures and two videos of her and now, here she was. The worker placed her in my arms and she buried her head in my neck. I was in heaven. We played and got to know each other and then it was time to leave. When I got home I was exhausted!

The next morning I was picked up at 9 a.m. to go back to the orphanage! On the way Galiya told me my court date was Thursday! That's the day after tomorrow! That means Friday, I get to bring my daughter, Alison, back to the apartment.

Unfortunately, Kazakhstani law requires a 15 day waiting period before the decision is final, so we're not leaving here for a while. However, we'll have a couple of weeks to get to know each other before we get on a plane to Moscow. Yes, Moscow. We have to go through the U.S. Embassy in order to enter the U.S.

11-22-2000

Today was the best day yet with my little girl. I brought her Cheerios and some baby cookies and she LOVED them. I wanted to give her a bottle, but being the brilliant newbie mom that I am I remembered the bottle but forgot the liners! Luckily, a friend gave me a sippy cup, which I did remember to bring. After lunch I had the happiest, funniest, cutest little girl ever. She wanted to play games, explore my face and mouth with her fingers, and walk around the room with me holding her hands up.

11-23-00 Thanksgiving

It truly is Thanksgiving. From now on this holiday will be extra special for me. Today was my court date to officially adopt my daughter. The judge allowed us to videotape the hearing, so Alison will be able to see it when she's old enough to understand!

The entire proceeding took only 10 minutes. First, the judge asked why I was there. I responded by saying I wanted to request the court allow me to adopt the child known as Maigul. The prosecutor asked many questions: Why did I want to adopt? Why specifically from Kazakhstan? They asked about my income, my housing situation, and many others things I can't even remember. It will be interesting to watch the video and experience it again. Then the orphanage director was asked some questions, mainly about Maigul's background and health, and a woman from the Education Department was asked for her recommendation. The prosecutor asked more questions about how I would deal with any potential health issues, and if I was aware of her background and diagnoses.

I was asked to make a final statement. I'm not sure exactly what I said, but I included something about today being Thanksgiving. I also promised I'd give her a wonderful life and love her forever! (It was during this little speech I lost it. I was able to hold back the tears until that moment.) The prosecutor approved the adoption. The judge then granted the adoption! I asked the judge if he'd take a picture with me. He reluctantly agreed. As expected, the decree isn't official until 15 days have passed, which unfortunately, delays my departure a bit.

I'll be picked up tomorrow morning to take Alison out of the orphanage for good. I'll have to bring clothes for her to wear, as she'll come to me with nothing. I will ask for something of hers from the orphanage as a keepsake. I have a questionnaire to give her caretakers, asking everything from her eating habits and nap times to her likes and dislikes. Hopefully they'll give that to me tomorrow along with her complete medical file.

Luckily I have found a pediatrician in Los Angeles who speaks (and reads) Russian and will be able to understand her history. This will be my last night as a childless woman. Tomorrow I get my daughter! I guess I'd better try to get some good sleep tonight. I may not have a full night's sleep for some time to come!

11-27-2000

I just got Alison to sleep. This is the toughest time of the day. She fights going to sleep, climbs all over the bed—no crib here—and sobs mournfully. I did a bit of reading on toddler adoption, and the children do go through a mourning phase. It makes sense. They are suddenly taken from everything and everyone they've ever known, and cannot possibly understand what's going on. They also cannot express what they're feeling.

For the most part, Alison is doing great. It's only at bedtime that she really has trouble. She is a very happy baby, and is absorbing everything like a sponge!

At the orphanage, it didn't even seem that she could crawl. However, in the three days I've had her, not only has she started crawling but last night she pulled herself up and, holding on to the chairs, walked around and around the big dining room table!

Bath time has been rough. The kids at the orphanage were only bathed once a week and I don't think they used bathtubs. I think it was just a sponge bath. Alison was terrified. She has gotten a little more tolerant each night. Tonight she actually sat in the water rather than digging her fingernails into my shoulder and trying to climb over my back. I think we're making progress.

My travel plans were finalized today. I will leave for Moscow on December 13 at 2 a.m. It's a three-and-a-half hour flight. Once in Moscow, we will check into a hotel, where a doctor will examine Alison (required by the U.S. Embassy). Then off to the Embassy for our interview. My flight leaves from Moscow on Thursday, December 14 at 7 a.m.

12-8-2000

My 15-day waiting period, required after court, was over today. So it was time to go all over Almaty to get new documents. We had to drive back out to Karakastek, the village where Alison's orphanage is located, to get her adoption certificate, and to the Almaty registration office to get her new birth certificate listing me as her mother.

A few interesting observations about 21st century life in Kazakhstan: The office that handles all certificates (birth, marriage, adoption, etc.) had no computers, so all the paperwork was done by hand. There was also no heat and it was freezing!

We then drove back into Almaty to get the new birth certificates. Although this building did have heat, it too didn't have computers! All the birth records were in archived books; pink for girls and blue for boys, filed by year. The woman working there looked up Alison's original record and wrote in my name and address, as well as Alison's new name.

12-12-2000

It's Tuesday, December 12, about 12:20 p.m. and I'm still in Kazakhstan! I should have been in Moscow by now, but Alison's visa didn't come through in time. So, I'll go tonight.

I spoke with Michael, the coordinator in Moscow, who told me not to worry, because he'd be able to get us in and out in one day. Let's keep our fingers crossed that my plane leaves on time tonight and we get Alison's visa.

12-17-2000

It's Sunday afternoon, December 17, and Alison is napping. So while I have a few moments on the computer, I thought I'd continue detailing the journey home while it is fresh in my mind.

We left Kazakhstan for Moscow on Tuesday night. We were picked up for the ride to the airport shortly after midnight. Sitting on the bus with Alison on my lap I felt it . . . that familiar warmth and rumble that let me know she had just pooped! I thought, "No problem, I'll change her at the airport, before we get on the plane."

Well, the bus took us right to the plane. We got off the bus and herded up the stairs and into our seats. The plane was packed.

I figured I'd change her as soon as the fasten seat belt light went off. The airplane bathroom had to be the smallest one I'd ever been in. There was no pull down changing table, so I closed the lid on the toilet, put down my little changing pad, and attempted to lay Alison down on it. Her reaction was similar to her first experience in the bathtub: screaming at the top of her lungs and clawing my neck.

We arrived in Moscow at about 5 a.m. local time and were met by our Moscow coordinator, Michael. We then drove to the hotel. How wonderful to be in a luxurious hotel! Michael explained the schedule for the day. He would come to our room and go over all our paperwork for our interview at the U.S. Embassy. I was told to be in the lobby at 3 p.m.

The doctor arrived at around 7 a.m. to examine Alison. He told me Alison looked pretty good, "examined" her for all of five minutes, took my $100, and filled out the necessary paperwork.

At 3 p.m. we were in the lobby waiting for the van to pick us up. When it hadn't arrived by 3:15 p.m. I got impatient and called a cab. I wasn't about to come this far only to miss our embassy appointment and have to wait another day to head home.

We got to the U.S. Embassy at 3:40 p.m. and went right in. At the embassy, I was asked a few questions and given all of Alison's original paperwork and a sealed packet to give to the INS officials when I reached the states, complete with Alison's immigrant visa stapled to the front of it. We were officially ready to come home.

So, we left Moscow at seven the next morning for the three-hour flight to Germany. This time there were no poopy problems on the plane, and Alison did just fine. We landed in Frankfurt and had just enough time to wander around the airport a bit and get to the gate for the 10:05 a.m. departure to Miami.

As I got to the gate, the attendants informed me the flight was delayed, and we'd be leaving at 11:30 a.m. We took off and 10 minutes into the flight, the captain came on and said something in German. Then he spoke in English and explained two systems had failed, that we were in no danger because of all the backup systems, but we had to turn around and land back in Frankfurt.

By the time we landed, disembarked, and got back to the terminal it was around 3 p.m. They said we'd board again at 5:30 p.m. for a 6 p.m. departure. At about 5:15 p.m I was told the new departure time was 8 p.m. I thought.I was going to die. I was exhausted and Alison was definitely way past tired and cranky.

We finally boarded the plane and took off. Though I was in coach, I had a bulkhead seat, and the airline had a bassinet that attached to the wall. It was a nine-and-a-half hour flight to Miami, and we arrived at about 12:15 a.m. on Friday morning, December 15 (only 10 hours later than scheduled).

We made it through customs and INS, and my sister was waiting for us at the gate! We got back to her house at 2:30 a.m. and the barking dogs woke my two-and-a-half-year-old niece, Lindsey. So we all spent the next few hours catching up.

Alison met her grandfather yesterday, and as soon as she wakes from her nap we'll visit him again. We'll be here until Wednesday, when we get to take our last plane ride (for a while) to go home!

12-22-00

It's taken me a while to write this adoption journal entry. Now that we're home I seem to have no time to get on the computer. Alison is doing very well, though I think she's a bit confused about where we are now (I keep telling her, "We're home!").

Our flight from Florida to Los Angeles was only delayed an hour (nothing after my Frankfurt experience), and using all my miles for a first-class ticket for our final leg was a great decision.

Alison slept for most of the flight and I was able to enjoy a decent meal and a hot fudge sundae without having to share it with her!

My friend, Dan, picked us up at the airport. I left the car seat at my house, and told him to install it before coming to get us. When we got to the car, I saw the seat installed rear-facing, sitting straight up. Needless to say, it was wrong. So, the two of us sat in the parking lot with the manual for the seat trying to figure out how to put it in while Alison sat patiently in her stroller waiting to go home.

We pulled up in front of the house and the first order of business was to go next door and get my dog, Sandy. Dan held Alison while Sandy and I said hello. I then introduced Sandy and Alison. Alison giggled at this big furry teddy bear. Sandy just wanted to lick her, but Alison didn't seem to like that. We're still working on that one.

Alison's sleep schedule is still a bit screwy. Just as she was adjusting to East Coast time, I brought her to the West Coast! She finally fell asleep at about 6 p.m. and it's now 9:40 p.m. I hope she wakes up soon so I can give her dinner and a bath, but I have a feeling she might sleep for awhile and I'll really be in trouble!

We went to the grocery store today and she was great for the first five minutes or so, then started fussing, fidgeting, crying, and screaming. She wanted me to hold her, which I wound up doing, while I pushed the cart and loaded it up. When we got home, I noticed she had another one of those annoying poopy diapers, so I'm hoping that was the cause of her outburst (though she doesn't like to be restrained, and would rather have mommy hold her than have to sit in anything).

The nanny starts on Tuesday, and I'll go into work for about an hour. I guess it's time for the next part of our lives to begin!

Biba Has A Family

by Anne Roberts

I am a wife, mom, and a clinical specialist. My husband and I have seven children who have come into the family via domestic and international adoption, and birth. The plight of orphaned children has become my passion.

One day this past week I participated in a ritual many American moms experience each day. I went to pick up my four-year-old daughter, Biba, from her daily four-year-old kindergarten program. I walked into the room to be met by the sounds of children finishing up their day. There was a chorus of little voices shouting, "Biba, your mama's here." My daughter looked up from the coloring table with shining eyes. She jumped up, ran to her cubby to collect her day's work, and ran to me with open arms shouting, "Mommy, mommy, mommy," eager to show me each colored paper.

I took Biba into my arms and gave her a hug when I heard the voice of the teacher behind us. She said, "Aren't those beautiful words? Biba, your mama is here!" I stopped, looked at Biba, and tears came to my eyes. Yes, they are beautiful words.

You see, only five months ago, my four-year-old princess was an orphan in the far away country of Kazakhstan. She lived in an orphanage with wonderful caretakers, but no parents. She had the company of other children but not of brothers and sisters. My little girl was waiting for her very own mama and daddy.

My mind began to race to a day in early September 2000. My husband, Rope, and I had left five children waving from the back porch of our home. We traveled to Russia and then to Karaganda, Kazakhstan, to be met at an empty airport by a vivacious MAPS (Maine Adoption Placement Service) worker named Kana. We were tired, but anxious to see this little girl who lived in our hearts but not yet in our home. Kana helped us settle into our hotel, gave us a pep talk, and we walked up the road to the baby home that had been Biba's shelter for most of her life. The anticipation was almost overwhelming.

We came to the orphanage, taking in the sights and forgetting our fatigue. Our little girl was behind those doors! We were led into the building, up the stairs, around the corner, through a door, and were met by happy children pushing their way towards us. A loving caretaker greeted us, then turned toward another door and opened it. I stooped down and Biba ran into my arms calling, "Mama, mama, mama." She flung her arms around my neck and laughed out loud the most beautiful laugh I'd ever heard. It was like the angels in heaven were laughing with her.

My husband was standing beside me waiting for his turn with Biba. Another little girl, Aida, had grabbed him around the leg in the hope that he was her papa come to take her home. Rope was experiencing the emotions of love for his daughter and grief for this little girl who so desperately needed a papa. He reached down to give Aida a father's love for a brief moment. They connected and then a caretaker took Aida away. It was not her time. She would have to wait. Maybe the next mama and papa would be for her.

Time stopped for us that moment. Biba turned from me to her new father. She jumped into his arms with the joyful cries of

"Papa, papa, papa," and that same joyful laugh. Rope took her into his big arms and held her to his chest. Biba had a family!

We thank God every day for our beautiful Kazakh daughter. She is part of who we are. How quickly Biba has adjusted to parents, brothers, sisters, English, home, school, and church. She participates fully in anything we do. Simple pleasures bring great joy: jumping in fall leaves, McDonald's, birthdays, bedtime stories (her favorites are *Curious George* and *Quick as a Cricket*) and pushing her doll stroller. Biba is home!

Rope and I would like to encourage anyone considering adoption from Kazakhstan to move forward. Yes, you will get criticism, questions, and have self-doubts. Yes, it is worth it all! We'd like to share some of the questions and concerns that have come to us from well meaning people and the answers we give.

1. **"How much does it cost?"**

Our answer is that it is a bargain; less than a new car. Anyway, Biba is worth millions and it is certainly less than that.

2. **"It's not fair to your other children."**

Our other children are compassionate and concerned for the lost children of our world. Four of our children have come to us by adoption and two by birth. Each of them is God's special gift. We are blessed beyond measure to share the bounty of our lives with each other. Our children know no prejudice towards other races or countries. We are a multi-colored family and love it! Besides, which of our children would be better off without us?

3. "You're too old."

Rope and I are in our 40s. We have decided as a couple that our children are where we want to devote our lives. Neither of us plans to retire. We are bucking our culture, so to speak. Experience is a great educator. Our teenagers will be the first to tell you we are more patient and encouraging as older parents. We're better off financially, too!

4. "What about time for yourselves?"

What is more rewarding than rearing children? Rope and I experienced a mid-life adjustment period last year. We made a conscious decision to strengthen our private relationship and enlarge our family. There are ways to nurture our marriage within the context of our family. The trip to Kazakhstan bonded us as a couple in ways we never would have imagined!

Yes, I am Biba's mama. She also has a daddy, brothers, sisters, grandmas, aunts, uncles, cousins, and friends. Our hearts continue to grieve for Aida, Diana, and all of the other girls and boys that are waiting in Karaganda. Can you go for them?

Where Did I Come From?

by Jane McManus

In many ways adoption is the experience of a lifetime, and I would not choose to build my family any other way. We have adopted internationally four times, and the adventure has been full of learning and growing, for the children as well as for us. In providing opportunities and structure for the children to discover themselves, we have found previously unknown qualities and talents in ourselves. We are one unit and it feels as though we have always been so.

As the mother of four children, adopted internationally past the age of four, I encounter many questions from others like me who are struggling with what to tell their older adopted children about their birthfamilies. This can crop up when a teacher assigns a family tree project or otherwise incorporates ancestry into a lesson. Questions can be raised by the children, their friends, or even complete strangers. How my children and family view our situation and define family is the foundation for how we respond.

Our oldest daughter was nine years old and home less than a year when she begged me to tell her she came from my belly. I gently explained that she didn't come from my belly. My belly doesn't work and can't safely carry babies. God knew this and so he put our babies in other bellies to grow so they could be born safely. They were always my babies, and so they grew in my heart and papa's heart until we found them. God helped us find each of them after they were born and living in orphanages. It took a longer time than we would have liked, so it was very hard, but they were still growing in our hearts. When we did find them, we were very thankful to God that he found a way to give us our children. Each of my daughters has been happy with this explanation and understands we are the family we were all meant to be. Family is not blood or DNA. This definition has also eliminated any of the questions about family tree or ancestry in their minds.

On another note, our oldest daughter was the oldest at adoption, and the second child to be adopted by us. She was nine years and ten months upon adoption in Russia. At that age you worry a lot about attachment. Of our three, she attached the firmest and the fastest, and absolutely treasures her family.

Here is a poem she wrote for a class project after she had been home 18 months :

I Remember.
I remember the time I came to USA.
I remember at 7:00 p.m. coming to my home.
I remember getting lost in the family room,
Seeing my own room, jumping up and down.
Seeing Nastia playing and then sleeping in my own bed.
Eating my first best breakfast ever, seeing my own dogs.
Yelling, screaming, jumping, running, playing, bumping.
I remember going to my lake home and riding on the jet ski.
I remember, I remember, and I will never forget.

Jane's daughter, Sera, has written "My Long Amazing Journey," *which can be read in Chapter Three.*

American Daughter Born In China

by Bonnie Loomis

*Until five years ago, when Brooke came into my life, I was
simply a single woman working and living in Harrisburg,
Pennsylvania. Now I am no longer "simply a single woman working
and living." I am a single mom happily and joyfully living life.*

Before my daughter and I became a family, in fact,
before my daughter was born, I was attending pre-
adoption workshops to prepare for the international
adoption experience. For four hours on four consecutive Thursday
evenings I was educated on the joys, pitfalls, and future issues that
may arise when adopting a child from another culture, most
particularly a child that had been "lost to be found," as in China.

During these sessions, potential adoptive families were required
to participate in work groups, focus groups, and honest discussions
about the realities of adopting a child from another culture. We
discussed such issues as: our responsibilities to the child relative to
bigotry, positive and negative biases, well-meaning and sometimes
intrusive questions about the multi-ethnic family, preparation for
the child's questions, issues associated with losing a birthfamily,
and the almost deal-breaker, the teenage years. I soaked it all in and
felt very well prepared and ready to bring my child home from

China and to be the best, most culturally nurturing, empathetic, and open-minded parent that ever walked away from an orientation.

Fourteen months later when I arrived in China to meet my daughter, the enormity of the responsibility and commitment I had made on behalf of this beautiful child took on a whole new meaning. Book smart just wasn't enough. Now I needed to learn to be street smart. As the only mom in our travel group who hadn't thought to bring Cheerios as an icebreaker, I wasn't having an auspicious beginning for either book or street smart.

After arriving home, I continued with and grew in my friendships with other single moms who had adopted from China. I watched closely as these moms introduced their daughters to Chinese language classes, Chinese dance classes, and Chinese New Year celebrations. As time went on, it became clear I wanted to put my energy into raising an American daughter born in China rather than a Chinese daughter living in the United States. I began revising my earlier vision of how to incorporate cultural diversity into our lives into a vision that was more compatible with our personalities and situation. As a family, Brooke and I have become very comfortable with our strengths and weaknesses. Brooke knows I won't be preparing mooncakes for her first grade class and I know Brooke isn't the kind of child who wants to take dance classes, be it Chinese or my most hoped for choice, Celtic.

However, I feel an enormous debt of gratitude to China and to Brooke's birthparents. I have decided this can best be paid by giving this American daughter born in China a sense of identity she can accept and embrace through self-esteem, pride in where she came from, humor for situations she finds herself in, and strength to handle any situation where humor isn't appropriate. This ongoing process requires introspection, empathy, and education.

I have kept a journal from the day I began the adoption process for Brooke to read. The journal is now almost three journals and hopefully will give Brooke insight into how and why she became my daughter. In order to give her a sense of why she is who she is, I've participated in two projects that provide specific information on your adopted child. One project, Asia Threads (www.asiathreads.com), provides adoptive families with as much information as possible relative to their daughters. This may include photos of the child's finding site, photos of the orphanage and staff, and maps of the city. In our case, I have irreplaceable photos of the village where my daughter was found. The photos should help give her a very clear understanding of some of the circumstances that led to her being "lost to be found."

Another smaller project I participated in was through BlessedKids (www.blessedkids.com). From this project, I have additional information about Brooke's first few hours before and after arriving at the orphanage. This information was very bittersweet but provides me with a starting point to talk to Brooke when she is ready to learn about her first year of life. In addition to the two projects, I have collected a large file of articles and information. My favorite resource book so far is *The Lost Daughters of China* by Karin Evans. I anticipate referring to this book for many of the answers to questions so far unasked.

I defaulted into probably the best arena for sharing Brooke's culture with her when we traveled to New York City's Chinatown. Although I wasn't expecting much more than an interesting day, it was an enlightening day for both of us. It was the first time Brooke had been anywhere when she wasn't the minority and where everyone looked like her. She became more relaxed and animated than ever before when we were in uncharted territory. This is a wonderful example of street smart versus book smart.

Probably the most emotionally satisfying tradition we have for embracing our family's ethnicity is an annual reunion with the eight other families who met in Hong Kong to become first-time parents.

From the moment of sharing the most joyful and exhilarating experience of meeting our daughters, our group became an extended family. Although we live in six different states, we meet every year for a reunion. Initially, our motivation was to provide our girls with a sense of history and identity among themselves. After our first reunion, we knew it wasn't only for the girls, but it was for us parents, too. At six years of age, our girls are sharing their American culture through Barbies, Lizzie McGuire, and Veggie Tales. At 10 years of age, we will be sharing our children's Chinese culture with a homeland tour reunion.

If we've raised any eyebrows as a duo-ethnic family, it has not been obvious. I haven't had to dodge any rude or insensitive questions or remarks and Brooke has been accepted lovingly and completely into our immediate family and friends, community, school, and church. In fact, I've been surprised at how effortlessly and automatically we are accepted as mother and daughter. There have been many questions about adoption and how we became a family and, without providing personal history that belongs only to Brooke, I have been able to answer those questions openly and honestly. The question that has been asked most frequently by Brooke's peers is, "Where's your daddy?" I heard her response once and knew from that moment on whatever preceded our Forever Family Day and whatever is to follow, we are truly a family. Brooke's answer? "It's just my mommy and me, and that's all I need."

A Mother's Thoughts On Cultural Pride

by Leceta Chisholm Guibault

Leceta has also written "Unsolicited Comments," which can be read earlier in this chapter.

I have been working on instilling cultural pride and a positive cultural and racial identity in my children since Kahleah (ten, from Guatemala) and Tristan (seven, from Colombia) were infants.

Our children are "different" in a sense. My husband and I choose to celebrate our children's differences and, of course, their "sameness" (for lack of a better word). Celebrating their differences will not make them feel more different. Most likely, as in our case, they feel less different.

It wasn't enough for us to introduce Kahleah and Tristan to other children who are also adopted from the same countries, although this, too, is important. I realized that fact when Kahleah was four and she thought everyone with brown skin was adopted. We had taken her to a large Latino community fiesta. She looked around and said with big eyes, "This is the biggest adoption picnic I have ever been to in my whole life!!!" That statement opened my eyes. It was a wonderful opportunity to discuss adoption, birth, and different types of families. She began to become aware at that point that, in that particular situation at the fiesta, mommy and daddy were minorities. We were white. Kahleah, Tristan and everyone else were different shades of brown! Cool.

I was so proud watching my children dance and play with the other children from the Latino community. As much as my kids are accepted and valued members of "our" community, I was well aware that I wanted them to feel a part of and comfortable in the Latino community. Right now, they don't feel "different" in either.

Like many families with minority children, we don't have the choice of where to live because of a job situation. We make the point to drive a distance once or twice a month to attend fiestas, Latin American restaurants, concerts, etc. The children love these outings now. Maybe when they are a little older they will reject this, but the seed of interest is planted.

We also decorate our home, not just the children's rooms, with artwork and handicrafts from Latin America or with a multi-cultural theme. We have piles of adult and children's books on multi-culturalism, Guatemala, Colombia, adoption, etc. We have made friends with families who have immigrated to our area from Latin America. I have learned so much from these people. They take great pride in taking my children under their wing.

We visit Kahleah's school to talk about Guatemala. She participates and beams with pride. Of course, everything we do is age-appropriate.

I hope I have shared a few ideas to help instill cultural pride without being a fanatic. Let your children take the lead. If they roll their eyes and say, "Not this again!", cool it!

The Joy Story
by Dawn Degenhardt

I am the founder and executive director of MAPS (Maine Adoption Placement Service). My husband, Ed, and I are the parents of nine grown adopted children of all races and several mixtures arriving from six weeks to ten years old. I have been a full-time volunteer for 25 years.

"Don't call me until they are on the plane and it has taken off," I said in utter frustration. Another postponement. How many had there been? It had been 12 months since we had heard we would be able to adopt Nguyen Thi My Lien, (Joy), three-and-a-half years old, from the orphanage at Cam Ranh Bay. The war was raging, and she was in one of the first groups to be escorted from Saigon and one of the very first children from the Cam Ranh Bay area.

During the Vietnam War, the conditions were dire. On one occasion 17 babies died because of measles. A group of us were known as the Cleveland group (COAC—Council on Adoptable Children). We were a parent group who wanted to find families for children waiting everywhere. Through Johanna Spicuzza we became involved with the orphans of the Vietnam War. She had adopted twins and was determined to save as many children as she could. She had arranged the adoption of our son, Vinh (now David). There were no agencies involved back then.

But I digress. This is Joy's (Nguyen Thi My Lien) story. I believe Joy was one of the many miracles coming out of this terrible war. How did it happen? While waiting for the processing of adoption to smooth out during David's adoption from Saigon, we heard of an Air Force Chaplain who just returned to the States from the Cam Ranh Bay area. We called him and asked if he would help us adopt a little girl from Cam Ranh. He listened to our story. We had two children, Freddie (age five) and Heidi (age three), both adopted locally. We were approved by INS for two more children and had a boy (David) assigned. The Chaplain said he and his crew had volunteered at the orphanage near the base and he knew Sister Mary Lieu (who ran the orphanage) well. He would write her a letter, call, and ask her to send us a little girl. We also wrote a letter to Sister Mary Lieu explaining who we were. Within a very short time she sent us a letter with pictures of two little girls, one almost four and one almost five. Since we already had a three and five-year-old, we chose the four-year-old and found another family for the five-year-old. Later that month another letter arrived from Sister Mary Lieu with 13 children she wanted us to find families for, and we did. In those days everyone was a volunteer and the total cost to adopt a child, including delivery to Cleveland, was $780.

There were several problems however. There was no safe way to get the children to Saigon for transporting out. They could not go overland because of the landmines. Through an informal network we heard that Roma Conroy (from a Utah group) had a son who had just returned from Vietnam. He had been stationed in Cam Ranh and was willing to return to help these children get to Saigon. He would also help escort them to the U.S. With the help of his buddies he commandeered a truck to take the children to the helicopter pad. They were smuggled onto the helicopter to the military airport, and then smuggled onto the plane for the flight to Saigon. This was the established procedure for all children coming out of the Cam Ranh area, and it worked.

It was August 9 when the call came to say that eight children, including our David and Joy, were in the air and on their way to Los Angeles. Friday evening, August 11, the red-eye special from Los Angeles arrived in Cleveland. As the parade of businessmen with their briefcases got off the plane they all waited to see these eight children meet their new families.

We had invited only family and close friends to come to the airport. With eight children arriving that meant a rather large crowd anyway. As the full plane unloaded we waited anxiously for the children to appear. At last the children deplaned. David was first off and Joy was second. I held David and Ed held Joy. We were all in shock. The crew of the airplane was helping to deliver the other

. . . every other day or so she would withdraw into her "trauma." Something would happen, we never knew what, and she would shrink quietly into herself.

children to their new parents. I wanted to meet them all. When the last child was placed in the loving arms of his parents, everyone waiting, including those tough businessmen, let out a cheer. There was not a dry eye in the area. Luckily, we have a short movie of this momentous event.

Joy was very small for her age. Although she was four-and-a-half, she wore a size three dress. She was this miniature person. The first month we spent a lot of time at the doctor's office. For a while neither child wanted to get into the car as it meant doctor's visits. Both children had several problems, which included: malnutrition, protein deficiency, parasites, lice, skin conditions, enlarged liver and spleen. David was very sick. Joy was quick to respond to treatment and very active. She was also very much in charge.

Oh, yes, I forgot to mention that on July 3 we had adopted Annie, a seven-year-old girl from South Dakota. We had been in the process of adopting an American Indian child long before our Vietnam involvement. We also were in the process of adopting a black/Vietnamese baby. Heather arrived on December 1. So we went from two children to six children in a five-month period. The oldest was seven; the youngest was 12 months. Two were very sick for quite a while and three were in diapers. Somehow it didn't seem difficult at the time. Now I look back and wonder how we did it.

There was no preparation for adoption back then. There was no training and no one with experience to teach us. It was truly on-the-job training. And without the parent support group (COAC) I couldn't have functioned. We were all in the same boat and learning from each other. Many of us are still in contact today.

Joy was very traumatized by all that had happened to her. She had been brought to the orphanage the day she was born. Her birthparents were young and both in the Vietnamese army. They had hopes of returning to claim her, but had not been able to. We had also been told they had both died. Life in the orphanage was difficult; not enough of anything for all the children. All the children had a job. At age two they helped with the washing and cleaning. At age three they were assigned a baby to care for. At four-and-a-half, Joy was very able to handle babies. She often told me I was not doing things right for Heather. She would sling Heather over her hip and take over her care and feeding. She had a special bond with David, even though they had not met until they got on the airplane in Saigon. If things didn't go her way she would threaten to take David and return to Vietnam.

Joy was acting normally within a few weeks. She ate all the

time, slept well, attended Montessori school, and played well with siblings and friends. However, every other day or so she would withdraw into her "trauma." Something would happen, we never knew what, and she would shrink quietly into herself. Her eyes would glaze over and become fixed and she was not in there. She would not allow me to move her so I would just sit and hold her hand. This would last 20 to 40 minutes and then large tears would silently fall down her face and she would join us again and be okay, until the next time. I could only guess what memories and nightmares she was reliving. These episodes lessened in frequency and in time spent "in her trauma." If I was not in the room when it happened one of the other kids would say, "Mama come quick—Joy's in her trauma." I soon learned the way to Joy's heart was through her stomach. She particularly liked pickles, popcorn, and potato chips. As her trauma became lighter, I would lead her to the refrigerator and give her a pickle and she would come right out of it. I only did this when schedules didn't allow the time it took for her to go to where she went. I felt it was important for her to grieve her life in this manner.

Within a month of her arrival she understood everything we said to her and was speaking some English. We had a visit from a GI and his Vietnamese bride. When Joy saw this lovely young woman she went right into her "trauma" and pretended not to understand or speak Vietnamese. I believe Joy feared that this woman was going to take her back to Vietnam. After she left, Joy came up to me and said, "Joy no Vietnamese—Joy Indian." Annie had been wearing an Indian headband around so we made Joy a headband and she became an Indian for a while. I told her not to worry; she could be anything she wanted to be.

Within 18 months we moved to northern Maine where our children were the only non-Caucasian children in the community. The children were very well-accepted, did well in school, and loved the great north woods. Joy had a rather typical upscale American childhood. In high school she sat first chair flute in the band and played on the state championship soccer team. At age 18 was ready to go off to college after graduation. She majored in early childhood education at the University of Southern Maine for two years. While there she realized that was not what she wanted to do. She

We toured the facility and it was devastating to see. There were post-polio kids sitting in rusty wheelchairs with nothing to do. It was a colorless, difficult existence.

transferred to the University of Hawaii to study Japanese and international business. We also felt it was important for her to be in a more Asian culture. She graduated in 1992. As a graduation gift she asked if I would take her back to Vietnam for a visit. I had always told all of my children I would help them, when it was possible and when it was safe, to visit their motherland. Through a very interesting set of circumstances we received an invitation from the Vietnamese government to visit orphanages and government officials. In August of 1992 we found ourselves on a plane to Hanoi. We were met by the Ministry people who had planned our itinerary. We were taken to a class D mini-hotel, where Joy exclaimed she couldn't sleep in that room or stay in that dirty, noisy place. We did stay, but asked to go to another hotel the following night.

What an adventure! Everywhere we went we were welcomed with interest and curiosity. I was taken to areas where they had never seen an American or a Caucasian woman. Joy was welcomed by all. Her story was told in several newspapers. She was the adopted child who had come back to see her motherland and to find her birthfamily. However, on that trip we were not allowed to visit the Cam Ran Bay area as it was still occupied by the Russians. It took two more years before Joy was allowed to go to that area.

Visiting orphanages became a daily occurrence. The day we were taken to Thuy An Handicapped Children's Center was unusual. We toured the facility and it was devastating. There were post-polio kids in rusty wheelchairs with nothing to do. It was a colorless, difficult existence. After meeting the children it was time to give them each a gift. As Joy was preparing the bag of gifts she looked up and saw all those beautiful children, smiling and waiting. She began to cry and covered her face with her hands. As everyone watched they all began to cry: the director, the doctor, the staff and the children. I went over to her and said, "Joy, please control yourself, the children are waiting for their gifts." I knew if I sympathized with her we would all become a puddle.

Later I asked if she had a flashback, as this orphanage was very much like the one she came from. She said, "No, mom, I told you I have forgotten everything about my early life in Vietnam. I looked at those kids and I felt so sad. I kept thinking what my life would have been if you and dad had not adopted me. Mom, we have to do something to help these kids." I said, "I know what I can do, honey. But what are you willing to do?"

We returned home, me to northern Maine and Joy to complete her last semester of college. She graduated in December and came home for the holidays. She was engaged, and had opportunities to work in Japan. While we were in Vietnam MAPS was asked to start an adoption program. Joy decided she would put her life on hold and volunteer for a year to begin MAPS' work of humanitarian aid and adoption in Vietnam. Joy has referred to herself as a V.A.P. (Vietnamese American Princess). She was used to the best and just expected it. I wondered how she would cope with living in Hanoi, not speaking the language, and with very little money in a truly foreign culture. She left January 17, 1993.

As Joy learned the language, the customs, and the work of humanitarian aid and adoption, she was frustrated by how long it took to accomplish what she had set out to do. She was also gratified by the difference she was making in the lives of the children being adopted and the ones left behind. MAPS first two children were placed for adoption in March of 1993. My husband Ed and I went over to escort these first two children home. That first year 12 children came home. Joy was very busy developing programs in other areas as the ministry asked us to: building new orphanages, funding and developing programs, and putting in water systems.

After Joy completed her first promised year she came home for the holidays and said, "Mom, we have to talk." After all her frustrations and loneliness I thought for sure she was going to say she was done and was coming home. She apologized that it had taken her so long to accomplish so little. She was determined to go back for another year. She is still there after twelve years, developing new projects and programs and is totally dedicated to the children.

On September 20 Joy, still single, adopted a little girl. She found her in one of MAPS supported orphanages and was in our sponsorship program. Vanessa Ha Thu Degenhardt was four-and-a-half years old when they found each other. This was the same age Joy was when she was adopted!! Imagine that.

On December 18 Joy and Thu will be home for the holidays. Thu will meet her new family, all 25 of us. Oh, yes, we adopted three more children: Jeanne, age nine; Tony, age ten; and Douglas, age eight. Now they are all grown. Thu is our eighth grandchild, and the first adopted. But I am sure not the last. What goes around comes around.

With continued support and God's continued blessing Joy will continue her work for the children of Vietnam.

From Social Worker To Adoptive Parent

by Deborah L. Cohen

I'm a 45-year-old single mother raising a son, 15; a daughter, 13; and the newest addition to our family, my adopted daughter Leiana, 20 months old. I've worked in the adoption field for more than two decades but now that our family includes Leiana I have a new perspective on my job and my life. I'd like to thank all of the adoptive parents with whom I've worked over the years, and Adoptions From The Heart for giving me the honor of assisting families in their adoptions and inspiring me to experience my own.

For 20 years I've seen adoption through other people's eyes. I've worked as an adoption social worker since 1984, and for the past nine years I've managed the Pittsburgh office of Adoptions From The Heart. My job has always been to help other families grow through adoption. Adoption wasn't something I ever planned for myself. As the working single mother of two biological children, I never dreamt that I would want to adopt a child.

But that all changed when I traveled to the People's Republic of China with adoptive families several years ago. Seeing the hope, anticipation, and joy that resulted from their experience gave me a new perspective. Suddenly, I imagined welcoming a child from that country into my own family. Five years later, I decided to adopt. I took off my social worker hat and put on my adoptive parent hat, completing all the paperwork, getting my financial requirements in order, and waiting.

For me, solving the financial part of the puzzle was the most daunting. When I first thought about getting $20,000 together, I thought it wasn't possible. But if you put a plan together and look at all of your options, you can make it happen. You scrimp, you save, and you work with a loan officer at the bank to get a line of credit, borrow against the house, and borrow against your 401-K. Many companies offer a cash payment as an employer adoption benefit, from $2,000-$5,000. If your company doesn't have that benefit, perhaps it would consider starting it. There's also the $10,000 federal tax credit to consider, which can be taken over one to five years. Now that I've been through the process, I think I'm better equipped to help other parents look at all the possibilities

Besides the financial side of the picture, there are many challenges that come with adopting internationally, especially for a single parent. China is one of the countries that offer a limited number of adoptions to single parents. I was lucky enough to make the "quota" when I was ready to adopt. Finally, my dream of adopting came true when I traveled to China in December 2003 and brought home my one-year-old daughter, Leiana Jeanne Xian Cohen.

For years, I've been asked the same questions by adoptive parents: will I love a child who isn't biologically my own? How will I blend my biological and adopted children into one cohesive family? What will I tell my adopted child about her heritage and about her history? What is it like to have a child from another culture in the family? Suddenly, I was asking all of those same questions myself.

Just like I had been telling parents for years, the answers soon became crystal clear. I took one look at Leiana's referral picture, and she became my daughter. And, when I brought her home from China, our whole family welcomed her and embraced her with love and unconditional support.

I found it very important from the beginning to involve my immediate and extended family in welcoming Leiana and learning about her culture. Even though she is only 20 months old, we've already started to set the stage for her to be in touch with her culture by reading everything we can about China, being in touch with other families with children from China, and celebrating Chinese New Year and other holidays. My family has joined other families in our local area to start a Chinese school for our daughters.

The stories that other families have shared will also help in addressing my daughter's questions down the line about her heritage and history. There will be stories about her abandonment that will need to be addressed. I have also already experienced people's sharp curiosity about her. While they mean well, some people's questions are extremely insensitive. "How much did she cost?" asked by a man in the grocery store is my favorite. These questions could hurt her as she gets older, and we will have to address this and help her "own" her story in a way that is comfortable for her.

Adopting Leiana has absolutely made me a better social worker. Now I personally understand and have experienced what I tell my families about, whether it's sleep deprivation from a long flight to the various phases of the adjustment period once everybody settles in at home. But as much as I value this professional benefit, adopting Leiana has helped me be a better person and a better mother in every way. It's an experience I'm thankful for every single day. My only regret is that I didn't do it sooner.

Thoughts On Adopting Older Children

by Linda Belles

Upon realizing our family of two biological sons was not complete, my husband and I adopted Katie from China in 2002 as a five-year-old. I spent years learning about the common emotional scars post-institutionalized children have before adopting which helped to prepare for the grief and trauma our daughter experienced coming to live with us. After Katie displayed symptoms of Post-Traumatic Stress Disorder, I started connecting with other parents who are dealing with this and Reactive Attachment Disorder. This is how I met Nancy Spoolstra, Executive Director of the Attachment Disorder Network, and became involved with the organization.

Adopting older children either domestically or internationally is not for every family. Please consider the following points carefully before investing time and money with an adoption agency.

1. **Read everything you can get your hands on concerning adoption.** Be sure to read books that explain what it is like to live with a post-institutionalized child, what issues face ANY

adopted child, and articles dealing with health problems common with these children. I can't stress this enough. Information in the books can be startling to read and may scare you. Keep reading more books, connect with parents who have been there and take time to digest it all. Please check Attach-China (www.attach-china.org) for its wonderful articles and terrific suggested book list. Even if you decide to adopt an infant you need to read up on all the issues. Preparing for the worst while hoping for the best is THE way to prepare for your child.

2. **Are you willing to put the child's physical and emotional health as your number one priority?** Adopting at any age requires that you be sensitive to the child's needs. These children need 100% (and possibly more) of your energy during the adjustment phase. They may need months of consistent, loving parenting with no babysitters, and no daycare (of ANY sort, no matter how briefly) in order to develop a strong, healthy bond with their new parents. Some older children need years in order to adjust. Are you willing to sacrifice your time, money, and possibly your career to help your child?

3. **Are you willing to accept a different race, culture, and language into your family?** If you are considering adopting a child of another

race than yours, you are going to get stared at. Even if you live in a large, diverse city, you will get noticed. Are you comfortable with your grandchildren being of another race? If the child is also from another country you will need to incorporate some of the culture into your family. The most popular way is to celebrate holidays, like Lunar New Year, for instance. Another way is to learn to cook various dishes from that country! Older adoptees may feel the need to continue using their birth language, which will require you to network with other people from her country. This is a wonderful opportunity to learn more about her country while creating new friendships.

4. **Are you willing to allow your child to keep contact with foster parents and/or birthparents?** This mostly applies to domestic adoption due to the fact that most international adoptees have little to no information about birthparents. Some older international children do like to keep contact with foster parents or their friends at the orphanage. They also like to donate money and clothes to their friends left behind.

5. **What are you financially, emotionally, and physically able to handle?** Not that I'm trying to scare everyone away, but please take time to seriously consider what you can handle. The

photo listings out on the Internet can really hook you; that is why agencies use them! If your heart is being pulled by a special needs child please make sure you are able to handle the special need. We turned down a few referrals not because we didn't like the children, but because they had needs that we were not comfortable handling.

6. **Love isn't always enough.** This goes with the first point above. Even if you are the most loving parent out there, sometimes the scars from the past need therapeutic help. The scars can be emotional and/or physical (malnutrition for example). Your child may need help with speech delays, developmental delays, attachment issues, sensory-integration problems, social delays, prior physical/sexual abuse, and exposure to alcohol in utero and various unknown medical problems that are not discovered until after you bring the child home.

7. **Children are very resilient!** Children from the worst backgrounds with every strike against them have flourished in the love and stimulation of a good family. Even if your child has issues that need professional attention the good news is that there is hope! These children can heal! By heal, I don't mean that every child will be perfectly normal. Damage caused by exposure to toxins while in utero (like Fetal

Alcohol Syndrome), is lifelong. Therapy will help the child to become more than he or she would have been at the orphanage. A very tiny percentage of children respond poorly to treatment and take many years of hard work to make progress.

8. **Are you willing to take a "leap of faith"?** Being a parent means you have to give up control. You can't say for certain what your child is going to be like, so don't make yourself crazy trying to. When pregnant, the only thing you have control over is what you eat, drink, and inhale. Adoption is much the same. You can scrutinize the medical information on a child, but in the end you have to take a "leap of faith" and trust everything will work out.

These are the main things that helped us deal with our daughter Katie's trauma when we got back:

1. **We were as prepared as possible.**
   Find out all you can on post-institutionalized children.

2. **We are Love and Logic parents!**
   Love and Logic is a parenting method that helps parents and children establish a rewarding relationship built upon love and trust. It focuses on raising responsible children using a win/win philosophy. You can learn more about it at www.loveandlogic.com.

3. We bottle fed Katie.

We followed several of the bonding suggestions from Attach-China (including bottle feeding) after consulting our social worker. The work paid off huge dividends for everyone. Katie attached quicker, her stress was reduced, and the family got back to normal quicker.

4. We had support from friends and family.

A support network was important to help us through the rough spots. You need a good friend to vent your frustrations to or your sanity and marriage will suffer greatly.

5. We had faith.

Prayer helped us before the adoption and became another source of strength after

6. We introduced new things/events slowly.

We had practically no guests for a long time, avoided loud, crowded events (reunions, parties), and gradually introduced her to church. Anytime we rushed into something she wasn't ready for, it backfired big time.

7. We cooked Chinese food.

Having familiar foods really helped her feel comfortable in her new home

8. We played Chinese CD's.

Any time she was having emotional problems I would rock her and play her music.

9. We created a Life Book.

This is a BIG one! I can't stress enough how important it is to make a book that is your child's life story. It doesn't have to be fancy. Katie had fun putting stickers all over hers. The late nights spent putting it together paid off big. When she is grieving the loss of her former life the book helps her reconnect, regroup, and move forward with confidence.

10. We helped her find a few friends.

It's daunting to make new friends, but when you have language, culture, and self-esteem issues it can be overwhelming. A couple of play dates gave her the confidence to try interacting with children. Now she is anything but shy!!!

11. We kept our sense of humor!

No matter how crazy everything gets, it helps to inject a little humor. Katie found it hard to have a tantrum if she was laughing. My husband is an expert in the humor department, I in the nurture department, so we complement each other nicely!

Linda has become very involved with Attachment Disorder Network (www.radzebra.org), a national organization serving children and families affected by Attachment Disorder. Their mission is to support families parenting children with attachment issues or Reactive Attachment Disorder through education, mentoring, advocacy, local/regional resources, and in child-centered environments (schools, doctors offices, foster/adopt community, legislative) to develop awareness of attachment-related issues.

Special Needs

All Children Need Love!

*"I seldom think about my limitations,
and they never make me sad.
Perhaps there is just a touch of yearning at times,
but it is vague, like a breeze among flowers."*

- Helen Keller

The Little Boy That Could

by Karen A. Hunt

My husband, Ronald, and I adopted Dima from an orphanage in Moscow, Russia. With our help and that of a fantastic attachment therapist, Dima has successfully resolved his attachment disorder. I have over 20 years of experience in the field of developmental disabilities and a wealth of volunteer experiences including being a Sunday School Teacher, Scout Leader, Support Group Facilitator, and Parent Advocate.

Just the other day my 11-year-old son, Dima, said the most amazing thing. He was spending a few days at his grandmother's. I called to speak with him and said I was considering coming that evening. Dima stated in a very panicked tone, "But mom, you can't come. I don't want you here. I don't even miss you!" Those words were like music to my ears. Before you think I have totally lost touch with reality, let me back up.

Dima spent the first three years and nine months of his life in an orphanage. He never knew what it was like to be cuddled when lonely or afraid, fed when hungry, or given extra blankets when cold. His life was like the movie *Groundhog Day*. Every day the same: no trips to the zoo, no beach, no Chuck E. Cheese, no McDonald's.

And then these strangers show up, spend a few days playing with him, leave a few toys and disappear. People said they were his new mom and dad, but they left and were gone for a very long time. Suddenly they show up again. With no time to get reacquainted, they dress him in strange clothes and put him in a *machina* (car) of which he is immensely terrified. Dima has to ride in that horrible *machina* all day to appointments all over the city. This, after never, even once previously, having left that orphanage. What a first day with his new family.

Several days later, this scared little guy is whisked away from the land of familiarity to what might as well have been the moon. Everything is different. For the first time ever, Dima sleeps alone. He is in a big house with no other kids, and a monstrous dog. He has two adults all to himself. The language, food, sights, smells, and sounds are all different. Everything familiar is on the other side of the ocean: the orphanage moms he knew; his bed and friends; those klunky blue shoes. He has lost everything, down to the shoes on his feet, to come to America. And he had no choice.

And Dima tries his mightiest to adjust to this new world. He appears to adapt well. What the grownups miss is that he has simply replaced the shifts of orphanage workers with a new mom, Headstart staff, and a babysitter. And it is not until his babysitter moves away one year later that this little guy falls apart. America is no better than the life he left behind. People here come and go, too. Nothing and no one can be trusted. He is all that he can count on. He is all that he can trust.

Like many others, Dima's journey to a diagnosis and treatment for Reactive Attachment Disorder was bumpy. Along the way were folks who said he had Oppositional Defiant Disorder and Attention Deficit Hyperactivity Disorder. But they could not help Dima. He did not trust enough to benefit from their type of help.

And Dima struggled to keep control. Control of these adults he could not trust. Control over every experience, every situation, so he could never be hurt again. Mom especially scared Dima. She represented all of his hurt, his emptiness, his rejection, his worthlessness. Too many moms had come and gone. Too many moms had already proven how insignificant he was by walking away. Never again would he trust one of these moms. Dima became obsessed with his new mom. Obsessed with controlling her, and being with her all the time so he could be aware of her every move.

So Dima would manipulate and con when it suited him. He perfected wearing that plastic smile because adults gave him what he wanted when he pretended to be fine. When the fear and pain overwhelmed him, he would try to stuff it deeper inside. Sometimes that fear would boil out into a fury of anger. He would attack, scratch, spit, hit, and do whatever it took to protect himself from any pain. Dima literally felt like he was fighting for his life.

From the moment Dima met Dr. Art, his attachment therapist, he did not like him. This guy was different. He knew all the games. He knew all the cons. Dr. Art could not be controlled. He could not be provoked to anger. How Dima wanted to anger him. And now Mom was different too. The tricks weren't working like before. Dima felt safest when he could control the emotions of adults around him. Push an adult to anger and Dima felt secure. Dima was in a panic because he could no longer recreate the familiarity of the harsh orphanage environment.

But despite all the pain and past hurt, Dima had this little spark that was still alive in his heart. It was a spark he had kept deep inside, well hidden from the cruel and unsafe world. Dima knew if he exposed that spark, it would get stomped out, and in the process stomp out his life. Dima hid that spark, and his fragile heart, behind a brick wall. Solid, to keep out the hurt and pain, but also to keep out the love.

As he settled into life in America, Dima saw many kids who had something he could not even imagine. Kids who felt safe. Kids who basked in the love of their parents. Could he risk it? Could he chance showing his mom that little spark of hope? It was a momentous leap of faith, when Dima shared that spark for the first time. He sat with Dr. Art in therapy, and briefly cried because he did not know how to love his mom. At first Dima would only let that spark out for a moment, then fear would tuck it safety back inside. But with each experience, Dima got stronger, got bolder.

Dr. Art and mom took care of that little spark. In their excitement to see it, they were careful not to blow on it too hard. They guided Dima to bring it out at a pace he felt safe with. They let him tuck it back when he needed to. They provided a world safe for that delicate spark to smolder and stay alive until Dima felt ready. And in the safety of that kindle, Dima was able to let his little spark slowly grow into a flame. He was able to risk loving and believing that he could be loved. At the age of eight-and-a-half, for the first time since early infancy, Dima knew he was a loveable person. And his soul burst forth, like a well-stoked fire.

And now, at age 11½, those flames burn strong and true. Dima is secure enough in his mother's love to talk about his problems, to admit when he has made a mistake, and to handle discipline without erupting into a rage of fear and anger (well okay, like any other 11 year old!). Dima is now secure enough in his mother's love and in his love-ability to be away from mom for a few days. And thus, the visit to grandma's this week. Dima was very excited about this trip. He was more than ready for three days away from home. Yes, he needed the reconnection of a phone call, but he wanted to show us and show himself just how far he had come. He can be away from the safety of mom's arms and yet know he is loved and will forever be loved.

And it was with this knowledge that I simply smiled and felt my own heart burst with the flames of pride when my son vehemently stated he was so secure in my love that he did not need to see me to believe it!

Dima's story would not be complete without sharing its impact on his family. I found myself, like most parents of a child with RAD, full of self-doubt and self-blame. Mothers especially bear the brunt of their child's fear and pain. Hence, it is typical for the mothers of children with Reactive Attachment Disorder to sometimes despise their children, and then feel tremendously guilty. I would highly encourage any struggling parent to reach out and find others in the same situation. The Internet has support communities which offer affirmation, advice, and encouragement.

Additionally, I would urge parents to listen to their instincts. If you feel things are not right with your child, seek help. Reactive Attachment Disorder does not get better on its own. Love alone cannot make up for a legacy of profound neglect. Sometimes it is mom, and mom alone, that experiences the impact of her child's pain. Others only see the mask your child carefully constructs for the outside world.

When seeking help, it is important to find a therapist experienced with adoption and attachment. Adoption therapy is truly a specialty field. It often takes an adoption expert to see the symptoms of something like RAD in behaviors which mimic more mainstream diagnoses such as ADHD.

Above all, I share my son's story to offer hope. Reactive Attachment Disorder is not a life sentence. With the right help, kids do get better and go on to have good lives. It does not take a super-parent, or a wealth of past experience, to help a child overcome RAD. More important is a willingness to learn. For me, my education and past experience were actually a hindrance. I needed to let go of my preconceived notions and beliefs in order to understand my son's perception of the world and how to help him heal.

Adopting A Cleft-Affected Child

by Dean and Beth Byler

God has blessed us with eight wonderful children! Four of our children came by way of adoption. This is a story about our daughter Rachel, who was adopted from Russia at two-and-a-half. Rachel was born with a unilateral cleft lip and palate that was repaired here in America, eight weeks after her arrival into our family.

Several people have asked us about what is involved in adopting a cleft-affected child. We hope that our writing will stir an interest in children born with this birth defect. We really desire to be a source of encouragement to those wishing to adopt a cleft-affected child. We have learned so much, and we are happy to pass it on to others!

First, I wanted to say we didn't always want to adopt a special needs child. We started the adoption process wanting a "healthy" little girl. I think it is a common misconception that special needs children are not healthy. In the five years Rachel has been home, she has been extremely healthy. Other than her cleft lip repair, she has had a few minor colds and a tonsillectomy. She rarely gets sick. She has grown by leaps and bounds and is a very active child!

So, we started the adoption process with the thought of adopting a "healthy child" and we had not considered adopting a special needs child. We actually filled out a form for our agency stating which special needs, if any, we would consider. Our list was very short. However, halfway through our adoption (prior to receiving a referral) we saw a news program on 20/20 about orphaned children in Russia born with birth defects. The program stated that these children are often labeled as mentally retarded even though they are bright, capable children! If they do not get adopted, they spend the rest of their lives in mental institutions. Dean and I cried throughout the program. We began to feel God was calling us to adopt a special needs child. We have good friends who adopted a little girl from Korea who was born with a cleft lip and palate. We started talking with them about their experience and what was involved in helping their child. Their little girl is just precious. I remember what she looked like before her surgeries, and today she has a faint scar above her lip. She is a beautiful child and such a sweetheart. It made Dean and I realize there are so many children out there who aren't even considered for adoption because of their special needs. So not only did we adopt a special needs child, we are now trying to educate others in hopes of finding homes for the "unadoptable."

A wonderful resource is Wide Smiles (http://www.widesmiles.org). It was started by a mother who adopted three Korean children, all born with cleft lip and palate. They have an Internet support group called Cleft Talk where several hundred moms of children born with cleft lip and palate, as well as adults who were born with the condition, belong to the list. It has been a great resource for us. There is information at the Wide Smiles website on how to join. Also, look through the photo gallery of the before and after pictures; you will be so amazed!

Something that we were concerned about was what expenses

were ahead of us for surgeries, dental work, etc. One source to turn to if your insurance does not cover the surgery expenses is Operation Smile. They are a not-for-profit organization that helps children all over the world who were born with facial defects. We contacted Operation Smile, and they were prepared to pay for Rachel's surgeries if our insurance didn't cover the expenses. Their website is http://www.operationsmile.com

Rachel had her lip repaired in August 1999, just after she came home from Russia. Because of her age (she was almost three), it was out-patient surgery. For younger children the stay in the hospital may be a day or two. The whole procedure took about 45 minutes! Rachel had minimal crying and discomfort after surgery and was up playing with her siblings a few days later. She really did great! Her stitches came out a week after surgery. She has not had another cleft surgery since then, but she is due to have her palate closed and a bone graft in January 2005. She has had some orthodontic work in preparation for this upcoming surgery.

Rachel is such a joy! She has adjusted so well in the last five years. We are so thankful to the Lord for leading us to our precious daughter! We are very grateful that Rachel has had the opportunity to have the medical care she needed, something she may never have received in Russia.

If you are considering adopting a child with cleft lip and palate, we would be happy to answer any questions you might have. Please see our family website at www.bylerbunch.com or feel free to email us at bylerbunch@yahoo.com.

Our Daughter's Arthrogryposis
by Barbara Burke

My husband and I have been parents for the past 24 years; 15 of those years as adoptive parents to six children. Four of our children have been adopted internationally from Korea and China. We invite other families pursuing adoption to visit our Christian family website at www.adoptionfamily.org which offers support and information on our children's special needs, adoption grants, resource books, and other adoption related information. Anyone with questions can write me at: barbaburke@comcast.net.

(Editor's Note: Arthrogryposis (Arthrogryposis Multiplex Congenita) is a term describing the presence of a muscle disorder that causes multiple joint contractures at birth. A contracture is a limitation in the range of motion of a joint.)

Our family has come in contact with so many beautiful children and families struggling with arthrogryposis. They have been such an inspiration and encouragement to us! My husband and I did some groundwork prior to accepting the referral of our daughter from the adoption agency. We attended a full-day seminar at our local Children's Hospital headed by Dr. Judith Hall, the leading expert on the subject. She has researched this condition for the past 20 years and has cutting-edge information. I also contacted parents who were raising children with arthrogryposis and found them most helpful.

We first heard of our daughter residing in a baby's home in Seoul, Korea, when she was four months old. At that time, she had been diagnosed as being born with a type of arthrogryposis known as amyoplasia, affecting only her upper limbs. Within 10 days of life, her biological parents placed her for adoption because they were given little hope for her future and felt unable to afford the needed care. We first met Soo (Excellent) Hee (Brilliant) through a picture at age four months. She was born with shoulders internally rotated, elbows fixed in extension, and flexion contracture of her wrists. She received range of motion by a therapist visiting her three times weekly in the orphanage. The U.S. doctors believe this saved her small muscles from atrophying.

Soo Hee arrived at our home when she was 10 months old. I continued the range of motion therapy by using music and movement. It was a nice time for bonding and exercising. I continued with this for 30-45 minutes a day until around the age of 15 months, when she balked at this type of therapy. I then used a different approach. I placed toys on high table tops to encourage her to reach. I bought a tabletop stove instead of one that stands on the floor for this reason. We used a TV table to play with toys on instead of the floor. I hid little dinosaurs and small surprises inside an egg of play-dough for her to dig out with her fingers. I first started with a very pliable play-dough so she wouldn't get discouraged. I made the play-dough myself, and over the months when we played this game, I would increase the stiffness of the dough.

She started seeing a private occupational therapist at one year, and also had her first pair of night splints fitted for her. Her therapist saw her one hour a week and gave me a lot of insight into what I could do in our home to continue therapy. I learned a lot from observing her therapist interact with her. It is really necessary for parents to instill these techniques on a daily basis in order for the child to fully benefit. She also attended our county's early intervention program, which she and I went to once a week. The school therapist also came to our home once a month. Although her sense of balance

She needed to learn adaptive skills like removing her coat, using the bathroom, . . . and needed to get experience dealing with her limitations among her peers.

was off, our daughter started walking within the normal time frame, 14 months. She was very cautious and took only a few falls. She had no protective reflexes but quickly learned to balance. Her legs have always been solid and muscular and eventually compensated in balance. She could run, jump, and pedal a bike all within the normal age range for her age.

At age two she was evaluated at an Arthrogryposis Clinic at a children's hospital. The doctors agreed hers was a mild case, finding all muscles present in her arms. They believed, over time and use, that the muscles would grow stronger (which they have). They did not see her as a candidate for muscle-transfer surgery. Her wrists, which were severely affected at birth, now have good flexion and function. At two she was able to draw, self-feed, turn pages, and carry objects with a fairly good grasp. She could drink from an open cup with two handles or a tiny shot glass with one hand. At that time, four fingers were somewhat affected. At age two she was learning to dress.

She seemed to have a mild case of this condition in her jaw. She drooled constantly during her first two years. She would chew only with her front teeth. She accepted my direction when I reminded her to chew with her back teeth. Chewing gum was good therapy to help wake up those sleeping weak muscles. In six months, these two techniques completely eliminated this problem in her jaw.

At 24 months her cognitive skills were tested by a group of doctors. Our daughter's scores were above the 36-month-old level. The report stated, "She is speaking in twelve-word sentences with pronouns. She knows all her colors, shapes, and her sex. She can stack a tower of 15 blocks and holds a pencil properly." At age three, she was tested and did not qualify for our county's developmental pre-school. She received a test score of 95% in gross motor and 90% in fine motor. We disputed these results, stating they were deceptive and that the test was too standardized for every child. She, in fact, has a disability and needed the developmental pre-school to learn basic skills for the kindergarten program. She needed to learn adaptive skills like removing her coat, using the bathroom, zipping a backpack, opening heavy doors, and needed to get experience dealing with her limitations among her peers. The school district paid for an outside evaluation. The recommendation was to place her into the developmental pre-school. She did very well. I withdrew her when she was four-and-a-half because I felt she had received all the benefits she needed from the program. Since they had made an exception in her case to admit her, I didn't want to abuse this, nor take up a space in the classroom when she no longer benefited from it.

When our daughter was five years old, she did not qualify for kindergarten because she turned five after the start of school. Instead, she entered a private, academic pre-K program three mornings a week. This was the first year she was in a class where she was the only disabled child. She was very excited the first day of school but worried about what the other children might say about her arthrogryposis. We decided if anyone mentioned it she could just tell that person she was born with arthrogryposis. This, in fact, did happen when a little boy asked, "Why are your hands different?" Our daughter relayed to me she simply said what we discussed and then she said, "and we thought no more about it, mommy." She was self-sufficient at age five and, other than a little more weakness in her arms, could do most anything any five-year-old could. We invested in a large above ground pool five years ago when her therapist suggested she would benefit from it. It has helped strengthen her arms and, at age four, she was again seen at the Arthrogryposis Clinic and found to have full rotation in both her shoulders. We believe the freedom of movement underwater was fantastic therapy. She is able to use a pencil, marker, or crayon, and her handwriting and coloring is better than the average student because of her perfectionist nature.

By age five she was completely self-sufficient in her toileting needs and brushing her teeth. She was able to fully dress herself, pull her socks on, and tie her shoes. Usually she can snap, button, and zip her clothes, depending on her mood and the difficulty of the snap, button, etc. One of the methods I used in teaching her these things was to have a large box of oversized dress-up clothes at her disposal. Initially, she needed me to stop whatever I was doing to aid in her changing into one of the outfits she picked out. Over time, I would slip some new, intriguing, glittery outfit in the box that required more difficult attention with snaps or buttons. Over a year she came to me less and less often for help. The first day of pre-K, I woke up to her standing alongside my bed at six in the morning. fully dressed and hair combed. She had awakened me and then waited for me to take her to school.

When she was to enroll in kindergarten, we had her tested and she qualified to skip kindergarten and entered the first grade as a five-year-old (soon to turn six). She had a wonderful year in first grade and was very popular and the tallest in her class!

At seven years old she was selected, based on her test scores, for a new, self-contained gifted program where she was in a combination class of grades one, two, and three taught at an accelerated pace with other gifted students. She was sorry to have to change schools to enter this program, but it was her decision to do this and she enjoyed the brand new school.

Our daughter is now 11 years old and a beautiful, capable, self-motivated young lady. She is the tallest in her sixth grade class at five-feet, five-inches, and the Talented and Gifted program she has been in has been an excellent fit for her. She recently cut off 13 inches of her beautiful hair and donated it to an organization called Locks of Love, which makes wigs for children undergoing chemotherapy. She aspires to become a writer and always has her head in a book. Recently, a special orchestra chair with elbow rest was designed for her and she is in her second year of violin. She volunteers in our Parish as an altar server, choir member, and lector reading from the gospel.

She is soon to travel with her father to China to meet her new brother. He was born with porencephaly and cerebral palsy and she is confident that she has a lot to teach him about living with a disability and reaching one's full potential in life. As a matter of fact, she auditioned and was selected for a spot in a Microsoft advertisement on developing one's full potential. She was tutored in Mandarin for this part and her line was, "I have POTENTIAL."

Our daughter's determination and gentle nature bring such joy to our family. We each feel we have grown knowing her and sharing our life with her. She reminds us constantly of what is really worth valuing in life, and she is a treasure beyond words.

Our Journey Through Attachment Disorder

by Nancy Geoghegan

I look back over the past eight years and am thankful for all my son has taught me. Because of our ongoing healing journey, I have been able to help other families through my website at www.attachmentdisorder.net. I am on the board of ATTACH (www.attach.org) which specializes in educating parents and professionals on the importance of attachment in the first three years of life and the consequences when a child's attachment is weakened. Adoption is a beautiful journey even through the bumpy times.

Our story began the day we brought our then-four-year-old son home from a Romanian orphanage. From the moment he came home, he was a whirlwind of hyperactivity: touching everything, defiant, destructive, loud, violent, and rageful. I noticed other strange behaviors: rocking back and forth and side to side, refusing to eat, lack of eye contact, a need to be in control of everyone and every situation, and a propensity to illicit angry responses from both myself and my husband, what we called "pushing our buttons." He had no fear of strangers, often just walking up to one, touching them, and talking to them.

He would hug me with his back when I went for a hug and he

flinched when I touched him. Yet he would be happy to give hugs to anyone not in his immediate family. I suppose the worst behaviors were the defiant ones: bossiness, arguing, and sassiness. No amount of behavior modification (sticker charts) worked with him. I read all the traditional parenting books and tried many different techniques.

Become as informed as you can about attachment problems but don't let it make you fear adoption or foster care.

Sometimes they worked for a small amount of time but inevitably we would end up back at the beginning.

I started to think it was my fault. That I wasn't loving him enough and that I needed to give him more time and be more patient. In kindergarten he was a constant behavioral problem. An insightful teacher told me to check the Internet for issues international adoptees face. That is when I stumbled across the Parents Network for Post Institutionalized Children. They have a newsletter that ran through many issues adoptees suffer from. Not only international adoptees but children adopted domestically, foster children, and even biological children can be diagnosed with attachment disorder. There was a list of symptoms for Reactive Attachment Disorder (RAD). At first I was excited as I thought "Okay, I'm not crazy this is real." But the more I read, the more frightened I became. It is a very serious illness and tough to recover from. Remember, not all children who are adopted will come to you with attachment disorder. A lot depends on the child's previous environment and their temperament.

This past year we adopted a four-and-a-half-month-old from Guatemala. I noticed a few signs of attachment problems: lack of eye contact and stiffening when being held, but I was informed and started working on the attachment process from day one.

Become as informed as you can about attachment problems but don't let them make you fear adoption or foster care. Some children may suffer from attachment issues, some from mild attachment disorder, and some from severe disorder as in my son's case. They all can benefit from treatment and therapeutic parenting and should receive both to help them become securely attached.

Our son was diagnosed with and received treatment for RAD and Sensory Integration Disorder (SID). It is important to find out if your child suffers from other disorders that may exist with RAD. He was also diagnosed with Attention Deficit Hyperactive Disorder (ADHD). He takes Adderall for the ADHD and Wellbutrin for depression and anxiety. I fought the idea of giving him medication for a long time but the neurologist explained my son's brain did not develop normally due to the deprivation and lack of attachment in his early years and that the medication would help him. The doctor was correct.

We found a therapist who specialized in attachment work. We traveled three hours each way but it was worth it. So we had the right kind of therapy in place for our son and then we had to learn therapeutic parenting. Typical parenting techniques do not work with attachment-disordered children. We used the parenting techniques designed specifically for children with RAD. I also found local and Internet support groups.

We started out with a boy who hated the world: a boy who couldn't love, obey the simplest request, trust, or be joyful. We now have a child who laughs, hugs, loves, smiles, trusts, and can live within the boundaries we set for him. It is an amazing sight to behold. God is merciful. Once you deal effectively with all the pieces to the puzzle—the parenting, therapy, medication (if needed), taking care of other disorders, dealing effectively with the school, and taking care of yourself—you can effect positive change in your attachment-disordered child.

Thoughts On Loving A Helpless Child

by Rosemary J. Gwaltney

I was born on the Alberta prairies and raised on a farm in Washington State. I married young but did not begin having babies at once. That marriage dissolved, and three years later, I began to adopt children as a single mother. I've been a mother now for thirty-four years, and have been blessed with twenty-six children. Most of my children have disabilities of one sort or another. All of them are dearly loved, greatly admired, and deeply enjoyed. They are mostly grown now, and I am a grandma of two baby boys! I am a published writer of non-fiction, many articles, and a chapter in a book about raising children with disabilities. I am now married again. We have seven adult children still home, all of whom have disabilities. So now, with so little to do, I have more time to write!

As the adoptive mother of twenty-six children, including children with a wide variety of disabilities, I've been asked many questions and I used to speak at adoption conferences. Everyone understood how I could love my beautiful, responsive children smiling in the picture frames, which I brought to show them all. But they would stop short when they learned about my daughter, Misty. I can't tell you the number of times I've been asked how I could love a profoundly retarded child.

Why is it so rare for people to love a helpless person? Is it fear of the unknown, fear of loss, boredom, indifference? Is it they have never known a child like this? That is quite likely. I'll tell you where to find many of them: in the photo listing books at adoption resource centers across the United States, waiting. And they are the fortunate ones. Some caring caseworker believes

Misty was a shock when she arrived. She was two years old and as limp as a cooked noodle. She did not babble or respond to anything we did.

they deserve at least one loving parent of their own, just like any other child. The less fortunate ones are tucked away in institutions. I know where many of them are, as well.

Is loving a newborn infant difficult? No, it is thrilling, precious, breathtaking, and natural. We just don't expect that newborn infant to remain an infant. We expect that infant to grow, learn, change, and mature. A profoundly retarded child needs much the same care as a baby, and is just as precious. It's just that he or she will remain helpless.

I think people's hesitation and avoidance might have a lot to do with fear—a very realistic fear, that perhaps this child could die young. After all, how many times in life do we give our love to someone we consciously, rationally, know we could lose?

I first began learning how to love someone I was going to lose when I became a foster parent. It was an excruciating experience. Every time a child moved on, my heart was broken. Some marvelous foster parents can love a series of foster children for decades, and survive the sorrow, even feel happy for the child when they move on. I could not. I began adopting.

Many years later, when I had experienced the deaths of several of my medically fragile children, having to pull myself together each time and continue loving and nurturing my other children, I began to think of these helpless children as rainbows. When the sun comes out, there is a lovely rainbow. Then it is gone. A fragile child is like a rainbow. It is terribly sad when the rainbow disappears. I have had periods of intense depression over my earthly losses. Between rainbows, I struggled and prayed to remain resilient, and to feel and continue to give joy! It is God who has healed my deepest griefs at last.

> *Those who give*
> *their love to fragile*
> *children must learn to leap*
> *from rainbow to*
> *rainbow.*

God gave me a helpless little daughter I named Misty Angelita. She was one of my lovely, fragile rainbows. Misty was a shock when she arrived. She was two years old and as limp as a cooked noodle. She did not babble or respond to anything we did. She was not in any way the little girl I had been told she was. The caseworker, who had never seen her, relayed the foster mother's words that she was a good eater, was learning to play with her foster sibling, and was beginning to crawl. But Misty could only drink from a bottle, and could not roll over, sit up, say a word, or play. As it turned out, she could not even see. She was not very much aware of her surroundings, unless startled or frightened. In my heart, I was terribly disappointed and full of sorrow. The doctors told me she was so globally damaged, she never would walk or talk, and they were correct.

Misty would never respond to me in the way I had expected. At first, when I learned how devastatingly limited she was, my heart was broken. A different break than I had ever experienced before. This child was not going to grow up and become largely independent like my other children. But I was outraged at the doctors' strong suggestions I send her back. She was not a defective appliance. She was a lovely human child. God had sent her. I always prayed He would send just the right child, so I knew that she was though I did not understand it. I had adopted her, and she was my own. Just as though she was born to me, I was keeping her.

To make a long story short, God put a love in my heart for this beautiful baby that had no explanation. I had lost the child I expected, but here in my arms was a helpless baby who needed me far more than any other baby could have. And loving her changed my whole life. Because I grew to love Misty with such a fierce and tender mother-love, I deeply appreciated the value and worth of children who were so completely helpless and went hunting for another one just like her to adopt. I never found another child just like Misty, of course, but in the decades that followed, I became the mother of ten helpless children. I adopted nine, and one was given to me by his loving mother. Each one was a unique individual, and dearly loved.

Loving anyone presents a risk of losing: any time, any place, under any circumstances. But imagine what life would be without love. A barren, selfish existence. Few would choose never to love. Even those who have been injured by losing love usually go on to love again in their lives. Maybe not the same kind of love, but love nevertheless.

Every kind of love is different. Even a parent of many never loves two the exact same way. No two children are exactly the same in personality or in the way they respond to others. Human beings are all different. Every relationship has its own characteristics and unique properties.

So it is with loving a profoundly retarded individual, exactly the same. Love is love. I have loved each one of my children in a different way from the others. Each love has been returned to me in a way just like none other. A relationship with a helpless person is very pure, because love has to be given unconditionally. It is pure in the way that it enriches the soul. I used to think that my love, as the mother, was deeper. But as the years passed, I began to wonder—is it really? Is my love, being the one who can express it, larger?

Consider the child who knows only one person, and whose entire existence depends on that one person. My Misty was such a child. This person makes the complete difference between life being a mass of confusion and life consisting of love and security. I think you might say this child's love is just as great as that of the person who is able to express it more. After all, simply being able to express love is not the defining element of its greatness.

Loving a helpless child is a blessing. It is not difficult. There is always something appealing and interesting, about every person, if you look hard enough. I think a person who never knows and never grows to love a helpless person is like someone who has never seen a rainbow. Love growing in a person's heart is enriching by itself, like a garden of exquisite flowers. The fragrance wafts into every portion of a person's life. Love is a gift, and a pearl of great price, to be treasured. Always.

Many Ways To Make A Family

Breaking the Mold

*"People ask me, 'What about gay adoptions? Interracial?
Single Parent?' I say, 'Hey fine, as long as it works for the child
and the family is responsible.' My big stand is this:
Every child deserves a home and love. Period."*

Dave Thomas
Founder of Wendy's

Bringing Jordan Home

by Jerry Windle

I am a Senior Neuroscience Sales Specialist with Eli Lilly and Company. My son Jordan is now six years old and in kindergarten. He is in the top of his class in reading and writing—and of course, in music and art. Jordan and I, along with Papa (Jason) live, in Miami, Florida.

In the spring of 2000, I sat in a physician's office and thumbed through several magazines when I noticed a copy of MAPS MUSINGS (the newsletter of Maine Adoption Placement Services). I read a listing of parents and their children and the date the child was placed with their forever families. In an instant, I was taken back several years to a time when I was on active duty as a Logistics Officer in the Navy. During my 12 years of active military service, I visited many countries and helped build playgrounds, repair roofs, and provide food to local orphanages. I knew long ago that one day I would like to adopt a child. I remember always having an affinity for Cambodia and its amazing history. Could it be that now was my time to adopt? This is where my journey began.

I contacted Karen at MAPS who put me in contact with Carol at the MAPS office in Florida. I told her I was a single man, and was interested in adopting a child from Cambodia. Carol immediately sent me a manila envelope of information including an application. "Am I ready for this? Can I really do it? I've wanted to adopt a child since my early days in the Navy, now is the time!"

While I made my way through the paperwork, I thought to myself, "Wow, this is a lot of work." Then I thought about the child who was waiting for me, possibly sick, in an orphanage in Cambodia. It became a race against time for me. I could not allow my son to wait one day more than was absolutely necessary. Even though I had no idea who he was, I knew he

Armed with a diaper bag, enough Cheerios for an army and a Pooh bear, we were off. Two friends and I were on a trek to Cambodia.

was there. I was in daily contact with Carol in Tampa. Within a couple of weeks, I was having my home study done. I received my checklist and, once again, I was off to the races. I had my physical, my background checks, and my employer records done. My INS paperwork was completed in record time. My dossier was complete in less than a month. Suddenly, I had a referral with a photo of my son. When I saw Pisey's face, I knew he was mine. His face was beautiful. Although he was nearly two years old, he was so small. Did he know that daddy was trying his hardest to get there to bring him home?

I called Carol and Karen over and over again. I always asked the same question, "Any word on my travel date?" As every parent who adopts a child knows, the wait is the hardest part of the entire process. Every night before I went to sleep, I stepped outside and looked into the sky and wished my little boy a good night. "Daddy will be there soon, and you will never be alone again." I took a photo of myself and placed it in a plastic photo protector and then fashioned it into a necklace. I asked MAPS if they could get it to my little Pisey so that he would know me when I arrived to bring him home.

To help with the wait I took my friend's advice and auditioned for a musical show and got the lead role as Professor Harold Hill in *The Music Man*. The two months of rehearsals had started. Just before the first night of technical rehearsals, I got a phone call from Karen at MAPS. "Jerry, it's time. We don't know how much longer the Cambodian program is going to be open, so you have to travel now." She told me I would be in Cambodia for approximately four days. I was so excited I couldn't speak. I called my friends and asked them if they wanted to take a trip—in two days!! They said, "Absolutely, let's go."

Then I looked at my watch and realized I had rehearsal that night! Oops! I went to my director and told her the news. After she recovered her composure and her breath, she reminded me I had no understudy and every performance was already sold out. The show was going to open in 10 days. I told her if she got the rest of the cast ready, I would be back from Cambodia with my son in time for the show. I would not let her down. Our entire cast of 35 actors and actresses maintained the faith. My colleagues and my fellow cast members even threw an impromptu baby shower for me.

Armed with a diaper bag, enough Cheerios for an army and a Pooh bear, we were off. Two friends and I were on a trek to Cambodia. It was almost five months to the week that I made that first phone call. We flew from Fort Myers, Florida, to Phnom Penh with an overnight in Bangkok. Youn, (pronounced Jon) met us at the airport. He was our driver for the next few days, but he would be a young man I would visit in Cambodia again. "We will go to the orphanage now," he told us.

As we made our way down the bumpy dirt road toward the orphanage gate, I felt my heart pounding. This was the moment I had waited a lifetime for. I was trying to memorize every emotion, every feeling. Youn honked the horn and a man slowly opened the gate at the Chom Chao Orphanage. My eyes darted everywhere. Then I saw two ladies standing at the door of the main building. One of the women was holding a tiny little boy. He was wearing a baseball outfit and green tennis shoes. Was he my son? They smiled and walked toward me. As they got closer, I saw my photo hanging from a small leather necklace around his neck. I reached out my arms, and Jordan Pisey Windle was mine. I held him against my chest and though I knew this two-year-old little "angel baby" was wondering who I was, I knew I was in love with him forever. We stood in the middle of the Chom Chao orphanage and I made a promise to him that he would never be hungry and he would never be alone again. Jordan loved his Cheerios and his Pooh bear.

I was concerned because I couldn't make him smile. I thought to myself, "I don't want him to be afraid." Youn spoke to Jordan every day, as did the hotel staff. They comforted him and told him I was his daddy. I remember thinking how desperately I wanted to be able to speak Khmer. On the morning of our third day, as I was preparing for my embassy interview, I dropped one of

We are father and son. We are best friends. I hear time and again how adoptive families cannot believe how perfectly they are matched.

the papers. Holding Jordan, I bent over to pick it up. As I leaned downward, the brightest smile I have ever seen beamed up toward me. Jordan smiled, then he giggled, and finally he laughed out loud. He has not stopped smiling since.

On the fourth day, we were ready to go home. We boarded the plane in Phnom Penh and headed for Florida. The trip home was more grueling. How did I ever think I would be able to study my *Music Man* lines on the plane? The show was going to open in only a day. Exhausted, we arrived some 24 hours later in Florida. We rested the entire day and the following day we went to the theatre. The cast was relieved that we made it home safely. Yes, I needed scripts in the wings on either side of the stage but we pulled it off without a hitch. It was a great show and I had my son!

For the next year, Jordan and I grew closer and closer. I taught him American Sign Language so he could communicate with me as he was learning English and I spoke to him in both English and Spanish. Jordan's teacher spoke fluent Spanish and at my request she spoke to him in both Spanish and English. In less than 15 months, Jordan was communicating in all three languages.

After a while, our life was pretty organized. Then the theatre called me to see if I was ready to take on another role. I said I would audition only if Jordan could be at the theatre during rehearsal. It was during this show I met Jason Edwards, a pianist and composer. He had been writing songs since he was seven years old and his dream was to produce an album one day. I listened to his songs and was immediately drawn to the magic of his music.

Jason taught Jordan to play the piano and in less than six months, Jordan and Jason were playing duets. When we have friends or family over, Jordan is anxious to sing "New York, New York" and play the piano for them. When he is finished, he hops down from the piano bench and takes his bow.

Jordan is an amazing five-year-old. Although we have been a family for a little more than three years now, most people think he is my biological son. His personality is so perfectly matched with mine. We have the best times together. We are father and son. We are best friends. I hear time and again how adoptive families cannot believe how perfectly they are matched. There is only one answer and it cannot be found here on earth.

In early 2003, Jason came to me and asked me to listen to something he had been working on for the previous year. It was a compilation of his work. The CD of his piano music was complete and was ready to be produced. He asked me what I thought about him titling the CD *For The Children* and donating a portion of the proceeds to MAPS to help feed and shelter hungry children around the world. He said that knowing Jordan inspired him, and he hoped others who listened to his music would also be inspired.

Jason's album is a beautiful collection of works that have spanned his entire life. His gift to the world in his music and his gift to the children of the world in his support of MAPS is a fulfillment of a dream and the promise of hope. Jason designed the CD cover with a photo of Jordan and Jason's niece, Braden. The CD itself has an image of Jordan in Cambodian silks with his hands together as he is offering the Cambodian greeting gesture.

If you would like to purchase a copy of Jason's CD, "For The Children," you can get more information by calling (305) 522-0753 or visit www.jasonedwardsmusic.com. A portion of every CD sold will be donated to MAPS and placed in a special fund to help feed and shelter waiting children around the world.

Of Band-Aids And Such
by Cheryl L. Dieter

I live in Iowa and am the mother of four children. Two of them were born in Korea. Adopting transracially/transculturally brings with it special responsibilities and obligations that we owe our children. It usually isn't until our children are home for several years that we begin to realize the magnitude of what this truly means. This story is meant to remind us of all the little things that we take for granted that our children may not, and how we can never just take things at face value when it comes to our kids.

I saw his face on a website. He needed a home and I needed a son. It should have been that simple but it wasn't. Love never is.

Transracial/transcultural adoption isn't easy. It isn't enough just to give your child all the love you have in your heart and soul. It isn't enough to just be there for them. It's about learning to think differently and in ways that surprise and astound you. It's about surrendering your thoughts of how you see the world and working towards seeing the world in the way that your child will view and experience it.

I began to understand this one Monday afternoon as my son drove his shiny red bike with its skinny black training wheels. The bike tipped one way and he went the other. The result was a three-year-old's tears as big as puddles and a scraped knee full of bits of rock and sand. After cleaning the wound, I carefully placed the bandage on his knee.

"Mommy," he said through his eyes still wet as dew on grass. "Those are bandages for people like you. Where are the ones for people like me?"

Ouch, he was right! The bandage blended in so well with my white skin while on his beautiful caramel colored skin it stuck out, drawing unwanted attention to the wound.

And that's when it happened. That's when the light went on and I began to see things a little clearer. For it was at that moment, that I realized I couldn't continue just doing things as I had always done them. This is because I had done things and seen them in a certain way based in large part because of the color of my skin. For him the world will be different. People will judge him using a different set of criteria than those used

. . . if he is to grow up feeling his skin "fits" just right, it will require more than just celebrating yearly holidays and attending a cultural festival during the summer.

on the children born of me. So while I will have to do the big things that will help him navigate the world as a person of color it will also be the little things I do that will matter to him in the future. Small things like making sure my CD collection is abundant with artists who have Latino and Korean names. Things like making sure my bookcase contains numerous books written by African Americans and other people of color when compared to that of my own race. And making sure the art that he sees around our house depicts people of all cultures and ethnicities.

As older adult adoptees have so graciously shared with me, I can't make my son secure in his own skin just by my own actions. According to them, if he is to grow up feeling his skin "fits" just right, it will require more than just celebrating yearly holidays and attending a cultural festival during the summer. It means that his life will need to be celebrated and embraced by people of color. It means that he needs to be surrounded by people "like" him. Showing him that I value him and other people of different ethnicities means searching out the services of professional people of all races. It means sharing meals with families that look like ours on a regular basis and living in neighborhoods in which there are other kids that look like ours. It also means providing opportunities for my child to learn racial pride and not tolerating racist jokes of any kind.

I hope that by witnessing his mother showing compassion, love, and tolerance to all people of all races and ethnicities he will learn to be tolerant of my mistakes as I navigate the new worlds that have opened to me through adoption. And I also hope that as he glances down at his Big Bird bandage he will realize sometimes band-aids do more than just cover over the problem; sometimes they open your eyes to them.

She Really Is Our Daughter!

by Valarie Gauntt

Through my whole life, all I can remember saying when someone would ask, "What do you want to be when you grow up?" was "I want to be a mommy!" When I got married we tried right away to start a family. It was not until we adopted that my dream came true. I recommend adoption for anyone that wants to be a parent and is unable to give birth to a child. You can truly love an adopted child just as much as one that you give birth to.

We had been married for five years and were unable to have a child of our own. We were still talking with a fertility specialist, but always knew that adoption was an option for us.

Our journey to adoption started with a friend calling to say a member of her family was pregnant and was considering putting the baby up for adoption. We were thrilled to be considered as parents for this baby.

We made arrangements to fly halfway across the country to meet this person. After a nice Christmas with her and her family, our friend informed us the girl had decided she needed to give the baby to someone that did not have a connection to her family. We flew home devastated.

I signed up to start receiving an online newsletter from American Adoptions. It was just an informative e-mail with information about children that needed homes. I received the e-mails for months without ever opening one.

On Monday, August 25, 2003, I got the American Adoptions newsletter and opened it. I read about a baby girl three days old in Florida that needed a family to love her. I called my husband at work and told him all the information the website had on her. She was a beautiful, healthy African-American baby girl. I asked my husband if I should call the agency, and he said, "Yes, of course."

I think if you are considering adoption, and think you can handle a few stares and such, you should consider adopting a minority child.

I called and spoke with the woman handling this case. I told her we were ready to go to Florida and pick her up. All they had to do was say the word. After a couple of setbacks with paperwork, we were on our way to pick up our daughter.

"Our daughter," what an amazing and scary thing. The baby was now a week-and-a-half-old. We packed and headed south. We had picked out a name, bought some bottles, and made arrangements to meet the birthmother.

I had several conversations with God during that time. Was I really the right person to be this little girl's mother? Could I really love her as if I had given birth to her? Could we as a white couple raise a happy black child? There were so many questions in my head.

When we arrived at the adoption agency in Florida and they brought in the baby, the questions I had all went right out the window. Yes, this was our daughter, yes, I could in fact love her more then anything in the world; and what did it matter what color we were? We were from then on her parents. The day after we picked her up, we met with her birthmother. We had spoken with her over the phone but she wanted to meet us in person. As much as I was not sure about the whole thing beforehand, now I know that it was not only the right thing to do but the only thing. We had a nice conversation with her, talked for about an hour-and-a-half, and parted. We send pictures and letters, but I know we will never meet again unless our daughter chooses to later in life.

I am glad we met her birthmother. We can tell our daughter a little more about her now. I can say to anyone that is nervous about meeting a birthparent, that for us, it was a closure in a way. I think for us and the birthmother, we each just needed to know where the baby was from and where she was going.

The next couple of months are a blur. We traveled the country to have everyone meet our precious baby girl. Our families took to her and accepted her as if we had conceived and given birth to her. We are very lucky. No one in our family has a problem with her being adopted or with the fact that she is not white.

I think if you are considering adoption, and think you can handle a few stares and such, you should consider adopting a minority child. There are so many children waiting for good parents. Who really cares if everyone in your family is the same color? The only thing that matters to us is that our daughter is right where she belongs. She will always know she is adopted, but she will also know that she is loved just as much, if not more, than any of her non-adopted friends.

Our precious "little duck" has never been introduced to anyone as our adopted daughter. Instead, we both hold our heads high and tell everyone this is OUR DAUGHTER. A silly dream come true for me; I can now sign Christmas cards in a way I was not sure I would ever get to do:

Love and Prayers, Valarie, Will, and Debra-Jane.

A Love Story:
A Single Parent Adoption
by Edith Rose

I stood on the sidelines for 20 years with empty arms while my siblings raised their children. Today I am raising mine in the beautiful Colorado Rockies. Not only are my arms full, but so is my heart and life.

After years of infertility and sorrow trying to have a baby, I turned to adoption. My husband and I were so excited. No more treatments, no more disappointments. We were going to finally have a family. And for me, no more empty arms. I had wanted nothing but a baby for 16 years. I was at a point where I could not go to a baby shower or church because it just hurt too much seeing mothers with their children. When I saw families, I was happy for them, but the pain ran deep.

It was 1996 when we started the process. We wanted to do a traditional domestic adoption. We did our home study and opened our whole lives up to the agency. They poked and prodded. They took fingerprints and did criminal checks. We even cleaned and set up a nursery. It was very hard to wait. Stress was very high. I still remember the day our caseworker called to say we were approved. Then the wait began. The agency we worked with would not tell us if we were matched. That way if it fell through

> *They told me I could still adopt, I just had to change my focus. I now would have a hard time doing traditional adoption.*

ahead of time, it would not cause more pain. But somehow I could always tell if we were matched. I swear I even nested, but they still fell through. As the years passed the wait got harder and harder. The stress grew. I would sit in the baby's room and cry, or rock in the rocking chair and read. It seemed like I would never become a mother. A common theme with other people was, "It will come when God knows you are ready." That made me crazy. Why would a 15-year-old in the back of a car be ready, but we weren't? Then someone sent me an e-mail that said, "Please be patient. Your baby wants you to wait for him/her." That helped me see we were waiting for the right baby, not just any baby. The baby meant for us.

In 1999 my life fell apart. My husband wanted a divorce. He used the reason of not knowing if he could love an adopted baby but I know that was not it. The stress of adoption may have added to the problem but it was not the cause. He had been excited and wanted to adopt. He even talked to our caseworker three days before and told her how excited we still were. Adoption comes at a high price; not only in cost, but in how it affects lives. I was crushed. With adoption you live, eat, and sleep adoption. It becomes as normal a part of your life as breathing. I felt he took my last chance to ever become a mother and tossed it out like a piece of trash. I cleaned out the baby's room and got rid of most of the stuff. I could not even look into that room until all the baby things were gone.

Feeling beat, I called the agency to tell them and the most

amazing thing happened. They picked me up, dusted me off, and told me I could still become a mother. They told me I could still adopt, I just had to change my focus. I now would have a hard time doing traditional adoption. I would now have to go with an older child, a handicapped child, or a black or biracial infant. To me, a baby that needs love is just that, a baby. Color had never mattered to me. I wanted a newborn so I picked an infant. But first I had to get my life in order.

It took me three years to get a better job, health insurance, and my life running smoothly again. On January 4, 2002 I called the agency to say I was ready to try again. The funny thing is they had turned down a baby girl that very day for lack of a family. A few calls later I was told to get ready; they had a baby for me. My paperwork would need updating and that would take two weeks. The baby would go into the agency's foster care until it was done. My joy was soaring. I told my family and friends. I contacted my boss and arranged for time off after I picked the baby up. I then started planning. Three days later I got the call: the birthmother had taken the baby home. I can not put into words how crushed I was. Maybe I was not meant to be a mother. Maybe this was telling me it was finally time to stop. Maybe it was time to let it go.

Once again the agency picked me up, dusted me off, and kept me going. They knew I was going to be a mother. They knew what was deep inside me. They were going to make it happen. They wanted me to adopt a girl. There was only one other couple waiting for the same type of baby I was. I remember that depressed me because they were a couple. I felt they would get picked first. And they were. Before they could even get all their paperwork done a baby boy came up. They worked hard and brought him home. And I waited.

In May of 2002, after a hard day at work, my phone rang. It was the director of my agency calling. She started with small talk.

I somehow just knew that this was the call. She asked, "How about 17 months old, red hair, green eyes, and light complexion?" I had a newborn in my heart. I was packed and ready for a newborn. After hearing her story I said, "Yes!" The person raising her had died. She had not been neglected or abused. This little one was the perfect match for me according to my agency. And I trusted them with my whole heart. After some communication back and forth between the two agencies I waited for the go ahead. The out-of-state agency wanted me there. My agency said I could not travel until she had been surrendered in court. I spent the weekend getting things done at home. I bought a red Teddy bear and an African-American baby doll. And again I waited. On Monday they told me the birthmother would not surrender until I was there and we had met. My agency said "Go!" It took a leap of faith. Praying she would like me and I would come home with a baby, I was going. I heard at 10 p.m. that night I had to fly out and meet the birthmother for dinner the next day. I bought tickets, contacted a friend to go with me, packed, and even got some sleep.

The next day, while driving to and waiting at the airport, I spoke with the out-of-state agency and learned more about my soon-to-be daughter. Then my cell phone rang non-stop with calls from friends and family. It seemed word was spreading. Most had believed adoption for me was just a dream. One told me she thought when I talked about it, it was like me wanting to be a rocket scientist: just a dream. Most had even stopped talking about it with me. But now, as I was about to take this leap of faith, I could not even answer my phone. I knew they were excited, but I needed peace to still my shaking heart.

As I walked into the restaurant that evening, six months to the day from when I made the call saying I was ready to start again, the first thing I saw was the most beautiful little baby in the world. She did not have red hair or green eyes, but I have never seen such a happy, beautiful baby. Then I met and had dinner with her, the birthmother, their case worker, and the director of the other agency. All too soon my baby was being carried out and I was on my way to the hotel. My prayers were answered and she did surrender the next day. We met and spent a few hours together, then she handed me my daughter and walked out the door. I felt like she was a part of my family, and in a way she always will be. My heart cried for her loss. And my heart hurt for the little one in my arms. This little girl lost everything she ever owned and everyone she ever knew, and found my heart. As I held this little girl, years of pain and sorrow melted away. My heart was healed. She is my child in every way. People tell me we look alike even though we are not the same race. An amazing thing is that I have only one dimple and I soon noticed she has only one as well—on the same cheek as I do.

On this six-year journey I learned many things. It was not me who was not ready. I was not waiting for God to find I was ready. I had to wait for my daughter to be born and be ready. I learned we don't make families; God makes families. No matter how hard we try to control our lives, we don't really have control. As I looked at my child that was supposed to be a newborn, I understood we do not always get what we want in this life, but we are given just what we need. Most of all, I learned to keep strong, have faith, and when the time comes, don't be afraid to take that leap. You will find joy well beyond what you ever dreamed or expected.

And the best part—the love affair has just begun. We have our whole lives ahead.

Brooke's Bridge

by Bonnie Loomis

*Bonnie has also written "American Daughter Born In China,"
which can be read in Chapter Six.*

My daughter, Brooke, is six years old. In my life I have never felt such intense love for another person as the love I feel for her. In 1997, when I finally decided to follow my heart and pursue an international adoption, I knew I would be going to China. Even though my decision wasn't made until 1997, Brooke's and my destiny were set in motion in 1994 when I was spending a quiet Sunday morning reading the newspaper. An article in the paper about a local family who had recently returned from China with their daughter was a revelation to me. I always knew I wanted to be a wife and a mother but becoming a wife was looking less and less likely to happen. I was getting older and becoming less interested in putting myself through more heartbreak. I began evaluating what it really was in life I wanted. The article in the Sunday paper made it very clear to me. I wanted to be a mother more than I wanted to be a wife.

I'll never forget the euphoria I felt that day when I so clearly understood what lay ahead of me. I still remember when I was ten years old and wondering what I was put on this earth to do and after almost 35 years, that question was answered. For three years I went back and forth about my ability to be a mom. I knew instinctively I'd be a good mom, I just didn't know how to make it happen. Financially I was in no position to take on the exorbitant adoption costs and if I couldn't even do that, how was I going to support my child when she came home? I visited the home of a couple who had just returned from China and watched as both mom and dad took turns getting up to take their newly-adopted Sara out of harm's way in one fashion or another. I went home with my head spinning. How could one person possibly keep a child safe? I pictured myself in the kitchen getting dinner ready as my little Brooke (yes, she was already named—actually named 20 years earlier) climbed on some furniture, fell off, and needed to be rushed to an emergency room. No, I just couldn't do this. It wouldn't be fair to my daughter to be raised by a parent who didn't have a spouse to be her daddy, whose financial situation was and would probably always be a struggle, and who it appeared was doubting her own instincts to the contrary.

Despite the number of roadblocks I put in my way, God continued to gently remove them. In November 1997 as I was walking into work, one of the security officers, Mike, who, with his wife, Faye, had recently returned from China with their daughter, pulled up beside me in the car and asked how my adoption was going. I told him it

To any single parents out there, my recommendation is not to travel alone. It's very lonely. . .

was on the back burner. He opened the car door and told me to get in. When I was in the car he pulled out photos of his Hannah. All the self-doubts I had been feeling melted away. He invited me to their house to meet Hannah and to watch their China video. When I got out of the car, he simply told me to do it. So, I did it.

I put myself in contact with the social worker Mike and Faye had used, which happily defaulted me to Holt International, and I was on my way. That was in November of 1997. My daughter was one month away from being born. I sincerely believe each of our daughters is meant for us through divine intervention. I know if I had followed my heart in 1994 I would have been matched with a daughter I would love as intensely as I love my Brooke. However, in 1994 my Lin Xiang was three years from being conceived, and so for three years I had to resolve my own issues about my readiness and ability to be a single mother. By November of 1997, there was not much time left for me to put the wheels in motion for this special baby girl from China to become the special daughter of this mama from the United States. In 1998 the wheels moved faster and my dossier was sent to Beijing on May 8. My referral of Lin Xiang was received on December 8, 1998. On February 23, 1999, Lin Xiang became Brooke Ashlin Xiang Loomis. She has changed the lives of everyone who loves her ever since.

When I saw this opportunity to tell a story and put a personal touch on adoption, my first thought was to share a portion of my adoption story that was a reality for me and might be a reality for others. Such a reality was an unwelcome source of much confusion and angst. It was what I felt during my first two weeks of being a mom.

I traveled to China by myself as there was no one to go with me. Having always been independent, I thought it almost would be preferable to travel alone. To any single parents out there, my recommendation is not to do this. It's very lonely and even after you've met up with your travel group, who in my case have become nine second families to Brooke and me, it is still lonely. There is so much joy, fear, apprehension, and blessings that you want to share with someone. When you get back in the hotel room, first without your baby and then with your new child, you need someone who knows you well enough to share all of the thoughts that are going through your head. Additionally, you don't have a videographer or photographer to preserve all of those memories for you. Thankfully, families of my travel group made copies of their own videos and sent them to me, so I do actually now have videos of that very special time, most particularly that moment when Brooke was placed in my arms.

The reality I spoke about was the reality of questioning my love for and adoration of my child. To use the cliché normally reserved for failed romances, "I loved her but I wasn't in love." How hideous of me and what was wrong? Did I love the idea of becoming a mother more than the reality of being a mother? I'm certain if I had traveled with someone who I obviously trusted with these revelations, I would have been reassured that it is normal. However, all around me I was seeing couples lovingly relating to their new baby. To clarify, I was very loving toward my daughter and she was my center but I couldn't escape the feeling that I was play acting this role of mother. It was as if I was watching someone else take care of this beautiful child because I wasn't worthy enough to do it myself. All I wanted was to get home with my daughter and begin life in familiar surroundings.

I was home for one whole week before the jet lag, the stress, the all-encompassing fatigue, and the cold I had brought to China with me finally dissipated and allowed me to fall irreversibly and completely in love with my daughter. From that point forward I have never considered Brooke anything less than an answer to my 35-year-old question: What was I put on this earth to do?

My Non-Conforming Family

by Arlene Lev

I am a social worker, family therapist, educator, and board member of the Family Pride Coalition. My books and articles can be accessed at www.choicesconsulting.com.

My arms are full of laundry when my eight-year-old son asks, "What's this book about?" He is lying on my bed, waiting for me to finish folding the laundry. I glance over and see he is holding a copy of Michael Moore's *Stupid White Men*. I put the laundry down and smile weakly. "It doesn't sound like a very nice book," he says, looking at me parentally. "You never let us say the word 'stupid,' but you have a book that calls people stupid right on the cover." I try to explain it's about politics and how people in government sometimes do very stupid things. "Are all the people in government white men?" he asks, innocently. Before he read the title of Michael Moore's book, "White" has always simply defined one of the many colors that people in his family come in. We are on the edge of something, and we both can feel it.

I take a deep breath and prepare to answer when I suddenly feel the rush of wind pass me as my three-year-old whirling dervish slides past, using a paper bag as surf board, and smashes into the wall overturning the laundry basket on the way. His Power Ranger underwear is hanging from his head.

I am an adoptive parent to two boys. My older son, at eight years old, stands near eye-level to me. In all fairness, I am barely four-feet ten-inches tall, and my son's birthmom is six-feet two-inches. All I know about his father is that he was "much taller." I often forget how tall my son is until I see him playing with his friends. He looks years older than them, standing nearly a head taller than the children a grade above him. He is quickly growing into a tall black man.

When we adopted our second son, a biracial boy, we expected that our sons would have each other as black men growing up in a house with white moms.

We have tried to raise him with a strong, solid self-esteem. He knows he is handsome, and he is proud of his African heritage and his kinky hair, flat nose. and thick lips.

We have never sheltered him from knowing about the harsher realities of the world. He is aware of racism and knows about slavery. But as parents, we have also done what we can to protect him from being a target of racism, as much as that is possible. The world he lives in is filled with people of many colors and ethnicities who respect and honor each other's traditions and cultures. He attends a school whose aim is to raise "multicultural citizens of the world." He has never experienced any major disadvantages simply because he is black, or at least none that he or I have been aware enough to recognize.

But at eight, some store clerks eye this tall black boy fondling the candy bars with suspicion, and he is about to face some ugly truths about being black in this society. It breaks this mother's heart to tell him the police will treat him differently than his friend, Jake, simply because he is dark-skinned. Although he's been raised to speak his mind ("You're not the boss of me!") the truth is dressing appropriately and speaking politely in certain situations might one day be a matter of life and death. Teaching a black man-child safety skills in a racist world is a tall order for white parents.

I remember when we first began this journey, much less grey. We were rushing through the mall when we suddenly became aware we were being watched. My partner leans into me slightly, whispering innocently, "Why are these people staring at us?" I catch a glimpse of our family in the mirrored sides of the escalator. In the reflection I see my handsome, butch, red-haired partner wheeling the stroller where our chubby-faced brown-skinned son is joyfully singing. My family, my precious, sweet family, the only home I've ever known, stands out awkwardly, noticeably. We are somehow odd, different, and only barely welcome in the malls of America—our gayness presents a dissonant picture to the suburban shoppers.

That we are different is not exactly news to us. I live in this world as a Jew and a lesbian. But there is a different danger now, as strangers' eyes pierce my son's glowing laughter, annihilating his presence with what looks like disgust.

When we adopted our second son, a biracial boy, we expected our sons would have each other as black men growing up in a house with white moms. But our three-year-old is barely a shade darker than his olive-colored momma. Everyone kept telling us he would darken, but it's pretty clear by now his rosy cheeks, slightly tan skin, and Irish nose are here to stay. Most people read him as white except for older black women, who stop me in the grocery store, lean in, and say, "He black, right?"

"Yep, he is," I assure them, and they pat me on the back, offering me both support and appreciation. I know they think his father must be black (which is true), especially when we are standing next to his darker-skinned brother. They, however, also assume I am partnered with my children's father. I suspect their support and appreciation might ebb if they met my very light-skinned partner whom the kids call mommy.

It is a challenge raising strong black men in this world, and a particular challenge as white, Jewish lesbians. It is an especially unique kind of challenge raising a strong black man whom most people will assume is white.

Living my life (to borrow Emma Goldman's words), I often forget how unusual my family really is. Almost everywhere we go we are different. Although we are not the only lesbian family at synagogue, we are the only lesbian multiracial one. Although we are not the only multiracial family at school, we are the only lesbian one. Although we are not the only transracial lesbian family at most events, we are often the only Jewish mixed-race family. Although we are not the only multicolored family at most events sponsored by people of color, we are often the only Jewish lesbian-headed family. The only place I have ever been with families just like mine was Family Week in Provincetown, Massachusetts, a yearly event sponsored by the Family Pride Coalition, where the beach is filled with gay couples raising children of all colors.

Although I live my life at an intersection of many communities, I find we are warmly welcomed almost everywhere we go. My family appears to be respected and appreciated. Nonetheless, I am aware of sub-text, and a sometimes underlying tenor of nervousness. My e-mail box is filled with people sending me kudos and hurrahs for speaking out at the PTA meeting about the lack of attention to Black History Month, or for my criticism of the barrage of white faces on all the flyers, worksheets, and biblical images sent home from Hebrew school (the Hebrew tribe lived in the Middle East, not the Midwest!). My letter to the editor on the way the word "adoption" is used as a synonym for unwanted ("I always felt unwanted in my family, as if I was adopted"), receives accolades, and my reminder to the African drumming instructor that not all blacks find salvation in Jesus, are met with thoughtful appreciation and apologies. However, the bottom line is that if I don't speak up, these issues are not addressed, and some parts of my family, some aspect of my children's lives, or some piece of our souls, is invisible once again.

Lesbian, gay, bisexual, and transgender (LGBT) transracial adoption exists at the intersection of three huge political and social issues. The first is gay parenting. It becomes tiring having to repeat over and over again that LGBT people are good parents that do not molest their children. Despite their children's immersion experiences at Gay Pride Events, we do not and cannot make them gay. Children seem to be growing up just fine in our homes, and despite all of our efforts to raise them with progressive values they seem to want to watch the same Disney movies and wear the same environmental hazardous flashing shoes. Ultimately, they seem to be all but indistinguishable from their peers.

The second issue at this intersection is adoption. It's not exactly the same kind of front-page issue as LGBT parenting, except of course when something goes wrong. I find even within families formed by adoption, there is often much silence about the topic. Hardly anyone I meet is opposed to adoption, but there seems to be an unwritten message that talking too much about adoption will highlight the differences of adoptive families from families not formed by adoption, possibly making adoptees and their families feel bad. Although most people will deny it, there is often a sense adoption is not quite real, that somehow these are borrowed children who really belong to someone else. A friend asks, "What do you know about his mother?"

"I assume you mean his birthmother, since you know his mother very well," I say.

"Oh, I didn't mean that ! You know what I meant."

Actually, I'm not exactly sure what she meant. This is not simply about politically correct language, nor is it about any resistance on my part to talk about or acknowledge my children's birthfamily, who are flesh-and-blood people in our lives. Adoption is riddled with assumptions about how lucky our children are. After all, where would they be if we hadn't taken them in? Every adoptive parent knows it is not

> *An African-American friend said to me, "The problem with you white parents, is you think you can protect your black children from racism." I admit, guilty as accused.*

our children who lucked out, but us; we are receivers of this great gift of love. Whenever adopted children act out, or struggle with issues, the question of genetics gets raised. Illnesses like bipolar disorder and alcoholism have a likely genetic linkage, but I'm not just talking about medical inheritance. I'm talking about what one man called "getting stuck with someone else's problems." Adopted children are expected to be more grateful and to be on their best behavior. Or what? Should we just return them?

The third issue that intersects the life of my family makes the two previous ones seem easy. Highly contentious, and far too large to tackle in one small article, is the issue of race and more importantly, racism. What can I say as a white woman, in one, two, or ten sentences, that would convey the relevance and weight of race on cross-racial family building?

I did not realize the earthquake of changes that transracial gay adoption would unleash. I expected homophobia from the patriarchal heterosexist mainstream community, and I also knew that many lesbian and gay parents felt unsupported within the gay community. I suspected that the Jewish community would struggle with accepting a child of color, and the issue of adoption would raise issues for my family. I expected resistance from both white supremacists and black nationalists whom I knew would find my family's very existence offensive.

Even after 25 years of anti-racism activism, I did not realize how much white privilege I had until it was revoked. I was not prepared for the multiple levels of issues that transracial gay adoption would raise, even for the most progressive of my friends.

An African-American friend said to me, "The problem with you white parents, is you think you can protect your black children from racism." I admit, guilty as accused. I do want to protect my sons from racism. What parent would not want to protect their children from becoming fodder for an angry white policeman's frustrations, or an elementary school teacher's prejudice? I also want to protect my children from schoolyard bullies and fast-moving cars, from electric outlets and large bodies of water. I want to protect him as well from poverty, homophobia, and anti-Jewish hatred. What parent would not want to do the same? The sad truth is that none of us can protect our children from the ravages and pain of the world.

I do not think that being the white mom of an African-American child and a biracial child has made me more conscious of racism. I do not think it has made me a better anti-racism activist. Being the mother of black children has meant I no longer have the choice of moving within white culture as if it were my own; it has made me an outsider.

I make my home on the borders of many communities: not quite a part of communities of color, a bit outside of the Jewish community as well as the white community, and as a parent within the gay community. It is a good home, however, filled with laughter and friends and my family.

The Changes In Life

by Sherry Armstrong

I am a 43-year-old woman who lives in Fairfax, Virginia. After working for several years in office positions after college, I went to law school and now work as an attorney for the federal government. While I am grateful for my education and career, one of my dearest dreams was to become a wife and mom. Adoption was a great way for both to happen!

I'm going to be a mother!! I can hardly believe it. When I started this adoption process months ago, it was hard to really grasp that at the end of it I would hold a baby that I would get to love, cherish, and nurture for the rest of my life!

Like many single women who reach their 40s, I wrestled with accepting that I might never meet Mr. Right and have babies of my own. I always assumed somewhere along the way I would find the man for me and we would marry and have children together. However, like so many single women that dream did not come true. For a few years, I had mulled over how I would feel if I never had the opportunity to be a parent. While I had a happy life, which was complete with a loving extended family and friends, I really felt a part of me would be unfulfilled if I never became a mother. I felt like I had so much love to share with a child, and while I looked for other opportunities at church and in my family to pour out that love on children around me, it was not the same as being a mother to my child.

I explored various options such as foster care and domestic adoption but quickly found international adoption was the best option for me. In Guatemala, single women were given the opportunity to adopt infants who were cared for in loving foster care homes and were generally healthy. I had great fear about whether it was the right decision but I met someone else who had done it and I was encouraged to at least take the next step. I have always believed that to have a rich and fulfilling life you have to take some risks along the way. I did not want to get to the end of my life and feel that I had missed out on something wonderful because I had been unwilling to take a chance! I did not know for certain if I could manage it all on my own, if I would have enough money or enough patience, but I knew this: I had enough love. Love that I wanted to pour out and lavish on a child. A child with whom I could share my life and the many gifts and blessings I had been given.

I found an agency in my area and decided that, while I did not know for sure adopting was the right decision, I would just take the next step, and the next step after that, until I was either sure I did not want to pursue it, or the doors closed. That never happened.

I completed my home study, signed a contract with the agency, and accepted a referral. The process has moved smoothly and rapidly. I went to meet my precious daughter a couple of weeks ago and it was such a joy to hold her and see her face. She is a content and peaceful baby who is receiving loving care from her loving foster mother, Nancy. I hope to return to pick her up in a few weeks but, until then, I have complete peace that she is well cared for and will come home to me soon.

As a side note, along the way, I met a wonderful man. That had not been my plan, as I was not seeking a relationship; but what an awesome surprise! While making a wire transfer at my bank to my attorney in Guatemala, the bank manager and I hit it off immediately. He was very interested in the adoption and we had a wonderful conversation. That conversation was followed by a date and we've been virtually inseparable ever since. He is a kind, loving, giving, and Godly man who has brought incredible joy into my life. I have loved sharing my life with him. To make a long story short, we will soon be engaged and will marry. He wants to be a father to Christina and she will be immensely blessed by his presence in her life. I know that I am!

What have I learned from all of this? While many lessons remain to be seen as I learn to be a wife and parent, this I know: I may not be sure that I am to take a certain step but, if I feel led in that direction, I must take a chance. The greatest joys in my life to date, my daughter and my soon-to-be husband, came from taking a risk and stepping out in faith. How glad I am I did!

My Adopted Sister

by Kate Dani

I am a 37-year-old mother with three beautiful children, Olivia, Alexander, and Amelia. I grew up in a loving family of two brothers and one beautiful, wonderful adopted sister. Adoption has touched our family, with the adoption of my sister and the adopting out of my brother's little boy.

Adoption is very emotional and can be extremely difficult for the child adopted, the natural parents who made a very courageous decision to give up their baby, and the adoptive parents who were given this incredible gift. However, sometimes there are siblings involved so I thought I'd write from that perspective. As a sibling, you often feel you are a spectator in an emotional drama. However, you have a minor role.

We always knew Anna was adopted. In fact, it gave her a very special place in the family. She was called "the specially chosen one," as mum and dad would say that "we were given to them by God but they got to choose Anna, which made her special."

As children, Anna and I would lie in bed at night and wonder about her natural parents. I was convinced she was really a princess and I would say to her I hoped she would remember me when her real parents came for her and she was famous.

I love having an adopted sister and it has always been special. Only once did it really cause me grief. It was when her natural parents found her. When I heard that, I thought I'd be excited and happy for her but I wasn't. I was scared and worried, which made me feel guilty. I didn't share it with anyone as I felt I was really on the edge of it all. I believed it was all about Anna, mum and dad, and her natural parents, which it was.

When I found out she had a half-sister, I was intensely jealous because I thought I was going to lose her as my sister. Again I felt guilty when I was relieved that she didn't want a relationship with them.

I didn't lose my beautiful sister and we have a wonderful relationship today. I am so grateful that God bought her into our family even though I know it has been hard on Anna from time to time.

Kate's mother, Janet McMillan, has written the piece "The Other Side Of The Story," which can be read in Chapter Five.

Waiting

by Laurie Barr

My name is Laurie and I am a 35-year-old single woman living in Portland, Oregon. Between the time I wrote this essay about waiting and the point of publication, I became a first-time mom through the miracle of adoption. I brought my 10-month-old son home from Russia in July 2004. Nathan is now a happy, healthy, and active toddler who fills my life with joy and wonder every day. Motherhood is everything I thought it would be!

I always figured someday I'd be a mother. I imagined I'd follow the same path most people do: find the right guy, get married, buy a house, and have kids. But I found myself turning 30 and someday hadn't come. After college, I had focused mainly on my career, finding fairly rapid career success. I had gone ahead and bought a house and created a home for myself. But I hadn't met the right guy yet. That 30th birthday made me start thinking about what I really wanted in life. Around that same time, my sister was diagnosed with a malignant brain tumor. After a three-and-a-half year battle with brain cancer, she died, leaving behind two young girls. Her death made me realize what was really important and what wasn't. During her illness, I also had some health problems and was diagnosed with Polycystic Ovarian

Syndrome; the leading cause of infertility in women. I might be able to have children someday but I might not. It hadn't ever really mattered before but suddenly now it did.

Why is it that human nature makes us want so badly what we think we can't have? At the age of 33, I found myself faced with huge life questions: If I were to die tomorrow, what would I have to show for my life? What's keeping me from being as happy as I could be? After a lot of self-reflection, I realized how much I really wanted a family of my own. I tried hard to find the right person; he just wasn't finding me. So I was faced with a decision: do I venture down this path on my own or keep waiting for him to come along? I realized that maybe the path most people follow wasn't the one meant for me. I could continue to wait, but I didn't want to find myself regretting that I did not have kids. So, as scary as it was, I decided to venture down the path alone. What I found is that I wasn't really alone.

For me, the choice of adoption was a relatively easy one. I knew I wasn't up for going through the expense and emotions of fertility treatments without a partner by my side. After a lot of research on my adoption choices, I eventually decided on international adoption and chose Russia as the place I would find my child. Then came the hardest part for me: telling my family. I was afraid that I wouldn't have the support from them I knew I'd need. I was afraid that my dad wouldn't understand why I needed to do this. I was afraid my parents would be disappointed in me because I wasn't doing this the right way, the way my brother and sister had, by getting married first. I was afraid my mom would think I was giving up on finding someone. What I found instead was an amazing sense of support from my family, from my friends, and from the adoption community in general.

I have to make two trips to Russia. My dad is going with me on the first trip and my mom and step-dad are going with me on the second. They have all been so incredibly supportive. I've also felt that support from my siblings, aunts and uncles, cousins, friends, and even co-workers. When I've started to have my doubts, they gave me encouragement. There have been times when I've felt completely overwhelmed with the paperwork and steps involved with getting my dossier together, with the financial implications that come with international adoption, and with the awesome responsibility I'm taking on. Even though I don't have the hormones of pregnancy, I'm certainly experiencing all of the emotions of impending motherhood: the fear, the excitement, the anxious anticipation, the doubts. I've had them all. And when I cry about it and share it, I have a circle of people who hold me up and cheer me on. And I know I'm not alone.

I know my child is out there in the world somewhere. I can't hold or comfort him or her and that is heartbreaking. But knowing he or she is in an orphanage somewhere in Russia just waiting for me to come gives me hope. I've already fallen in love with the faceless, nameless little wonder that right now is in some ways so real, and in some ways a figment of my imagination. The room is ready. I am ready. Now I just wait for "the call." I know my life is about to change forever. And I can't wait.

That's My Sister

by Patricia Younce

Patricia has also written "Our Two Open Adoptions," which can be read in Chapter Five.

An issue I want to address which raises many myths in society is adopting a child of a different race and color. Some waiting adoptive families might be struggling right now with this question: "Can I give a child of a different race from my own what he or she needs to become a healthy young adult?"

My husband, Matt, and I prayed for an answer to this question. We were still uncertain until the day in May of 2001 when Adriane (the birthmother of our daughter Rachel) called and told us she wanted to select us for her baby. Adriane is African-American and so is Rachel's birthfather. Within minutes of that very long initial call I knew I loved Adriane and I could not wait to pour my love into her baby. Color was not important, although Adriane and I discussed it immediately. She said she selected us because she knew we looked like a big, happy family and that was what she wanted for her baby.

Adriane and I still feel a connection to each other almost like sisters. We talk about everything together and race often comes up because there is no doubt that Rachel looks different from me and Matt. But different can be great! It can be celebrated! Different is a challenge that can be embraced!

Our son Erik is biracial. His skin is lighter than Rachel's but many people ask us if they are birth siblings. All of our children will grow up more fortunate than most because they will learn all the stories from their birth traditions. There are negative influences in both the white and black cultures that we want to shelter our children from. We want them all to learn to love who they are; their skin color is only part of that beautiful combination of traits.

We now live part of our year in Vermont and we have discovered that any combination of a family seems to be accepted and celebrated in that wonderful state. However, in other states adoptive families who adopt a child of a different race might encounter less progressive views about "family." I think it is good to prepare yourself for what you might find and be ready to respond in easy-going ways.

For my children's sake, I know we all need to learn to respond to others' comments, especially when our children are with us. Matt and I try to keep an open mind and we say things that help people understand that we are a family by choice. Our daughters totally love each other and Mary (our daughter by birth) does not hesitate to tell the world that the black child holding her hand is her SISTER!

Special Moments

Our Lives Will Never Be The Same!

*"Life is not measured by the number of breaths you take,
but by the moments that take your breath away."*

- Unknown

He's Yours—A Finalization Story

by Cheryl L. Dieter

Cheryl has also written "Of Band-Aids And Such," which can be read in Chapter Eight.

"I will not cry" became my mantra as we drove to the courthouse.

"You will not weep," I admonished myself over and over again as we climbed the gray granite steps to the building.

"I will not shed a single tear," I told my husband as the judge entered the courtroom.

Now, normally I'm not a crier but you couldn't tell that to anyone who knew me for the last twelve months for everything about this adoption had made me cry. Absolutely everything. The day we got the call from Kathy that we had a son, the tears started flowing. While pictures may say a thousand words, hearing the sounds of, "I've got good news . . . you have a son" was worth a million bucks. I cried as if I'd won the lottery . . . because I just had.

I cried when the plane took off as we headed to Korea to pick up our new son. I bawled the first time I saw his beautiful face, and tears of joy mixed with laughter ran down my cheeks when I first glimpsed his "stick 'em up" hair. I sobbed when I first held him and fed him his bottle. I cried buckets when it was time to take Karson (our son) from his foster mother and I cried at the airport knowing that I was taking this precious boy from the only family and country he had ever known. I blubbered the first time he called me "mama," during his first steps, and when his first tooth appeared, as well as numerous times in between. In short, the last year has been an endless river of happy tears but today I vowed I wasn't going to cry.

Not a tear was shed when the bailiff swore me in nor did they fall as the judge examined the paperwork, making sure that everything was in order. I didn't cry when she asked me to tell her his name, what he liked to do during the day, and what kind of baby he was.

"So far, so good," I concluded. It was then, just when I thought I was in the clear, that the judge sideswiped me.

"Now tell me what it has meant to you to have Karson in your lives," the judge said quietly. "Uh-oh," I thought as I bit my bottom lip to keep the tears in check; the judge had unknowingly just crossed the line. I looked up at her and with an incredulous look on my face reflecting on the fact that there were no words I could ever use that would adequately express what in the world this boy, my hopefully soon-to-be son, meant to me. Yet, we had made it this far and, as far as we were concerned, we were already a forever family. I knew I couldn't blow it now.

"The sky is bluer," I suggested quietly, thoughts swirling in my head.

"Since we have had Karson the mockingbird is more melodious, the colors of the rainbow are brighter, and a baby's laugh is sweeter," I replied, as my voice cracked and I bit down on my lip just a little harder. Tears on the horizon threatened to take me out to sea.

"The sunshine is a little sunnier, the grass is greener, snowflakes fluffier, and the wind whispers softer," I stuttered, desperately grasping for the right words that would explain just how precious our son was to us.

"Our love is deeper, our hearts are stronger, each minute is more miraculous, our joy more profound. . ."

"You need not say anything more," came the voice from the bench with a tear glistening in the corner of her left eye. And at that moment time stopped and the silence became deafening. And then, finally, the judge looked over her bench, a soft smile gracing her lips and declared, "He's yours."

And with that pronouncement I did the unthinkable. . .
I smiled. . .
I laughed. . .
I jumped up and down. . .
We posed for pictures. . .
And later that night. . .
I cried.

Meeting Aaron

by Courtney Rathke

Courtney has also written "But Why Not A Baby?" which can be read in Chapter Six.

Flying into Guatemala City that Sunday night was like every other step of our adoption, somewhat veiled from our sight and a little fuzzy on details. But my husband and I knew in the daylight we would see all the details of our son's birth country. We couldn't see much from the plane windows, but we trusted, as we had for the last four months, that all was well. And we knew when the sun rose the next day it was also rising on the rest of our lives as a family of four.

We wanted so badly to soak in every detail of this trip, but in the Guatemala City airport, at 11 p.m. on a Sunday, there wasn't much to absorb. It was an airport, not a museum. There were long, plain hallways, one baggage claim that moved far too slowly for our sense of anticipation, and customs agents who were friendly but businesslike.

Finally, we dragged our suitcases into the waiting area, where, even that late in the evening, vans from various hotels awaited travelers and family members waited anxiously for their reunions. A little tired, and a little apprehensive, we looked for someone, anyone, holding the Clarion Suites sign to give us a focal point to begin this last leg of our journey.

Instead, as we passed slowly by the roped-off crowd, a man reached out and touched my husband's sleeve. "Rathke?" he asked, rolling his 'R' in a deep melodious voice. When my husband nodded, he smiled widely and announced, "I am Feliciano!"

Feliciano! We dropped our suitcases and embraced him right there. This was the director of our son's *hogar* (orphanage) and we were touched beyond belief that he would meet us at the airport, especially since our flight was hours late. He smiled, helped load our suitcases into his van, then told us he had to wait for one more family.

Once we were all safely tucked inside his van, he drove us to our hotels and explained he would be back the next morning to bring us to Nuevo Amanecer to meet our children.

The next morning was such a blur. I suppose we slept. I know we woke, dressed, had a small breakfast, and waited for what seemed like hours in the lobby of our hotel for Feliciano and his van to reappear. The drive from our hotel to his hogar was not more than half an hour. It seemed so surreal. It was our first real glimpse of our new son's homeland. I remember the sun shone. I remember narrow traffic lanes and small European cars as well as trucks, vans, and "chicken buses." There were vendors selling wares on the streets, beautiful flowers and bushes in the boulevards. We passed a store selling brightly colored children's bicycles. My husband mused that we should buy one for our new son, and then we chuckled, realizing it would be impossible to try to bring one back into the United States.

And then we turned onto a quieter street; the buildings were all behind gated walls. I remember the walls were turquoise, yellow, and lime green. Feliciano stopped and unlocked a door which seemed to have no other markings around it. We walked into a vestibule, down a hallway to a reception area with a Winnie-the-Pooh mural painted on the wall. We could hear children playing, as one would hear in a daycare center. There was banging and laughing and musical toys tinkling away. There were voices; many, many children's voices. Feliciano opened one last door. There they were, children of all ages. At one end of this large, central room, there were three or four women wearing scrubs, caring for the infants. Beyond them were a few toddler-sized mattresses in case someone nodded off during play. One child was slumbering peacefully among all the racket, her thumb tucked in her mouth and her knees tucked under her little bottom in the classic "baby sleeping" pose.

I sat down right on the floor and opened my arms, too. He flew into my lap and nestled there as if he knew he belonged. And of course, he did.

A little further down, a few other toddlers, all boys, were playing with cars and trucks. One little fellow was so small he was kneeling in the back of a Tonka dump truck and busily pushing himself along with his hands. Feliciano looked at me and asked, "So, which one is yours?"

It took no time to find our Aaron; he was the one in the truck. "That one," I said, pointing. Feliciano beamed.

I would have been happy to simply have watched him for a few moments, to observe how he handled himself and others, to realize our road had finally reached its destination. This child, this beautiful little boy, would be part of our family forever.

But as soon as we identified our new son, an older girl, about nine years old, rushed over to Aaron, gently took his shoulders, and turned him towards us. "*Esta es tu nueva mama,*" she said excitedly, pointing. There is your new mama.

We had been prepared for our new son to react with trepidation and to be frightened, and even for us to have to carry him away kicking and screaming. We were not prepared for him to scramble out of the Tonka truck and scurry across the floor as fast as his pudgy little legs could carry him, laughing with his arms outstretched and a smile that lit up his face, as if to say "Here you are! I've been waiting for you!"

I sat down right on the floor and opened my arms, too. He flew into my lap and nestled there as if he knew he belonged.

And of course, he did.

The next days flew by. He loved riding in the stroller as we walked to a nearby shopping mall to buy him new shoes. He was less impressed with a bubble bath since he had always had showers at the *hogar*. He loved the treats brought to our room by the concierge and housekeeping staff. They spoiled him endlessly! We took him to the zoo one afternoon for the first time in his life and spent a day sightseeing in the city of Antigua, where we shopped and watched the nearby volcanoes smoke both day and night. At night we could see the mouths of the volcanoes glowing beneath the clouds of smoke and steam. We made our required visit to the U.S. Embassy, which gave us our final approval to bring Aaron into the United States on an immigrant visa. We obtained his Guatemalan passport and vaccination records.

And then, four days after our arrival, it was time to return home. Again we were amazed by our son's resilience and interest in the world around him. We were so concerned about his reaction to his first ride in an airplane but he belted himself in, having become used to seatbelts at the *hogar* when the children would visit Feliciano's *vinca* in the mountains. He very calmly pressed his hands to his ears to alleviate the change in pressure as we took off and was happy to stand on daddy's lap and look out the windows at the passing clouds.

In Houston we cleared Customs and had just enough time before our next flight to have lunch. Aaron had his first fast-food meal; the hamburger was all right, but pickles? "Blech," he said, and placed them at the farthest corner of the paper wrapper. The french fries were practically inhaled, which was a good thing as it was time to board the plane for the final leg of our trip home.

We couldn't wait to get off the plane in Minneapolis. I think those last few minutes of waiting to deplane at the gate are always the worst, but this time we knew our older son, my mother and sister, and my husband's sister and her family were waiting for us. We couldn't seem to move through the hallways to the baggage claim area fast enough.

Finally, we went down the last set of escalators. "There's Laura!" I said, pointing to my husband's niece. But no, it wasn't Laura; Laura was off to the side. It was Abi, our neighbor, with her sister Emily, their mother Sue, and our neighbor Anna and her mother Colleen. All the families who had walked with us through the adoption journey were there, with "Welcome Home Aaron" signs, balloons, and flowers. I started crying. My friend Sarah, whose daughter Anna was adopted from Romania 12 years earlier, was one of the first to greet us, holding on as tight as she could and laughing through her tears, "You did it! You did it!!"

We will never forget those moments when Aaron met his nana, his cousins, his aunts, and his uncles. Most importantly, we will never forget when he finally met his big brother for the first time. I will never forget how my oldest boy simply looked and looked at his new baby brother, soaking in every detail of his little face, and then turned to my husband and I saying, "I feel like crying, too, but I don't know why!"

It's good to be a family.

Love At First Sight

by Candace Abel

People outside of the world of adoption often have trouble understanding the profound connection that occurs between adoptive parent and child; the adoptive parent experiences the same soul-altering, fiercely protective, and emotionally-charged link as biological parents do with the arrival of their child. I wrote this story to offer a window into this unique and unwavering bond.

I believe in love at first sight. You know, that wonderful, giddy love that occurs in an instant when you least expect it. You look across a room and see a face that lassos your soul in a rush of warm emotion. Friends and family would argue that a life-long commitment had to be based on rational thought and common values, not instant attraction. Nonetheless, there was nothing rational about the love I felt when I first met my husband. I simply looked up, felt my heart stand still, and was his forever.

I remember experiencing love at first sight when I held my newborn babies for the first time. With each new baby, I stared with wonder; I was unable to look away from their perfect faces. I watched them as they slept, inhaled their heady scents, and dreamed of their soft cheeks at night. To my amazement, the same held true when my husband and I began our journey of adoption.

With each official letter of match came the photo: beautiful and haunting eyes stared out from little round, hopeful faces that made me weak in the knees and caused my breath to quicken. I trembled with the pure joy one knows when they are looking fate in the eye; my child, my beautiful child, waiting a world away. There was nothing rational about loving a photograph, but rationality had nothing to do with what I felt. And when I held my children in my arms for the first time, whether at an airport or a foreign hotel lobby, I experienced the dizzying rush of overwhelming love.

After marrying the man of my dreams and parenting three beautiful biological babies and six wonderful adopted children, I believed my love-struck days were over. As a woman in her forties, I wanted only to watch my children grow and experience all their firsts. It was to experience such a first that my beautiful 16-year-old Vietnamese daughter, Mai-Lynn, and I traveled to her birth country. As we explored fascinating sites and historic areas, Mai rediscovered her heritage. Having adopted her at age eight, I watched with wonder as she embraced Vietnam the way one does an old friend. Her face glowed as she excitedly recognized places she had been or always wanted to visit. I listened as her Vietnamese language skills quickly honed into fluent prose from her conversations with local people. She shared stories, both funny and sad, that had long lain dormant inside her. I watched her open up and blossom and realized I did not know how much her soul had hungered for her culture.

Along the way, I realized we had made lifelong relationships with our fellow travel companions of adoptive families. Somewhere else along the way, I realized Mai-Lynn experienced love at first sight. During the tour we visited a number of orphanages where some of the children had lived. When we toured Mam Non II outside of Ho Chi Minh City, we were treated to a beautiful show by the children at the center, when Mai-Lynn looked over and was struck by the "sweet look of Alyssa's face." After the show, Mai-Lynn shared a few hours of chit-chat with Alyssa before they exchanged addresses and we went on our way. Over the next couple of days, Alyssa was all Mai-Lynn talked about.

Mai-Lynn told me Alyssa had been in the orphanage eight years, was a good student, and was soon going to be 15. Mai clearly identified with her. Both their mothers had mental health issues and she understood how it felt to want the love of a family. With some earnest begging from Mai, we traveled back to the orphanage so Mai could visit Alyssa once more before we left. As I watched them embrace, I recognized the look of fierce love on their faces. They had become soul sisters. Before I knew it, I was traveling back to file the adoption papers.

All went well on my first trip to file Alyssa's adoption papers in Vietnam. As I strolled through the special needs baby room, one of the caregivers handed me a sweet-faced, delicate baby girl. As an experienced romantic, I should have seen it coming. I held her in my arms and fell in love. I barely heard the director tell me she was blind and premature. I handed her back and left, trembling; but it was too late. I tried to rationalize: I was too old to parent a sick baby, I already had a house full of children, and I knew nothing about the visually impaired. In the end, it did not matter. Emily had captured my heart. Friends thought we were crazy and our parents cautioned us, but on the day before Thanksgiving we brought home our two new daughters. Alyssa and Mai were reunited in a tearful embrace and Emily was greeted with a million kisses from her excited siblings.

To this day, curious people ask about our motivation to adopt Emily and Alyssa, and about the rational thought we must have put into it. I answer—there was nothing rational about bringing home a nervous 14-year-old and a blind and frail 14-month-old. I simply looked up, felt my heart stand still, and was theirs forever.

Meeting Our Daughter

by Lisa Scott

As a first-time adoptive mom, I read every personal adoption story I could find. I had been a mom for 14 years to two sons, but meeting a nearly year-old child who had lived in an orphanage all of her life was a daunting thought. Would she learn to love us? What if she didn't? When our China referral came, we received three pictures of a beautiful little girl who would be 11 months old by the time we met her. We traveled half-way around the world to finally set eyes on her. This is the story of meeting our daughter, Abby.

January 6, 2004 - 3:30 pm
Grand Sun City Hotel
Changsha, Hunan

The phone rang. I jumped to answer it. On the other end, our facilitator said, "They are less than ten minutes from the hotel." She continued, "You can go down to watch the babies come through the lobby, but come back to the 18th floor to meet your daughter." My heart raced. This is it. We were moments away from meeting Abby.

I put the phone down and told my husband, Mitch, the babies were on the way. We walked to the elevator lobby to find the other families in our group. We were all giddy as the elevator headed down. Calmly, with cameras in hand, we stepped out and looked around. About a minute passed before I heard Mitch say, "They're here!" as he saw people with babies getting out of a van. A hush came over our group. The video cameras started rolling, as did the tears.

The very first baby carried through the door, dressed in a hot pink marshmallow suit, was our Abby. I was sure. She was wide-eyed and curious as she looked around at the shiny, bright hotel lobby and the group of people staring back at her. It seemed at the time as if they walked by in slow motion, but the caregivers moved through the lobby quickly. They saw the ten Americans watching them. There was no mistaking who we were and why our cameras were pointed at them. The elevator doors closed; our girls were on their way up. Our group caught the next elevator. What an emotional ride it was. Some of the group laughed, some still had tears in their eyes. The elevator door opened and there they were: our daughters.

The next few minutes were chaotic. We walked around looking at the girls, waiting for someone to make a move. The caretaker with that beautiful girl in the hot pink marshmallow suit looked at Mitch and said, "Kui Yan?" and he said yes. Before I knew it, little Guo Kui Yan was in his arms and she was not very happy about it! A photo from an early moment of Mitch meeting Abby has become one of my favorites from the trip. It is one of him holding her, trying to comfort her, but it clearly shows the great fear she experienced being handed to him.

We walked around the elevator lobby and talked to her softly. She was the only one of the five girls who was visibly upset. We were called to our facilitator's room to meet the orphanage staff and ask questions. Abby was upset with us and hot from being dressed in three layers. I went blank; I only wanted to get her to our room, get her down to one layer of clothes, and calm her. We took pictures with the Zhuzhou Children's Welfare Institute staff. They gave us a bag of formula, a box of rice cereal, and a new bottle for Abby. We were touched by their gift; they have so many mouths to feed. We said thank you and returned to our room.

For a little over an hour, Abby cried. She went to me more willingly than to Mitch and calmed down with me. If he looked at her or talked to her, it set her off again. We put her on the bed and laid out the toys we brought: colorful stacking cups, a small inflatable beach ball, a teething ring, and a soft pink bear. They caught her attention. She chewed on the stacking cups and looked at us with great uncertainty. Mitch put the teething ring on his head and let it fall off on the bed. Was that a faint smile on her face, I wondered? He put the stacking cups and the teething ring on his head over and over, letting them fall to the bed at her feet. A tiny smile spread across her face. He did it again, and she giggled softly. Within a couple of minutes, those giggles were belly laughs and we saw for the very first time that our daughter had dimples! Her smile melted our hearts. Our life together was underway. Since daddy made the breakthrough, he was her favorite in China, although she did tolerate mom's attention for feeding and diaper changes.

Guo Kui Yan, now Abigail KuiYan—thank you for opening your heart to us. I am so incredibly honored to be your mom.

A Child's Journey To Parvuli Dei

by Karen A. Hunt

Karen has also written "The Little Boy That Could," which can be read in Chapter Seven.

I would like to share a bit about my amazing son and his journey to Parvuli Dei (a Catholic Cub Scout Religious Award). I am so proud of him, and I just wanted to put my thoughts into writing and share them with you.

Just three short years ago, my son was a very angry and hostile child. The thought of doing any extra work would have been impossible. He completely lacked the ability to trust the adult world. He lacked the basic building blocks of morality and conscience development. He would have never been able to tackle a project like the Parvuli Dei Activity Book.

My son lived in a Russian orphanage for almost four years. By the age of six he was diagnosed with several disabilities due to his early years of profound neglect. These included Sensory Integration Disorder, Central Auditory Processing Disorder and Reactive Attachment Disorder. When linked with properly trained therapists who specialize in the treatment of foster and adopted children, my son began to shine. His turnaround has been remarkable.

Reactive Attachment Disorder is very debilitating. It steals away a childhood and a future from many neglected and abused children. My son truly had to have the desire to heal. I could not provide this for him, nor could his therapist. My child needed to have the ability to put forth a tremendous effort to face the demons of his past. To learn to trust adults, and especially a mom, he had to be willing, figuratively, to jump off a cliff and trust that I would catch him. He had to do this despite past experiences with adults who pushed him over that same cliff and left him alone to wither in his pain.

I am still completely in awe of this little boy, who could actually have the Herculean strength to do all that was required to become attached. It was gut-wrenching watching him struggle in therapy and at home, learning to trust and feel worthy of love. My little boy thought he was the lowest form of life possible, lower than the dirt on the floor. His early life had taught him he was inherently worthless. Yet somehow he had the strength, at such a young age, to rise above all this and heal.

I now have a 10-year-old son who is excited about his faith. He is proud of his Russian heritage and proud to be an American. He loves being part of a family. He has wisdom beyond his years, and knows what it is like to be hurting and in need. I have seen him use this wisdom to reach out to another hurting child. Yes, he will bear the scars of his past for life. He still struggles with simple things that other kids take for granted, like jumping jacks or handwriting. He is more sensitive and more easily hurt. But with encouragement, he carries on and perseveres. It is so exciting to watch his future unfold. I can only imagine what a positive impact his past will have on the life he is embarking on.

Camille

by Dan Pierce

Fifteen years ago my wife Sue's biological clock started "ticking" loudly. Her chances of ever becoming a mother were gone as a result of stage four Hodgkin's cancer. Years of radiation and chemotherapy had rendered her reproductive process inoperative. She often mentioned adoption, but her pleas were falling on my selective hearing process with no result. I was 63 years old, had five grown children who prospered, and I looked forward to a day off. Sue and I had worked with Corrections for years and recognized most criminal/juvenile offenses were the result of deprivation, translating into substance abuse, no goals, and despair. We had more than we needed and elected to support another at a personal level. Our decision (Camille) has paid off way beyond our most fervent longings. She is, truly, a remarkable individual with talent, happiness, and self-confidence. She is Camille.

Our daughter will be thirteen this month. Twelve years and eight months ago, I walked into Dawn Degenhardt's MAPS (Maine Adoption Placement Service) office in Houlton, Maine, on a matter having nothing to do with adoption. As I entered the room, Dawn was on the phone. She regarded me quizzically and said to the party on the other end, "I'll call you back."

My wife, Sue, and I had previously applied for the privilege of adopting a child. We had been interviewed, attended prospective adoptive parent classes, and had our home study done. We were waiting and hopeful.

After Dawn and I had completed business, she told me she knew of a three-month-old child just abandoned for the third time. The child's birthmother had used cocaine heavily. When prospective parents considered the risk of possible brain damage to the child as a result of her mother's drug abuse, they elected to wait for a risk-free child, and the infant was passed over again and again. Sue and I elected to commit to Camille, and Sue flew to Kentucky to retrieve her.

Three-month-old Camille arrived in Houlton with a bag containing a letter from her birthmother. She was giving her up not because she didn't love her but because she did. She was just too sick, she wrote, to ". . . take care of you. I can't even take care of myself." In the bag was also a picture of Camille's birthmom embracing two half-siblings. There was a tiny pair of booties and a couple of small things from the couple who had cared for her the three months following Camille's birth. The only other thing Camille had when she arrived in Houlton was a catastrophic case of colic. Sue had fed her milk when she boarded in Kentucky, but the milk was cold, and Camille was hurting. Sue and Camille had barely entered our home when a friend pulled into our yard (real late at night) and, upon hearing Camille's grief, told us, "I have a nurse in the car." (Talk about providence!) The nurse cared for Camille, and to this day (nearly 13 years later) Camille has never complained about anything.

Camille is a high-honors student and has produced "A" school work through the seventh grade. She plays the piano, cello, and flute well enough to accompany other performers. She regularly plays in church and is being groomed by her teacher to play the church organ. She is the cello in a quartet, and she and the others are about to perform their first "gig" (for money). She plays cello in two orchestras, and she was first flute in the All-Aroostook (County) band this year. She has a new piano, a new (170-year-old) cello, and just this month a new, six open-hole flute (professional).

Camille owns and rides four horses; one Morgan registered in her name, and just last month, an Appaloosa registered in her name. She performs in local horse shows and has accumulated many first place ribbons. This summer Camille has signed to a three day horse camp as well as the same strings camp she attended last year for a week at the University of Southern Maine (at Gorham).

In the winter she downhill skis, as well as studies ballet and jazz dancing, and she swims all summer in her new in-ground pool. She has been on the softball team and takes tennis lessons. She figure-skated in Canada for two years and a whole bunch of people in both countries like her a lot.

I think the best gift one can give another is a feeling of self-confidence, and we have been so fortunate to have been able to put Camille in the presence of people who genuinely care about her. She is a beautiful, gifted, and happy child. Sue and I are blessed to have been given the chance to offer an opportunity to another human being. We are privileged to be instrumental in helping another life to become all she has every right to be.

Thank you MAPS and especially, thank you Dawn, for being on the phone about this incredibly, wonderful, delightful young life the day I walked into your office nearly thirteen years ago.

Our Forever Day

by Manon Bougie

Born in Hawkesbury, Ontario, I'm the oldest of two children. I was married at 19 years of age, and divorced nine years later. Born from my first marriage are Patricia and Jean-Philippe. I met Denis in 1994. He knew I had children and has been an INCREDIBLE DAD ever since. I have been an Executive Secretary for a dealership owner for 20 years. I love being a mom; our children bring so much joy to our lives. We have been blessed with four beautiful children and are praying that God will guide us to our next child or children.

Sunday June 20th, 2004

By the time we arrived at Guangzhou airport, excitement was on all the parents' faces as we were one hour away from meeting our babies.

Arriving at the Gitic Riverside hotel, we rushed out of the shuttle bus, which 10 couples and two guides had been sharing for what seemed like a forever ride. We had less than an hour to receive our luggage in our rooms, unpack and get a diaper bag ready.

The guide gave us the key to our room and Denis and I rushed upstairs to the 19th floor. We had so many emotions that we couldn't even talk to one another except to try to concentrate on everything we had to bring.

The doorbell rang; our luggage had arrived. We opened the luggage throwing half the stuff on the bed looking for the formula, bottles, rattles, baby snacks, baby sweater, and baby blanket. We took a final look through our backpack to make sure we had our adoption papers. We looked at each other, grabbed the video and camera, and proceeded back to the lobby of the hotel, where all the parents were meeting at 3 p.m.

We were the first ones downstairs, but in a matter of minutes the lobby was filled with our group of parents fully equipped to get our babies. "Everyone ready?" said Connie the guide. Ready? That was an understatement—get us there NOW!!! Denis had turned to me 10 seconds prior to tell me he forgot something in the room. In what seemed to feel like hours later (but was really a few minutes), Denis was finally back and we were getting on the shuttle bus ready to take us to the Center of Civil Affairs, where the adoption was going to take place.

By the time we were in the front of the Civil Affairs building so many emotions were running through us that we couldn't say much. As parents were taking the elevator to the fifth floor of the building, Denis and I, with two other couples, waited to get on last. We saw nannies walking in the building with three beautiful babies, then I LOST IT. I was crying, shaking, and sweating. So were the other two mothers. However they were not our babies. They were for another group.

Nothing could have prepared us for what we were about to experience up on the fifth floor: the smell of humid corridors like a hallway with classrooms on both sides; crying babies; crying parents; cameras; the smell of baby vomit; the smell of sweat; people everywhere; and a heat that was indescribable. I felt dizzy and sick to my stomach as we walked into a small room filled with parents in tears and babies not wanting to be there at all. I could not stop staring at a couple receiving a two-year-old behind me.

The heartbreaking cries and kicks of that poor little girl was making me sick to my stomach. I was trying so hard to look at Denis to try to concentrate on keeping my cool and not pass out. My attention was drawn to two other couples whose babies seemed to have settled down. At least I had something to focus on.

Five minutes later the room was full of parents (about 25 couples) and five babies. The guide walked in the room and told us our babies were here. My stomach was in a knot, the sweat was dripping down my face and entire body as the temperature of the room was 40 degrees Celsius (104 degrees Fahrenheit)

We tried to make her laugh and play with some toys, but she seemed emotionless looking at Denis and me. So, I decided to play UP in the air with her, putting all the energy I had left . . .

with a humidity index of 100%. Our baby's name was cried out. Denis and I stood in the middle of the other couples as a man walked over with our little Baby Hope. I was trying so hard to smile at her and we tried talking to her gently so she wouldn't be too scared. The man held her out to me, and my heart stopped; tears were falling on my face as we held our daughter for the first time. She was so tiny and looked exactly like her picture. She started crying and I just wanted to get out of there and be alone with Denis and Hope. I asked the guide if we could take her for a walk down the corridor while other parents were receiving their babies. Denis stayed behind to help with pictures and videos for the other parents as they helped us with ours.

I walked to the end of the hallway with Hope. She was sobbing. I wanted so much to take a good look at her but didn't want to scare her more than she already was. I finally got her to stop crying as we looked out a screenless window at the busy street below.

She was not reaching for the toys or snacks we brought her and didn't want me to touch her hands. She pulled them away. Still looking out the window, she was concentrating more on the traffic than what was going on around her. Holding my little girl in my arms, looking up in the sky, I said, "Thank you God for our beautiful daughter. Please let her biological mother know she is loved and she has give us a precious gift: a baby girl. God, make sure to put peace in her heart as I hold her close to mine. Amen."

As we turned away from the window and looked towards the end of the hallway, I saw parents crying, all sitting on the humid carpet trying to get their little girls to play with the toys they brought. Nothing seemed to work for them. My heart was in pieces to hear the voices of these babies as they were making it clear that they were afraid and wanted nothing to do with us.

We saw Daddy come over. What a relief! Denis really had been my strength throughout this day. We tried to make her laugh and play with some toys, but she seemed emotionless looking at Denis and me. So, I decided to play UP in the air with her, putting all the energy and expression I had left to make it fun. IT WORKED. I said, "Up Baby Hope," clapping my hands as I pushed her as high as my arms allowed me. Then I told her, "Mommy is going to kiss your tummy" and she started laughing. Denis and I played "Up" for about 45 minutes, then gave her a bottle of hot formula which she accepted without any problems.

It was now time to leave for our hotel, not soon enough for the both of us. We were totally drained of our emotions and the lack of food didn't help either. Back in our rooms, we needed to get ready for adoption papers in the guide's room at 6:30 p.m.

Not an easy task to do. Little Baby Hope clearly let us know she did not want to be here and threw up from crying so much. In the 30 minutes we were in our room, she was sick three times and we couldn't calm her down at all.

I brought her close to the sink and ran the water playing with a clear plastic cover to get her attention. She was quiet and I wanted to get her out of her smelly clothes and wash her gently. Daddy stayed in the room with her and I went to the guide's room to do some paperwork. I sat on the floor but I got dizzier every minute. I fought hard to concentrate on all the paperwork but my head was with Daddy and Hope. I told the guide I wanted Denis to fill out the forms and bring them back. When I got to our room, Daddy was lying on the bed and Baby Hope was sound asleep in the crib next to him. Clearly, we knew supper was just not meant to be for us tonight. But I really needed to get something in my stomach, as I felt really weak by then. Denis went down for a quick supper and brought me some snacks that are still on the table beside the bed. I think I obviously needed sleep more than food.

From that moment until now (4:54 a.m.) she has been VELCROED to us. She still won't look us in the eyes and is afraid when looking at us. We can't put her down anywhere as she just wants to be held. Poor little baby, she must have gone through so much and clearly is grieving the loss of her Chinese nanny.

Denis was able to put her in her crib around 9:45 p.m. Then she woke up at 3 a.m. and now she is asleep on the big bed across daddy's bed. We need to tag each other for sleep; if not, we will never be able to stay focused on our journey to return home with our daughter.

Pat, JP and Sidné, we miss you so much and can't wait for you to meet your tiny new little sister.

Hugs everyone from Daddy, Mommy, and Baby Hope
Totally exhausted but extremely happy parents. xxxxx✍️

Manon's husband, Denis, has written "Thank You For Your Support," which can be read in Chapter Ten.

What's Worked For Us

The School Of Experience

*"The only thing to do with good advice is pass it on.
It is never any use to just oneself."*

- Oscar Wilde

Advice From A Birthmom On Dear Birthmom Letter

by Nicole Strickland

Nicole has also written "Doubly Blessed," which can be read in Chapter Four and "Phone Call Tips By A Birthmom," which can be read later in this chapter.

As a birthmother, I have never had to write a Dear Birthmother letter. But, while in search of adoptive parents for my son and since becoming active in the adoption community, I have read many, been asked to read many, and have openly given adoptive parents ideas and suggestions on ways to improve their letter.

The letter you write to potential birthparents has to be one of the hardest letters you will probably write in a lifetime! I can only imagine how difficult this might be! You're writing a letter filled with hope, emotion, and vulnerability. You're opening up and sharing personal information, all with hopes of having someone get to know you through your words.

There is no right or wrong way to write a Dear Birthmom letter. There is not a certain format to follow. Just write it in a style and way that is comfortable for you!

If you are using an agency, be sure to check with them to see if they have any guidelines or requirements before you begin to write your letter. Some agencies require the couple to each write separate letters, while others may not be as picky about content.

Here are some of my ideas for Dear Birthmom letters:

Greeting

Personally, I do not like the greeting Dear Birthmom or Dear Birthparent, even though it is the most common greeting in these letters. My opposition is because, technically, a woman does not become a birthmother until she signs the papers relinquishing her rights. Up until that time, she is simply a mother-to-be making plans for her unborn child. Instead of having a Dear greeting, you could simply say Hello or Hi or even Welcome. (Welcome would be especially good for a letter used on a website.)

Body

After the welcoming, you will start the body of your letter and the paragraphs of the letter to tell about your family. There are many ways you can do this. I will list ideas for paragraphs below, but remember there is no right or wrong way. You can include as many or as few paragraphs as you want.

Introductory paragraph

This is where you introduce yourselves and your child(ren) if you have them! You can also tell about your intent to adopt and a little bit about what you're looking for in adoption. It is also standard to say something about the decision the birthmother is trying to make. If you struggled with infertility before turning to adoption, it is okay to mention this here, but only mention it briefly.

Individual paragraphs

It is customary to have individual paragraphs about the couple. Talk about each person's life, family, childhood, education, occupation, hobbies, interests, significant events in your life, etc.

As a couple

Tell about how you met, when you were married, things you love to do together, family life, etc. You can also have each person tell about the qualities they admire in their spouse.

Children

If you have a child or children, tell about them. Are they biological or adopted? If they are adopted, tell about their adoption. Tell what your children like to do for fun, if they are in dance or play baseball—that sort of thing.

Where you live

Talk about where you live, your neighborhood, schools, parks, culture, etc.

Adoption

Talk about what you're looking for in an adoption, how you feel about adoption, how you might tell your children about adoption, what your child's birthparents roles might be, etc.

Family

Talk about your family and your spouse's family. Tell the reader how your extended families feel about adoption, how active they are in your lives, any traditions you may carry out with them, etc.

Religion

You may wish to talk about your faith if it is important to you and involves how you would raise a child. Include information about your church, activities you may do there, etc.

Parenting style

If one of you will be a stay-at-home parent, or you're currently very involved in your child's schooling, you can discuss that in this paragraph.

Closing

In closing, you can thank the reader for her time and reading your letter, wish her luck, and offer your contact information. If you're presently working with an attorney, you can mention that here. You can sign your letter any way you like—Sincerely, Warmly, and Best Wishes are good examples.

Do's and Don'ts

Do speak from your heart. Let the reader see the real you!

Do write the letter as if you were speaking to a friend—not trying to secure a business deal.

Do be up front with the kind of contact and adoption you are comfortable with. For example, do not make vague statements such as "we can agree to some form of contact we are all comfortable with." If you are not comfortable with visits and a particular potential birthmom has her heart set on visits, then there is no need for her to read further. Instead, try wording it similar to this, "We would love to send you pictures, videos, and letters over the years."

Don't talk about how you understand what a potential birthmother may be feeling or that you "feel her pain." No matter how sympathetic you may be, unless you have been in an unplanned pregnancy and face the decision of how to best care for your unborn baby then you do not truly understand what a potential birthparent may be feeling. This is not meant to be mean; it is just how it is. On the flip side, I will never understand what its like to be infertile or to wait for a birthparent to choose me.

Don't make promises or suggestions in your letter that you cannot or do not intend to keep! If something makes you uncomfortable or you don't think it is something you can really follow through with (visits or sending pictures once a month) then do not promise it to potential birthparents!

So much importance and emphasis is placed on this letter. Many times it is a potential birthparent's first glimpse at who you are and what you are about. But, if you can put that in the back of your mind and write from your heart, the real you will come across. No fancy words are needed; just your everyday lingo and expressions. Sit down with your paper or at your computer, turn on some relaxing tunes, and write! It's not how you say it that's important, it's what you say!

Nicole has authored an informational CD-Rom for couples hoping to adopt entitled "Adoption Pointers, Advice from a Birthmom's Point of View." This CD gives tips and suggestions on writing your Dear Birthmom letter, advice on your adoption profile, guides you as to what a birthmom does NOT want to hear, and more! You will also find a few tips and suggestions on how to handle things after the relinquishment papers have been signed. You can find out more about this CD at http://www.wishuponaweb.net/cd.htm.

What Birthmothers Want To Know About Adoptive Families

by Michelle Wellwood

Michelle has also written "The Choices We Make," which can be read in Chapter Four.

Every birthmother has an ideal picture in her head of what she wants for her child. Birthmothers search for an adoptive family who can raise their child and give him everything in life they wish they could have provided. As a birthmother, and having worked with birthmothers, I have come up with a few different topics birthmothers want to know about the adoptive family they are choosing.

I grew up the oldest of five children and, therefore, I wanted my child to have siblings. That was important to me. I wanted the adoptive family to have other children or be open to the possibility of expanding its family in the future. It was also important that my son be able to play sports, go on family vacations, and spend holidays with family. These are all experiences I had that were very meaningful and I wanted my son to have those same opportunities.

Religion was another important factor. I grew up Catholic and wanted my son to grow up with a similar belief system as myself.

Although some birthmothers do not have a preference on the religion of the adoptive family, it was something important to me.

Another characteristic I looked for were the hobbies and interests of the adoptive family. I chose my son's adoptive family not only because they are wonderful, genuine, loving people, but also because we shared a lot of common interests and I knew my son would be able to share some of those interests with them as well. I was raised in a very athletic family and I knew my son would be naturally talented when it came to playing sports because both his birthfather and I were both involved in many different sports. I wanted his adoptive family to embrace his talent and allow him to explore all the sports he wanted in order to find out what he enjoyed playing. He has been able to do that and now plays basketball, soccer, and baseball.

Education is a value that was very important to me. In my family it was not a matter of whether or not you were going to college but instead where you were going to college. My son's adoptive parents both went to college and have their degrees. I was also able to finish my college education and I hope one day my son will do the same with the support of his parents.

I wanted my son to know who I was, always know he was adopted, and the reasons I chose adoption. I want him to know I love him and think about him all the time. My son's adoptive family is very open in discussing adoption with him. He has a wonderful mother and father who love him unconditionally; he knows he is adopted; he knows that Michelle is his birthmother; and he knows I love him. I could not have asked for a better adoptive family in the world.

I feel it is very important for adoptive families to know the needs and wants of their birthmother. I believe that when the time is right every adoptive couple out there will be given the opportunity to raise their child and have their family. If you paint a detailed picture of what life will be like if you are to have a child of your own to raise then the right birthmother will come along and find you. I truly believe things happen for a reason, and although it was not my plan to become pregnant when I was 17 years old, the plan was for me to provide such a wonderful gift and bundle of joy to my son's adoptive family. I feel truly blessed to have had that experience and to have all of them in my life.

The following is an outline I've come up with to let adoptive parents know what I think birthmothers are interested in and to help you write a Dear Birthmother letter.

Good luck to all of you who are planning to adopt.

1) **Sibling information**
   a. Do you have siblings?
   b. What are some of the activities you do with your siblings? What activities do they enjoy doing?
   c. Do they have children?

2) **Paint a picture of a holiday with your family**
   a. Include activities, food, who attends, games you play, songs you sing, etc.
   b. Make the birthmom feel as if she is there participating or can see her child participating.

3) **Vacations**
   a. Share vacation stories; special trips your family takes every year.
   b. Talk about trips you would like to take when you have a child to share the experience with.
   c. Description of the perfect vacation with the both of you and the child.

4) Religion

    a. Rather than sharing all the details of your religious beliefs, include thoughts that pertain to the child.

    b. Examples: "We feel as if positive reinforcement and treating people as you would want to be treated set a good foundation for bringing up a well-rounded person."

5) Hobbies/Pastimes

    a. Do you have favorite sports teams?

    b. Did you have a favorite game you liked to play as a child?

    c. Are there specific activities the two of you enjoy doing together such as exercising, washing the car, eating dinner together as a family?

6) Education

    a. Do you have a school near you that you see the child attending in the future?

    b. What are some good qualities you would look for in a teacher or someone who was watching the child? Example: responsible, fun, playful, nurturing, energetic, etc.

    c. What were some areas in school you were particularly strong in? Example: math, science, history, etc. Relate this to how you would help the child with school work.

7) Future

    a. Dreams for the child

    b. Example: "I really want them to grow up knowing how much both of us will stand by and support any decisions they make. I want them to know how much you love them, how strong of a person you are, and how much we respect you and appreciate all you went through for us."

    c. What are some activities you plan on doing with the child? Example: Coaching their sports teams, putting together puzzles, learning to play an instrument, etc.

    d. Are you going to be a stay-at-home mom, have a nanny, daycare, or babysitter?

    e. How much interaction have you had with children? Do you babysit for nieces and nephews?

    f. Do you feel it is important for the child to know they were adopted and to know who their birthparents were regardless of whether or not a picture/letter contract was signed?

!!!!!! Bottom Line!!!!!!

Paint a detailed picture for the birthmom of what life will be like for the child living in your home. Include some stories, dreams of having a child, and always remember to thank the birthmother as she will be thanking you in return. And one last thing: Be totally honest in all you write.

Here is a sample of a Dear Birthmother letter I've put together based on the outline. I've used the names Bob and Stacey as the prospective adoptive parents.

Dear Birthmother,

Thank you for taking the time to look over our profile. We are very excited to learn more about you and truly believe you will make the decision that is best for you and your child.

We have a very close family and enjoy doing many activities together, such as attending baseball games and birthday parties, going to the zoo, and having family picnics and Sunday gatherings at grandma and grandpa's place. My sister has two children of her own, and we enjoy spending time with them when everyone gets together. There are 15 nieces and nephews ranging from ages 6 months to 12 years old.

Bob and I have always wanted a family. We dreamed of having that special little boy or girl in our home, bringing laughter and joy to our lives every day. We thought about all the family vacations we would take to Disneyland, the beach, the mountains, and even the country. We are very fortunate in that we have very stable and secure jobs which allows us to travel and enjoy all the wonderful adventures of the world. We recently took a trip with my sister and her two kids to Kansas City, where we went to Worlds of Fun and Oceans of Fun. The kids really enjoyed riding all the rides and playing in the water. It would be so amazing to be able to take our own child there as well. They have a duck pond where the child can choose a duck and win a prize, the tea-cup ride, and even a mini roller coaster. We ate pizza, cotton candy, got wet from the rides, and had a lot of fun. My sister and I have already decided this is going to be something we do every summer.

Bob and I also enjoy holidays with the family. On Christmas Eve we go to grandma and grandpa's house and have dinner together. Grandma loves to cook and always makes the best mashed potatoes. After dinner we gather around the Christmas tree and all the kids get to open one of their presents from their parents. After all, Santa doesn't come until Christmas day. Bob and I usually buy a gift for our godchild who is his brother Jim's little boy. After the children open presents we all have dessert and go home to get ready for Christmas Day. On Christmas Day I can picture our sweet little boy/girl running into our room, wanting so badly to go sit in front of the tree and open all the wonderful things that Santa has brought for him/her. It would be a wonderful day!

Bob and I also enjoy spending time watching baseball. We travel to Chicago to watch the Chicago Cubs but are also huge Nebraska football fans. Bob has recently picked up golfing and I am learning to sew blankets and make other household items. We both really enjoy country music and dancing.

We really want this child to feel as if he or she is not only a part of our family, but also a part of your life. Sharing with them your talents, hobbies, and possibly physical characteristics can help them to understand their background.

Bob and I are strong believers in positive reinforcement and treating others as you would want to be treated. We feel this sets a strong foundation for bringing up a well-rounded child. We would want this child to appreciate all that is offered in life and also to learn from every experience and accept people for who they are.

Bob and I will do our best to provide this child with all the love, security, and happiness we have to give. We really want this child to grow up knowing how much both of us stand by and support any decision he or she makes and that we will love him or her unconditionally. We also want the child to know how much you love him or her, how strong of a person you are, and how much we respect and appreciate all you went through for all of us.

Thank you so much for reading our profile and allowing us to express our dream of having a child to share our life with. You're in our hearts and prayers and we wish you the best in this difficult decision you are faced with.

Thank You and Take Care,
Bob and Stacey

A Sample
Dear Birthmother Letter

by Kitty Stockslager

Kitty has written "Two Hearts Joined Together," which can be read in Chapter Five.

Once we were ready to get started on our Dear Birthmother letter we looked at sample letters to give us some ideas. We then made a list of things we wanted to stand out about us, such as: how our relationship started, how long we were together, our thoughts on adoption, what it meant to us to become parents, what we looked forward to when we became parents, and the things we liked to do. Then we took the list and wrote about each thing individually. After we had everything written we formed it into our letter. We tried to write it so whoever was reading it felt like we were talking to them.

Don't count on getting it right the first time. It takes time. We did ours several times and had others read it to give us advice on making it better. It took a lot of patience.

For our final Dear Birthmother letter (the one the agency sent to birthmothers) we used a light blue, marbled card stock. On the front we put a four by six close-up picture of us. On the back of the letter we included smaller pictures of us and our family and friends. We also decorated it with stickers. We wanted it to be eye catching to a birthmother without being too flashy.

This is our Dear Birthmother letter:

(Front Page)
Hello!

We are Chad and Kitty Stockslager. We are very excited (and nervous) that you are reading our letter to consider us as adoptive parents for your child. We understand the love and courage it has taken you to consider open adoption and we respect you for your decision. We also feel it is very important for you to be able to choose and get to know the parents of your choice.

Our life together began when we met in 1990 at a grocery store where we both worked. We were married in 1993. From our first date our love for each other has grown stronger and we continue to grow as a couple that is very happy and in love. We are truly each other's best friend!

After a few years of marriage we wanted to start our family. Through dealing with infertility, we have come to realize it's not important to us to have a biological child; we just want a child to give our unconditional love to and through open adoption we can make this happen.

We are committed to building our family through open adoption. Through this we know love and closeness are possible, and we are looking forward to sharing a relationship with you. Since we started the process, we have been so excited knowing that some day we will become parents through this miracle. We can't go shopping without the baby furniture, baby clothes, and baby items catching our attention. Often we find ourselves already buying something for the baby that he or she will need when it arrives. We are dreaming of the special times to come with our child: reading its favorite story, baking chocolate chip cookies, playing and learning together, the first day of school, and especially the holidays. We realize there are a lot of responsibilities in raising a child, but we promise to be fast learners!

We live in Troy, Ohio, which is 30 minutes north of Dayton, with our dog, Midnight. Our home is a brick ranch with a large fenced-in yard and the perfect spot for a swing and play area. Our community has an annual Strawberry Festival that is filled with lots of food, crafts and various events. The festival is a great time, and we can't wait to share this event with our child.

Our thoughts and prayers are with you as you read our letter and we look forward to the opportunity to meet and get to know you. If you would like to know more about us, we would love to talk with you. Please feel free to contact us toll free at _____ or call our Adoption Counselors at the Independent Adoption Center toll free at 800-877-6736. You can also e-mail us at:_____

With our love, your friends,
Chad and Kitty Stockslager

(Back page)

Family & Friends

Grandparents, aunts, uncles, cousins, and even friends, most of whom live within an hour's drive, excitedly await the arrival of a new addition to the family. Family is very important to us! You will find us at each other's family more than we are at our own home. We enjoy gathering with them for cookouts, weekend adventures, and especially the holidays. Everyone has already offered to babysit anytime, but we don't think they'll be able to get the baby away from us.

Our Time Together

Evenings are the best time of the day because it gives us the time to sit down at the supper table and discuss our day, sharing all of our thoughts and feelings. You will often find us working together in the yard mowing grass and pulling weeds from our flower beds. On the weekends we enjoy going to church, spending time with family and friends, or just relaxing at home watching movies. We also enjoy taking walks with our dog, Midnight. She loves people, especially children. The walks tend to be long because she has to stop and make friends with everyone. We also enjoy traveling to different places, whether it is to watch a sporting event or take a relaxing vacation.

About Chad

Chad is a very loving and caring person. He is always easy going and ready to help others when in need. He loves to watch football and is looking forward to having a little boy or girl by his side for the game to cheer on their favorite team. Chad has his associate's degree in Engineering Design. He has a stable and flexible career as a machinist for a successful pump company. Our nieces find him irresistible! I think they have him wrapped around their little fingers. When we are visiting them, you can often find him playing hide and seek, tag, or relaxing on the couch reading them their favorite stories. When I see him with other children, I can't wait until we become parents because I know he will be a great father. Chad is just a big kid at heart himself. Besides Chad's one-of-a-kind sense of humor, what I love most about him is his warm smile and big bear hugs. He is always there when I need him, whether it is to laugh with or to give me a shoulder to cry on.

-Kitty

About Kitty

Family is a very important part of Kitty's life. She is the oldest sibling in a family of four. She truly plays the role of big sister. Her loving and caring ways can be seen by all, from helping take care of her nieces to lending a shoulder to cry on for those in need. Her family all lives reasonably close, and Friday evenings is a must at mom and dad's for supper. Working as a medical assistant in a pediatrician's office couldn't be a better fit for her because she is able to help care for children of all ages. Although Kitty loves her job, she plans to take an extended leave when the baby arrives. She is looking forward to putting all her time into taking care of our baby. Her warm and loving heart will make her a wonderful mother. In her spare time she enjoys making crafts, either for our home or for an upcoming craft show. Evenings are also spent making her popular baby blankets for either friends or relatives who are expecting a baby. A wide variety of blankets already await the arrival of a baby in our home.

-Chad

Questions To Ask A Potential Birthmother

by Karen Ledbetter

My husband and I are parents to a 10-year-old daughter, adopted at birth through an open adoption. I stay busy as a full-time mom, part-time medical transcriptionist, part-time writer, Sunday School teacher, and volunteer librarian at my daughter's school. I am also the adoption host for BellaOnLine. Please stop by my site at www.bellaonline.com/site/adoption. I may be reached via e-mail at scahs@alltel.net or adoption@bellaonline.com.

You've completed your home study, mailed out adoption resumes, passed out adoption business cards, and maybe even advertised in newspapers. You had a special baby telephone line installed. When you're least expecting it, that special number rings and your heart pounds. You take a deep breath, then answer. You're talking to a woman who is making an adoption plan for the baby she's carrying. What questions do you ask?

Below is a list of questions I compiled during the months of research and reading I did before successfully adopting our child. Perhaps this list will help you, too.

1. How are you feeling?
2. Have you seen a doctor?
3. When is the baby due?
4. Where do you live?
5. Do you work? Go to school?
6. How old are you? How old is the baby's father?
7. Does your family know about this pregnancy and your adoption plans?
8. What do they think about adoption?
9. Is your mother emotionally supporting this plan?
10. Have you talked to other couples?
11. Are you married?
12. Does the baby's father know about the pregnancy?
13. What are his feelings?
14. Is this your first pregnancy?
15. Why are you considering adoption?
16. Would you like to call our agency/attorney?
17. Do you want to think about this and call me back tomorrow? Do you want me to call you back sometime?
18. Do you mind sharing your phone number?

Karen's daughter Courtney was interviewed in "Interview With An Adoptee," which can be read in Chapter Three.

Phone Call Tips By A Birthmom
by Nicole Strickland

Nicole has also written "Doubly Blessed," which can be read in Chapter Four, and "Advice From A Birthmom On Dear Birthmom Letter," which can be read earlier in this chapter. She is also the co-founder of BirthmomBuds, www.birthmombuds.com.

So many couples hoping to adopt have told me the first phone call a potential birthmom makes to them is very nerve racking. But remember: the potential birthmom is just as nervous as you are! I think it is a good idea to have a small notebook and pen near the phone. That way you can jot down important things she says. Also, keep a list of questions in the notebook; that way, if you are nervous you won't be fumbling for words or what to ask. Show an interest in her well-being as a person, not just the person who is possibly going to give you a child. On the first phone call, you don't want to ask too many questions or get too personal. Save those for another time.

Questions and things to say during the first phone call:
I'm so glad you called. How are you feeling?
Have you had a good pregnancy so far? Have you
been getting prenatal care?

When are you due?

Is this your first child?

Tell me a little bit about yourself. Are you a student, do you work, live with parents, etc??

How old are you?

Where are you from? Have you lived there long?

What is your family like? Do you have brothers or sisters? Is your family supportive?

What about the father of your child: Is he involved? What's he like?

Have you had a chance to talk to any professionals or others about your decision?

Do you have any thoughts on what kind of contact you would like after the baby is born?

Do you have any special requests on how you would like your child to be raised?

If the conversation goes well and you feel comfortable you could then ask her:

If she would like to meet before the baby is born

If she would like your attorney or agency's information

To send you (or the attorney or agency) proof of pregnancy

A few more tips:

Get a toll free number so potential birthmoms can contact you directly.

Keep in mind that a potential birthmom could call any time of the day or night.

Usually potential birthmoms will feel more comfortable talking to the female of the couple.

Be yourself and be honest and open.

Treat her with respect and know that she may be very confused and may know little about the adoption process.

Keep the conversation friendly.

If things go well, set up a time to speak again.

A few things NOT to do or say:

Do not pressure her to choose you or make a commitment before she is ready.

Do not patronize her.

Do not try to impress her with your achievements.

Do not say things you think she wants to hear just so you can adopt her child.

Do not be too pushy or overbearing.

Do not pressure her for more information than she is willing to give you at the moment.

A lot of these same questions and tips will apply to communication via e-mail. E-mail is a little trickier though. It is less personal and your questions may bombard her. On the phone, you can ask a question, talk about something else, and then ask another question. In an e-mail, your questions may look a little more threatening, so try to limit the number of questions to about three to five an e-mail. Try to write about something else in the e-mail so it is not only questions. Write about your life and what you did that day, then ask your questions. Some hopeful adoptive moms communicate with potential birthmoms (after the initial e-mail) via a messenger service such as AIM. This might be an easier way to communicate via the computer if the potential birthmom seems reluctant to move to the phone.

So the next time your adoption phone rings, just relax!

To Tell Or Not To Tell (The School), That Is The Question

by Karen Ledbetter

Karen has also written "Questions To Ask A Potential Birthmother," which can be read earlier in this chapter.

I asked for feedback about whether or not to tell the school, daycare, or preschool of a child's adopted status. I received several interesting and thought-provoking responses from others which I'd like to share:

Telling people our children were adopted was always something that came very naturally. Of course we didn't go into long explanations for every stranger in the supermarket who made a comment about the babies, but we did with those people with whom we were likely to have an ongoing relationship. It was something we never made any secret of. It was how our family was formed, and something that made us all very happy.

When it came time to fill out the first form when signing our daughter up for preschool, the question was right there in black and white: Was this child adopted, and if so, did the child know it? It really didn't occur to me not to answer the questions honestly. Being adopted is part of my children's life experience, and I didn't see any reason to withhold the information. I figured the school must have had a reason for asking, although I can't remember any situation ever coming up where it would have made any difference if a teacher knew or not. I certainly don't feel either my son or daughter was ever treated in a negative way because they were adopted.

I don't remember the question being on the applications for the private elementary school they now attend, but I know I eventually mentioned it to the kindergarten teacher at the first parent-teacher conference. Again, there were no negative effects, no labeling as possible problem children, etc. When each child was in first grade and had a week of being the class VIP, I made it a point to go in and visit the class and read an adoption story to the children. Some of them already knew my children were adopted. The teacher also made it a very positive experience.

I guess the decision about whether or not to tell the school is a very personal one that each family must come to after careful thought. I don't think there is any right or wrong answer. What's right for one family isn't necessarily right for another, and with these types of situations there are usually a number of different factors to consider before making this decision. **Miriam, NY**

While I'm open about adoption, in the past few years I've become open only with those I know share my interests. I didn't want my son known as "the adopted kid," nor did I want problems that might arise to be labeled "adoption issues." I came to this conclusion after witnessing this type of thing happen to friends with adopted kids.

I only told the school after he had been there for nine months. We went to adopt our daughter and I only told them then because

I had to explain things. I now regret that decision. Once his adoption became known, the questions started. Did I meet his "real mom?" (ARGH!!!!!) What was wrong with her that she had babies and then gave them up? Is he like his "real mom?" and so on.

Then, when he started to act up and act out from boredom and from problems in having a new sister it was immediately labeled an adoption issue. Boredom was never considered, not even when I brought it up. No, the "expert" teacher concluded; he knew he was adopted and was angry about it. Sibling rivalry? Nah. The fact my son had undiagnosed pneumonia (we thought it was asthma) wasn't considered, either. Nope, everything was adoption. One teacher went so far as to suggest my son's "real mother" did drugs and/or alcohol, and therefore, my son had fetal alcohol syndrome; right before she admitted she knew nothing about it!

When I enrolled him in his new school, one of the questions on the application was, "If your child is adopted, does he know?" I left it blank. I don't think it's their business. In time, perhaps I'll tell them, but most likely, I won't. If he chooses to tell, and I'm asked, I won't lie. I'll even offer to come in and talk about it to the kids, just to see how progressive and open minded they are. But volunteer the information? Absolutely not. **Barbara, NJ**

My husband and I have decided not to share our daughter's adoption information with the school, at least for now. We feel that her conception, birth, and how she joined our family are private matters (not secret) that have absolutely nothing to do with how she'll perform academically, so the school really doesn't need to know this. We feel her teacher and classmates need to get to know her for the unique little person she is, without any stereotypical misconceptions regarding her birth history. Plus, we feel it's HER story to share, not ours. If she chooses to share this information with her teacher or some of her classmates, that's okay.

She knows it's okay for her to tell others she's adopted, but so far I've only heard her mention it twice: once to my mom and dad, and again to the nurse at her doctor's office. She also has been told once she shares this information with someone, it cannot be taken back.

By not sharing this right now, we don't feel we're being dishonest or secretive. We're just not sharing what we feel is private. We realize at some point in the future we may have to share this information with a teacher and will take that opportunity to educate others about adoption; but for now, it's our private family business. I also realize if a child is a different race or nationality from his/her parents, or if a child was adopted at an older age, these issues are entirely different. Also, I feel there are no right or wrong answers here. Each family has to do what they feel is best for them and their child(ren). **Karen, NC**

When my daughter entered preschool, the school application had this entire section on whether your child was adopted or not. When were they adopted? Do they know they are adopted? Do they have a sibling that was also adopted? When did they find out they were adopted?

My mind was truly boggled the first time I read this, which was over two years ago. Why would they want to know? What difference could it possibly make? I have read numerous books and magazines on the issue. Some said tell, others said do not tell.

My husband and I made a joint decision not to tell. Quite simply, our children's adoptions are not secrets, but (the information) is private. We crossed out the section on the application. We did not want our child to stand out for any reason in these people's minds, whether it be positive or negative to them.

The one question that stood out the most to us was the one that said, "Do they know they are adopted?" For the life of me, I can't understand that one! Why would I tell the school they (my children) were adopted and not tell my own kids? It makes you wonder what is going on in their minds to ask such a question in the first place!

Our hope has always been that if either child feels like sharing his or her adoption stories, it would be a wonderful thing! So far so good, as our daughter has shared some of her adoption regarding her birthmom and birthfather with others!

Again, there is nothing that we are more proud of than having these two beautiful children. And truly I will talk to anyone about adoption anytime until I am blue in the face on how it is the best thing that could ever have happened to us. However, my husband and I do not share our children's birth histories with others. These are our children's own stories and theirs to tell, not ours.

I would have to say that not telling has been a positive experience. I really hate to even use the words "not telling" because that denotes a secret, which of course, it is not and never will be. So we don't answer their questions regarding adoption, but even if they find out, so what? Again, why are they asking in the first place? That is the million-dollar question!

Michelle, IL

The Toothbrush Monster And Other Silly Strategies To Parenting Success

by Mollie McLeod

I am the mother of two sons who joined my family through adoption from foster care in the United States. I believe that having fun with our children is a very important part of parenting.I'm also a board member of Families Adopting in Response (FAIR), an all volunteer organization that provides support to pre-adoptive and adoptive families. FAIR's website is: http://www.fairfamilies.org

My son, Jay, joined our family when he was five-and-a-half years old. There are many benefits to parenting a child who can talk and express himself. Initially, it was helpful to know he liked lobster, soup, and the beef sticks that are sold in the checkout stands in grocery stores. The lobster he enjoyed at a foster home once, the soup was a fond memory of when an older sister took care of him when Jay was sick, and the beef sticks? Well, I guess that's just one of those taste sensations that he enjoys.

There were definitely food issues in our house with Jay. He wanted assurances he could have a "feast" everyday after school or

Y-childcare. For a period of several months, Jay wanted to know exactly what his snack would be the following day, and he wanted it put out for him or in a special spot in the refrigerator. Under periods of stress, Jay needed additional reassurances and proof that there would be enough food for him to eat when he was hungry.

As a parent, it is my role to be aware of Jay's verbal and nonverbal signals about his needs, hopes, desires, and fears. I must be responsive and create routines that support our cohesion as a family. Mealtimes, bedtimes, and other routines are useful for establishing the framework of family life. Children need consistency. Adults show they are dependable and trustworthy by creating certain expectations in children and meeting their needs again and again over time. This is particularly important for children like my son.

After mealtime, or his feast, I wanted Jay to brush his teeth. Dental care was an especially big issue with Jay. When I first met Jay, his front four teeth had shiny silver caps on them. There were caps on the top left side of his mouth and more on the bottom right side. However, the dentist that installed the caps (baby root canals) did not properly size them. Food particles wedged under the protective metal plates, trapping them, and rotting those teeth.

During the first year Jay lived with us, he had six teeth pulled. Unfortunately, there is only one pediatric dentist in our county that accepts MediCal and Jay's teeth did not always break during office hours. I held his hand as Jay stared off into space each time a dentist had to remove another tooth. Once, the rotten tooth disintegrated and numerous small pieces had to be fished out of his mouth while Jay lay rigid.

Tooth brushing in the McLeod residence began to resemble a battleground. Tensions would rise as I tried to make Jay brush his teeth and he refused. As he flailed about in the bathroom, Jay cried out, "I'll call 9-1-1." When I asked "Why?" he responded, "Because you're making me brush my teeth!"

We both dreaded the conclusion of mealtime and the inevitable bathroom power struggle. I began to feel like an ogre.

Then, one morning, I stepped back into the hallway, got down on my knees, crawled toward the bathroom door, and began to make loud growling noises. I popped my head around the door jam and announced, "I am the dreaded toothbrush monster!" Jay put his toothbrush in his mouth, and I let out a screech. I pulled my head back into the hallway, waved my arms dramatically like I was choking, and said, "There is nothing quite as terrible to the toothbrush monster as the dreaded spit." Jay looked intrigued. I explained, in my persona as the ogre, the "dreaded spit" was when the toothpaste became creamy from being brushed on every part of each tooth. Jay began moving his toothbrush rapidly and thoroughly around his mouth. With a glint in his eye, Jay took aim into the sink and gave a loudly satisfying spit of frothy toothpaste. I moaned and groaned and collapsed onto the rug. Jay cheered and asked if we could do it again. For a few weeks, I played the toothbrush monster almost every morning. I still do encore performances at Jay's request.

Another time, Jay was reluctant to get dressed in the morning so I put his pants on his head. Jay put his shirt on his feet. We looked in the mirror to see how silly Jay looked and then checked to see how he looked with his school clothes on the right way.

My experience feeling like an ogre and transforming these monstrous emotions in a positive way taught me the benefits of silliness as a parenting tool. Now, I reserve five to ten minutes in the morning to play together with my son. We have pillow fights, play with stuffed animals, and use our imaginations. From trial and error, I realized our family is more relaxed and closer if we make time to play together each day. Whenever a new challenge comes up, I try to think if there is a fun way to approach the situation. As the saying goes, laughter really is the best medicine.

Welcome Home Woo Hyuk!
A Toddler Adoption Story
by Barbara Burke

Barbara has also written "Our Daughter's Arthrogryposis," which can be read in Chapter Seven.

There are many types of adjustments and reactions from children coming into a new family because each child and family is different. I feel for all adjustment issues, there are three key factors to consider in deciding if you're capable of handling the adjustment of a child through adoption, especially of a toddler over an infant.

1. Can you allow a child to adjust at its own pace?
2. Can you set limits when appropriate?
3. Can you justly discipline the child when these limits are broken?

Our son arrived home from Seoul, Korea, at 21 months of age. He was a very exhausted, sullen little guy, who had a trying trip. He had a difficult time separating from Oma, his foster mother, and spent most of his flight pacing the plane, calling out her name.

He was brought into a totally new environment with different people, language, and a culture other than he had known.

Our little guy went through all the classic stages of adjustment we read and prepared for in dealing with a toddler adoption. The book *Toddler Adoption—The Weaver's Craft* by Mary Hopkins-Best gives a detailed description of why toddler adoptions are unique. I highly recommend this book to anyone adopting a toddler between the ages of one and four. Please keep in mind the situations in this book cover all areas of difficulties, so don't become alarmed over some of the experiences told by parents.

For the first three days Woo Hyuk experienced terrible grieving for his foster mother. He spent much of his time going to all the doors and windows in our house, looking out and crying for her. He would constantly carry his shoes around in hopes we would take him to Oma in Korea. On his second day with us, we were in our front yard and he turned to me, waved goodbye, and walked down the road with no intention of coming back. Woo Hyuk was sure Korea was just around the bend. He only had one thing on his mind: finding Oma.

His first night was spent crying inconsolably for three hours between my husband and me on our bed: very unhappy, scared, and uncomfortable. He would not accept comfort and would push our hands away repeatedly. His sobs were heartbreaking. His mournful cries were the same as those of someone experiencing the death of a loved one. After about three hours, he suddenly stopped crying, crawled off our bed with an exhausted but determined attitude, and climbed into the toddler bed next to ours. Somehow he knew it was his bed. He curled up and was soon fast asleep. After that first night, he needed either my husband or me in the room to fall asleep. Falling asleep often took close to an hour or more. Occasionally, he would cry out from a night terror but never fully awaken. My husband or I, usually both, would stay close to him, saying soothing words, and rubbing his back. He never seemed aware of us being there but I think our presence was felt.

There are many ways your child's sleeping habits can be changed as they are becoming adjusted to your family. In our case Woo Hyuk remained in our bedroom in a toddler bed for a year-and-a-half before we moved him at age three to the lower bunk in our teenage son's room. Some people may think that was too long to transition him, but we felt our son needed that much time. We feel it's a good idea to consider having your child sleep with you, or in your room, at first and gradually introduce them to their own bed over time. Allow the child to lead and you will create more security and independence in them down the road. Now he sleeps soundly through the night, seldom waking. A great help in accomplishing this was the many routine rituals we followed before bedtime. He needed his bottle of water, his music box, a good night kiss from everyone, his bath at the same time after dinner, and a little play before going to bed. If one element of this routine was missing he'd let you know! Rituals are still followed now that he is three, but we don't have to follow them as strictly. Children are such creatures of habit, at this age, and routine is really the foundation for rebuilding the security they lose when removed from their accustomed surroundings into new ones.

... routine is really the foundation for rebuilding the security they lose when removed from their accustomed surroundings into new ones.

Sleeping during the day was very hard for Woo Hyuk. We did not press him to take a nap at this part of his adjustment because it was too upsetting to him, even though I could have benefited from a daily nap! We felt it did more harm than good forcing him to nap during the day. We tried, but found him to be very upset for hours after, so we gave up. Maybe that is why he slept well during the night.

Over the first couple of weeks Woo Hyuk challenged each and every one of our family routines, as if to say "Will you still love me even if I am THIS bad?" This testing phase is often described as a period of time where a child misbehaves on purpose to see if the adopting parents will continue to parent them anyway, despite their behavior. Although it can strain the patience of the adoptive parents, most parents do survive this period. Finally the child will assimilate into the family and seem like a regular member, not overstressing the family but making reasonable demands on it. A very useful tool to learn about this phase is *The Encyclopedia Of Adoption*, by Christine Adamec and William L. Pierce, Ph.D.

My husband and I decided to use a team effort with Woo Hyuk. Since I have always been the full time caregiver, the children tended to go to me over dad in most incidences. I knew I would need more help since Woo Hyuk was our sixth child, so my husband and I worked through his adjustment as a team. My husband had taken two weeks off from work and this was crucial for us to form a routine for Woo Hyuk and also to take care of the other children's needs and not disrupt their routines.

Those first couple of weeks Woo Hyuk needed to be watched very carefully or he would run into trouble. He had not formed a full attachment to any of us and could easily slip off in public. He was more than willing to go off with another person and not look back. He was exploring his new environment and was into everything! I would clean up his recent mess in one room, while he was in another making a new one! We restricted him from parts of the house to keep my sanity by closing the doors of bedrooms and bathrooms. Luckily he had not mastered doorknobs at this age!

He had a frenzied way of going about, never really playing with any one thing fully. We felt his restlessness was a result of feeling unsettled in his new surroundings. Children can experience a great deal of frustration during the adjustment period. They can

I think parents who have children in the home really need to prepare them for rejection from their new brother or sister at first . . .

exhibit changes in moods, especially when required to do something different than what they had been doing. They can have temper tantrums, be hyperactive, restless, and even exhibit what may be considered vulgar activities. These are partly frustration and partly survival mechanisms. A lot will pass when your child learns to trust you and learns some English.

We all wondered where the "angelic" child the Korean agency workers described was. We had a couple of exhausting weeks I thought were straight out of hell. I think the hardest part is to spend the entire day with a child, nurturing and caring for his needs, and getting nothing in return. There were a couple of moments I wondered what in the world we were thinking of, adopting this child. Dinner hour was especially hard. Trying to get dinner on the table and hearing the loud disturbances between Woo Hyuk and another sibling, and having him underfoot as I tried to work, was a challenge.

My youngest daughter, who was five at the time, was in her second day of adjusting to the first grade when Woo Hyuk arrived. She had confusing feelings. In retrospect, I can see where I should have prepared the children in the family more regarding Woo Hyuk's initial reaction into our home. The children waited with anxious anticipation for his arrival, and had no knowledge he would at first not be accepting of us. My daughter cried a lot those first couple of days. She thought she was not a good big sister and blamed herself for his unhappiness. I think parents who have children in the home really need to prepare them for rejection from their new brother or sister at first, and to explain the new child may initially be very unhappy because they are sad over the loss of what they had to say goodbye to in their birth country. You may see sibling rivalry and/or jealousy by both your newly adopted child and/or a child already in the home. Most expected, by the child closest in age to the new child. The new child naturally receives a great deal of attention at first. The other child may respond by clinging or being moody or acting out. On the other hand, the newly adopted child may begin to experience sibling rivalry when they realize they are competing for attention. A child that has been in an orphanage among hundreds of children, suddenly receiving a great deal of attention in their new environment with only a limited number of other children, can be confused. They have probably had to be aggressive to survive in the orphanage. They know how to get attention, and competition has been greatly reduced. In our son's case, as in the case of many foster care children in foreign countries, he came from an environment in which he was the only child and therefore received heaps of time and attention from his caring foster mother. Foster mothers are often very grandmotherly to the children in their care. Our son was rather spoiled in that way and needed time to learn what it was like to be one of others seeking parental attention. I kept telling myself this too would pass and this was just another part of his adjustment into our family. Nonetheless, we had our share of trying days!

He started to fall in love with each member of the family, one at a time. When this happened, it was genuine and real and there was no mistaking it. I was first, since I was his full-time caregiver. This is the way it happens with many children. At first, they feel secure with only a few members of the family or even one.

When Woo Hyuk came down with his first cold this started a positive change of events. I think it was probably because his tolerance was down that he came to me and accepted more cuddling and rocking. He was tired enough to take a nap without putting up a struggle. That was his first nap and he has continued to take a nap to this day. He sleeps two to two-and-a-half hours every afternoon and still has no problem going down at 8 p.m. When he woke up from his nap the first day he was sick, he immediately called my name. I also overheard him in bed that night whispering, "mommy, mommy…" in a loving way. After that day, he settled in and the phase of testing seemed to diminish.

Firmness and consistency were the key to getting to the point we are at today. I knew he was testing the water and had no idea what we'd tolerate from him. The only way he could learn was by trial and error. Somewhere I once read, a child has to taste a food nine times before he is comfortable with it and learns to like it. That seems to hold true somewhat with discipline. It was only through consistency that he was able to abide by the family rules. Things became easier with his acceptance of us because he was more willing to want to please.

My advice as a parent for the past 22 years is pick your battles and much can be accomplished by finding alternative ways of allowing your children to make independent decisions, like giving them choices you decide on. They soon learn from your compromise that they too, can compromise.

I am sure there is a huge variation in language with children the same age, or any age. Woo Hyuk was a verbal child right from the start. He was very language oriented. When he arrived from Korea at 21 months of age, his reports said he was speaking in simple sentences and spoke well for his age. He understood everything said to him. He was talking in our home from day one and would chant things incessantly in Korean, trying to get us to understand him. This in itself can be difficult because a toddler isn't savvy enough to understand that you speak a different language. They want what they want, when they want it. And that's usually now!! Woo Hyuk wasn't initially interested in understanding us, but rather wanted to be understood, and would chant the same thing repeatedly. My eldest son was dating a girl whose mother was Korean. Her mother helped a lot with interpreting what he was trying to say. This was hard for her at times since much of his speech was baby talk. He would ask for food, for drink, to play, but mostly, "Where is Oma?" "Take me to Oma!"

We have picked up many simple words in Korean and we'd play games with both the English and Korean words. He seemed to gain comfort by me repeating whatever he said in Korean. I guess it made him feel understood just to hear me repeat the words. This seemed to comfort him. His foster

His adjustment is an ongoing process and we felt it wasn't fully complete until he reached being with us for almost 21 months.

mother gave him two large, musical trucks when he left Korea and he spent endless hours the first few weeks pushing the buttons, hearing the Korean words and music. I would notice him run from the TV room into the living room with a determined look and choose one of the trucks to listen to over and over again. It seemed to me he needed to hear the Korean words for comfort when the English spoken on the TV got overwhelming for him.

When he made the transition of acceptance, it was visibly obvious that he no longer wanted to hear Korean spoken to him. He stopped playing with the trucks during this time, and when my son's girlfriend's mom came over and spoke to him in Korean, he refused to look at her. I asked her to ask him something he would have a hard time not responding to. She asked him if he was hungry in Korean. He made no response, remained motionless, and looked downcast toward the floor. I asked in English and he jumped for joy saying, "Yum! Hungry," running to the snack bar.

After two months in his new home, he had all but caught up to what he spoke in Korean, only now he was speaking in English. He was putting four to five words together to form sentences, understood all that was said, and did not use any of his Korean. This is very advanced for the common child, but Woo Hyuk tended to be very language oriented. Now, at age three-and-a-half he is more open to hearing and speaking Korean. We have a number of Asian Markets in our community where we shop weekly. Woo Hyuk is happy to hear his native language spoken there, especially when he knows this is the store we buy his beloved *kim-bop* for our weekly Korean meals!

Our son, Woo Hyuk, celebrated his second birthday three months after he arrived. His adjustment is ongoing. In many ways, he is like any average two-year-old. He is curious and active, filled with wonder over every new thing, delightful, verbal, fearful, self-centered, giving, loving, challenging, and a joy in our lives. He runs with exuberance for hugs and kisses at bedtime, and whenever he needs an "owey" kissed away. He loves with passion and lets his opinions be known with utter defiance.

Woo Hyuk has formed a strong attachment to his older siblings and runs to greet them when they come in from school. He is back to the "angelic" child described of him in his Korean child reports, and is very loving and affectionate. He asks, "Okay?" ("Are you okay?") with concern when anyone gets hurt. He seldom challenges the family rules. He is an accepted member of our family, participating joyfully in family activities. He does his share and helps out by feeding the family dog dinner every night. He picks up his toys and is often heard singing the Barney clean-up song as he works without being reminded. He stays close to family when out in public, and calls for mommy to come and get him up in the morning, even though he can get out of the toddler bed independently. When he does need redirection, he always tells us, "good boy, I am" (meaning, "what a good boy I am!"). His adjustment is an ongoing process and we felt it wasn't fully complete until he reached being with us for almost 21 months. Is that a coincidence, since he arrived at 21 months of age and spent that long in Korea with his foster mother? I don't know. But it did seem to be the magical turning point in our lives. Now, as a three-and-a-half-year-old, he is doing super! He sleeps through the night, shares a bunk bed with his older brother, and seldom awakens during the night. He is fully potty-trained and goes to bed peacefully with a story, good-night kisses, and a drink of water. He loves to be independent. He climbs his dresser drawers and selects his own underwear, socks, pants, and shirt, and dresses himself before heading into the bathroom and brushing his teeth. He loves food and hasn't fully mastered neatness. He is a bit of a messy eater because he eats with such exuberance, but eats independently and gives me the best compliments on my cooking. He rides a two-wheeler with training wheels, swims well with floatees, races around, jumps, recites the ABC's and 123's, and models professionally for a talent/modeling agency. His language continues to be amazing and his natural musical gift of rhythm and love for reciting the words to every song he hears demonstrates that love for language. We went through our typical terrible two's issues, along with the extra fears and insecurities adoption as a toddler brought upon us. Now we are well into the remarkable three's and marvel at the tremendous love a child this age has for his family, especially his mommy and daddy. We must be told a hundred times a day that we are "the best mommy and daddy in the whole world!" He is a joy beyond words in our lives and a gift from God to which we are exceedingly thankful for.

He is loved. He is cherished. He is family. And he belongs!

Building A Child's Self-Esteem

by Rosemary J. Gwaltney

Rosemary has also written "Thoughts On Loving A Helpless Child," which can be read in Chapter Seven.

I am the single mother of twenty-six. I have built my family mostly through adoption. Most of my children, who have disabilities, are very active and capable. Over the years, I have put much thought into trying to raise each one as though he or she were like anyone else. I don't see my children's handicaps when I look at them. To me, they are simply children. Children with strengths and weaknesses like everyone else. I want each one to be aware of all their strengths first, and not to feel badly about their weaknesses, or worse, to try to use them to get out of things! I tell them, every living person has weaknesses. The things you can't do are not as important as the things you CAN do!

A disabled child's self-identity and feeling about himself can be very fragile. He will be disinclined to try to progress if he believes himself incapable, a failure, or unimportant. Particularly vulnerable to this is the child who has experienced being in the foster care system. This child feels worse than useless. He has also been unwanted, maybe by numerous families, and knows it. Being in the foster care system, he has never learned how to be helpful.

Almost always he comes to his adoptive family bringing virtually nothing. He has no happy feeling about himself inside. He is a human child who feels miserably like a non-person.

Building a child's self-esteem is very important. The best way to do this is to make the child feel needed.

What makes a child want to help? Being appreciated! A child with cerebral palsy, who has intelligence enough to want to join his or her siblings in their play, is able to learn to help. I searched my brain year after year to find tiny things such a child could do to feel needed. A child, with a weak body but a willing heart, can do many of the following things:

1. Put away small cans, or light dishes, on a shelf the child can reach.
2. Carry something from one part of the house to another in his or her wheelchair.
3. Shake a bag with chicken and shake 'n bake.
4. Pour salad dressing on a salad.
5. Sprinkle candies on cookies someone is baking.
6. Stir the stew with a long wooden spoon.
7. Come to tell the parent if a certain child gets out of bed.
8. Tell a parent if the coffee is ready.
9. Tell someone the kitchen timer has gone off.
10. Drive around the house telling everyone that dinner is ready.
11. Smooth their own quilt on their bed.
12. Turn a light, a tape deck, a TV, or any number of things, on or off. Lamps can be bought that turn on and off with the touch of a finger.

13. Cover up a sleeping sibling whose quilt has fallen off. (Only a child who won't wake a sleeping sibling!)
14. Watch over a pot until it boils. (Only a child who is safe around boiling water.)
15. Possibly open curtains, with an object fastened to the end of the cord for grasping.
16. Help load or unload the dishwasher.
17. Pulling frozen food out of the freezer onto the tray of a child's wheelchair so it can defrost is a job everyone loves.

Of the twenty-one children who are still living at home, sixteen are able to help.

Usually my children's first job in life is picking up their own toys. From there, I teach them to put away their own clothes. Almost any child who is able to open and close a drawer can learn this skill. If they can't open and close drawers, I get wide, sturdy shelves for them.

My daughter Cherise has severe cerebral palsy (spastic quadriplegia) and normal intelligence. She is very careful and responsible. She gives her younger siblings rides around the house on her power chair. She holds them in her lap, lets them sit on her footrest, and lets them stand behind, hanging on to the handles. I remember how Cherise helped comfort several of my babies when they were fussy. I would put the baby in an infant backpack, and fasten it to the back of her chair. She would move around like she normally did, and the baby would be happy. This was a valuable help to me, and delighted Cherise beyond words! Cherise is helpful carrying things from one part of our huge house to another. All of Cherise's help is done from her power chair, as she is unable to move around the house on her own.

My son Tony has severe cerebral palsy (spastic/athetoid diplegia) and poor vision, and is most stable on the floor. He prefers the floor to his power chair, as he can reach things better and move around more. Tony makes good and positive use of the intelligence God gave him, though he has moderate mental retardation. He has a very sweet and helpful personality, thinks about others, and has a helpful spirit. He sweetly and patiently picks up toys and the numerous things that end up on the floor on any given day. He remains the winner as my best floor picker-upper! For Tony, dressing himself is a chore. But he can do it for the most part, and though it takes him a long time, he knows that it is a piece of independence he can accomplish.

My son Chad has cerebral palsy (spastic hemiplegia) and severe mental retardation. He only can use one hand and walks unsteadily. Chad can set the table (non-breakable items, as he falls easily), make his bed, and clean his room. He can vacuum his own room with some success. He can load and unload the dishwasher, washing machine, and dryer, with someone watching that he doesn't over-fill them. He sorts clothing into bins as well. I must admit he has broken the door off the dryer many times by falling on it, and he has been known to break a washer by stuffing it too full. But all the help he has given, and his independence and feeling of success, far outweigh the damages.

My adult daughter Priscilla has severe cerebral palsy (spastic quadriplegia) from being hit by a car when she was nine. She has normal intelligence. Her body and hands are very weak. She was a meticulous and accurate sock sorter before she grew up and moved away. Believe me: a family can always use a good sock sorter! In our family, it's a huge job, too, and few had the patience to do it. Thank you again, Priscilla!

My daughter Skyla has spina bifida (partially paralyzed from the waist down) but is very strong, nimble and quick, with a cheerful and brave spirit. She has normal intelligence. It is very difficult for her to get things out of the dryer without breaking the door off. But she has found a way to do almost everything else. She can pull herself up onto the kitchen counter to get something out of a high cupboard, or put it away. Skyla is capable, willing and extremely helpful with her younger siblings. When they were tiny, she was an expert diaper changer, a patient toddler-dresser, a loving rocking-chair comforter, and a tender band-aid putter-oner. She has an abundance of energy and the sweet spirit of helping others with it.

I could do it myself in a quarter of the time, or less, but she would be deprived of the chance to be a winner and the chance to experience success.

My daughter Cathy has Down Syndrome. She is very low functioning. But even she can help clear the table, and put away her toys and clothes!

My two other daughters with Down Syndrome, Julianne and Starr, have helpful intelligence and able bodies. While they were growing up, I noticed they had weaker hands than a normal child. I don't notice that any more. Juli and Starr still live at home, and are independent and magnificent helpers. Both of them know they are important to me and feel good about being needed. Both Juli and Starr, along with Skyla, change diapers and help a great deal. Juli and Skyla are dependable and truly enjoy helping. They are fun to work with. Starr tries her best to escape chores. She does not enjoy helping but she does bask in my approval! Starr takes literally hours to sweep and mop a floor. But when she gets done, the job is excellent. Clean and dry, it is a beauty! I could do it myself in a quarter of the time, or less, but she would be deprived of the chance to be a winner and the chance to experience success.

My two little daughters Sarah, and Sheena, who have hemiplegia, but normal intelligence, can already sweep a floor at six years old! They work together. One sweeps, the other helps push the dirt onto the dustpan and dumps it in the garbage can. Each daughter can only use her left arm and hand for this. They make a great team!

My daughter with fetal alcohol effect, Katie, and son with fetal alcohol syndrome, Jordan, both have an enormous amount of energy. This energy can be harnessed in positive ways, by keeping them busy. They are both good at outside things, which take a lot of running, and inside things that take a lot of walking. They are the best ever at unloading a van full of groceries! They are right in their element with filling wagons, and pulling them up the ramp into our house, and going back for more. Among the things that get dropped, I always hope it's not five dozen eggs, a gallon glass jar of dill pickles, or a quart of jam. And if it is something messy, I hope it happens outside! Katie and Jordan both do any job very quickly, though it won't be done very well. Neither one is able to slow down sufficiently to pay close and meticulous attention to details. If they exhibit a good attitude and get things done, I don't complain too much about the quality of the work, if I can help it. God loves a cheerful giver. So does mommy.

Billy, a 19-year-old living with us for a year who has Down Syndrome, has never been taught to work. At first he would not help in any way, though he has a strong and able body. He would stand with his arms folded across his chest and a frown on his face, and watch my children working together. Since he also has a mental illness, I did not try to change him at first. My children were amazed at him! They had never seen anyone who would not help, but just stare! Yet even he picked up a more helpful spirit as the months went by. He progressed from total refusal to spending a lot of time watching my children work together with apparent amazement and quite a bit of interest. Now he joins in for one or two small jobs and has his own name on the job chart, getting lots of praise from me! The way I got him to join in was to finally require he do a small chore, like carry the milk cartons to the table, in order to be allowed to eat. And he really enjoys eating!

Some jobs can be successfully accomplished with two or three working together. For instance, Julianne counts with Cherise's help, and stacks the dishes onto Cherise's wheelchair tray. Cherise drives them over to the table, and Chad, who has to lean on the table for balance, takes them one by one from the tray and puts them on the table, one place for each chair. It would be so easy for me to skip Chad and Cherise and just have Julianne set the table. But what would Chad and Cherise do then? They would just sit and watch Julianne achieving, while they felt incapable, or worse, unneeded. That is not an option in our family.

Each person has a basket in his or her room for dirty clothes. Every day, as it is written on the chart, it is two or three people's turn to wash their clothes. When the clothes come out of the dryer, Skyla and Chad, or any combination of children, sort them into the basket on the shelves to wait their turn to get put away.

Putting away clothes is a job that works well with a group approach. I sort clothes fresh out of the dryer into baskets. Each basket has a name on it. When it's time, Cherise carries one basket at a time to its appropriate bedroom and the child whose clothes they are, puts them away. Then Cherise comes back and carries the empty basket back to me. If someone isn't there, or doesn't want to put them away, she comes to tell me and I go see what the problem is. This doesn't happen too often. Cherise saves me a lot of walking, as our house has eighteen bedrooms.

Skyla saves me tons of time, doing wheelies in her chair around the house, changing diapers, putting away clothes. You name it and she does it. And her bubbly, cheerful attitude is a tremendous blessing! She is the only one who is able to go to the store for me at this time, unless her grown siblings are home. The store is a block away, and she can be there and back in just a few minutes. She gets good exercise and also enjoys this very much!

Tony is good at handing me clothes out of the basket on the floor by the washer. His face lights up when he hands me each handful because he knows he is helping. It would be so much faster if I did it alone, but then how would I help that feeling bloom, that he is a capable and needed member of his family? He is gentle and passive and would just sit and smile all day long, if I didn't encourage him to join in. But I want him to grow up and have the spirit of helping. That way he can possibly have some kind of job, even if it's a sheltered workshop, and maybe won't become bored or unhappy. Maybe he'll keep that sweet smile and his own ethics will let him know he is doing something important, no matter how small.

> *Helping children learn to help is giving them a gift they will keep for a lifetime.*

I have a rotating chart for all my children's jobs. It is kept on the refrigerator. My grown children, Noelle and Kyle, who do not have disabilities, have outside jobs, and Noelle is in college. They are marvelous in transporting some of their siblings to a store or to an appointment in their cars. They also help drive them to church. My young sons who also do not have disabilities, Matthew and Michael, are on the job charts like Noelle and Kyle used to be.

It sometimes takes considerable patience for me to wait for chores to be done. But it is important to the child's self-esteem. A parent could do these things in a flash, and never give it a thought. But even a child who is very weak and can move only with effort needs to be needed. A good way to tell if a little one is ready to start helping is if he or she is beginning to try to play alongside another child. The beginning of desire for playing with other children is a social developmental point. It comes at roughly the same time as the ability to cooperate in helping, when taught how. It's a point most normal children reach by 18 months old or so, when they begin to help mama wipe a table or try to sweep with a broom. An older child with mental retardation will be more mature by this time in some ways than an 18 month old normal child, though similar mentally. I am specifically NOT talking about a child with profound retardation here. These children will not be able to progress to the helping stage in any significant degree.

A child with mental retardation will be three, four, five, or more when they reach the ability to start helping. My daughters Juli and Starr, with Down Syndrome and mild-to-moderate retardation, could pull out drawers, put clothes in the right drawers with pictures taped on the drawers, and shut drawers when each was three years old. I began with cheerful coaching and hands-on help. By four, they did not need any coaching. By six, they did not need the pictures on the drawers. My sons, Tony and Chad, both with moderate and severe retardation, were five when they were ready to begin. Tony learned faster, because he was slow and he thought about it. Chad took longer because he was hyperactive and couldn't keep his attention on it. Helping children learn to help is giving them a gift they will keep for a lifetime. This gift is more than just learning a skill; the children blossom inside with a happy, fulfilled feeling. Nurturing that gift develops the belief that they are helpful people, which the child will continue to hold.

A parent needs to use creativity to discover things a weak child can do. It is a wonderful thing when a child can know he or she is needed, and appreciated, like everyone else. Then, within each child, is set the cornerstone for a happy and confident future success!

Thank You For Your Support

by Denis Benoit

Born in Manitouwadge, Ontario, I'm the oldest of four children. I attended college in Ottawa, Ontario. I met my wife in 1994 and we've been together ever since. I have four beautiful children. I'm a District Manager for an inventory service and my hobbies include photography and website design.

One year after our third biological child's birth, my darling wife Manon and I started talking about a fourth child. We discussed our true want, our true need for another child, and the repercussions it would have. The only obstacle was Manon's age. Although she is in perfect health, a woman, regardless of her health, runs several risks going through childbirth after 35. Risks that would possibly affect both Manon and the child. It was then that we started our research on adoption.

Our first look was at South America. Then we looked at European children. For one reason or another, we never confidently decided on any until we saw a couple with a Chinese baby girl. At that moment our minds were made up.

Manon's desires and wants were the driving force in gathering an enormous amount of data on adoption through China. In a short amount of time we found an agency in Montreal, Canada, ideal for our needs. Through them, we received more information than we could imagine and devoured every tidbit written or suggested. So was the start of our dossier.

The process of putting together a dossier was more arduous and time consuming than anything we had ever encountered. Manon had registered with several on-line support groups which consisted of people who had already adopted, were in the process of, or were simply thinking about adopting from China. Those that had been to China had websites displaying their trips, with pictures and information on their adoption. Our two-year process of putting together our dossier was made possible by those who had unknowingly supported my Manon, with glorious pictures of their newly adopted family members. I credit these sites, and their stories, to our continued persistence in getting our dossier ready. I thank everyone who took the time to build their labors of love. These sites helped us, as well as hundreds of others, complete the journey.

It is because of this simple fact, that we've built our own site; http://clanroundtable.homestead.com/hope/hope.html upon our return from China.

We've received over 100 remarks on our website. To see the kind and generous words of those who are in the midst of their voyage and who take inspiration from our journey makes the circle of selflessness complete. We've touched others as others touched us. They kept us going and hopefully, no, definitely, we've returned the favor and helped others as well.

Our two year wait is over—now the rest of our lives are about to start.

Denis' wife, Manon, has written "Our Forever Day," which can be read in Chapter Nine.

Baring Your Soul: The Home Study

by Richard Gold

My wife and I came to adoption after years of infertility treatments. We are now the proud parents of a three-year-old son, who is our joy and the love of our lives.

One of the first things you'll face after applying to adopt is completing a home study. At first it might strike you as unfair. Just think, anyone can become a parent as long as they can "make" a baby. But you, because of some flaw in your biology, must undergo an inspection that puts every aspect of your life under a microscope. That's the law in every state, so whether or not you think its fair you must be prepared and cooperative. Put your ego aside. If you approach it with a positive attitude you'll not only find you have nothing to worry about in regards to being approved but you'll discover things about yourself that will be very enlightening. Keep focused on the goal—bringing a child into your family. Try not to be intimidated. Everyone is working in the best interest of the child. Here's a brief overview of our home study experience to help prepare you and allay some common fears.

Be prepared to bare your soul. Between our written application and the interviews, pretty much everything about us was revealed. I actually learned things about my wife I didn't know before.

We were asked about our parents and siblings and how we were raised: How close were we with them as children? How close are we as adults? How much contact do we have now? What role will they play in our child's life? How do they feel about adoption?

They asked about our extended family: How often do we see them? How much do we like them? What will their role be in our child's life?

We were asked about our relationship: How did we meet? How long did we date? What attracted us to each other? What are our strengths and weaknesses as a couple? What do we agree on? What do we disagree on? How we make decisions? How do we communicate and handle arguments? In one interview I thought we were in marriage counseling. They also asked about my previous marriage. What went wrong? What did I learn from it? We had to supply birth certificates, our marriage license, and my divorce decree.

We were asked about our education and employment history. They wanted to know: If I liked my work. If I had plans to change jobs. Was I was happy with my education? What were my personal goals? What accomplishment was I most proud of? What was I least proud of? I felt like I was in therapy.

They asked my wife if she planned to work once the baby came. Since she planned to be a stay-at-home mom they explored whether she'd resent giving up a career for the baby.

We talked about other people who play or played significant roles in our lives. We discussed our beliefs and feelings towards religion. We spent a long time talking about why we wanted to adopt. What kind of child were we looking for? When will we tell the child he or she is adopted? How did we feel about communication with the birthmother? We were asked if we resented the fact we couldn't have biological children. How would we handle questions from relatives and friends?

They also wanted to know our expectations for our child and what experiences we had with children. They gave us some hypothetical situations about child rearing and asked how we would handle them. This was a tough one because for the most part you're sitting there thinking how they want you to answer the question. The bottom line is answer honestly and from the heart. Don't be afraid to say, "I don't know."

Some other things they wanted to know were: How did we spend our leisure time? What activities did we participated in? What were our hobbies? What kind of neighborhood did we live in? How close were we with our neighbors? Are there parks close by? Did we have pets?

They took a complete health history of us and our immediate family. A physical examination with a chest X-ray was also required. We were told they wanted to be sure we had a normal life expectancy.

Also included in the home study was a financial statement. They checked our income tax forms, bank accounts, investments, mortgage, car payments and then some.

And just when we thought we had done everything, we had to have our fingerprints taken for a criminal and background check. No, they didn't take a mug shot.

The application asked for three references. We picked people who knew us well (and more importantly who liked us). We talked to everyone we listed before we put their name down and told them we planned to use them as a reference. We wanted to make sure they realized how important this was to us and to make sure they had the time to write a letter. We didn't want the process held up because someone procrastinated with the reference. Our references included my wife's best friend, my employer, and our Rabbi. Not only did we feel they knew us well, but they represented a good cross-section of the people we knew.

One of the requirements of the home study was participating in a series of workshops. There were four other couples in our group and we discussed and explored all aspects of adoption. Different alternatives were presented: domestic, international, older children, special needs. We explored our feelings and fears on open adoption. We talked about issues we'd face as parents of an adopted child. We walked away with a better understanding of the adoption experience. Just when you thought you knew it all someone comes up with a question you hadn't considered.

And what would a home study be without the social worker's home visit. Talk about anxiety. I wanted to get a professional cleaning crew to clean the entire house but my wife talked me out of it. She wanted the house to feel lived in. She was right. The social worker wanted to see the layout of the house, the baby's room, and different safety features. She checked our swimming pool cover and had us test all the smoke alarms. Then she asked about our plans for childproofing the house. We didn't have all the answers, but that wasn't a problem since she offered some good suggestions.

It took three months from beginning to approval. The process was relatively smooth partly because we filled out the forms and collected all the necessary documents quickly. If I had to do it again I'm sure I wouldn't be as nervous as I was. No one is perfect and the person conducting the home study made us realize that. I'm sure you've heard this before but it's true: be honest with your responses. If you stay honest you won't run the risk of contradicting yourself from one interview to the next. It is very intimidating and overwhelming at first but if you take it one step at a time you'll do fine. By going through the process we learned a lot about adoption and our motives for adopting. Now we are the parents of a wonderful three-year-old boy and couldn't be happier.

Enhancing Attachment And Bonding With Your Child

by Karin Price

I have 25 years experience as a professional social worker and educator. I am the adoptive mother of a daughter who joined our family at age one through international adoption. I also have a son by birth and a daughter by marriage. At age two, I moved with my parents to South Korea where they provided a home for orphaned school-aged boys. Upon graduating from high school, I returned to the United States to obtain my degree in social work. As an interning case manager, I observed adoption cases for the county juvenile court.

A question I am frequently asked by prospective adoptive parents is, "What can I do to help my child attach?" Thus, I decided that compiling a list of activities, which other adoptive parents and I have used successfully, to enhance our children's adjustment after they arrived home would be beneficial to new adoptive families as they began their journey of parenting an adopted child.

As you read the following suggestions, please keep in mind your child's age and/or developmental stages, his life before he came into your home, his personality, and his temperament.

Your temperament and your expectations of him will also influence the attachment process between you and your child.

1. As soon as the child arrives, take a family picture, enlarge it and place the framed picture where all can see. This will show your child and your family that you belong together.

2. Follow a daily routine and have a set bedtime ritual. Children feel more secure when they know what is going to happen next.

3. Limit the number of visitors in the home. Your child will attach quicker to individual family members if only the immediate family is at home. Regular visitors may hinder attachment. It is okay to invite friends and family to the airport when your child arrives. Everyday there are many people at the airport, so either way your child will be seeing a large crowd at the airport.

4. For infants, leave your child for short periods of time, beginning with a few minutes, in another room. When you return, your child will learn that a parent leaves but will come back. For an older child, begin with leaving for a 15-minute period. Leave the child in your home with a responsible adult that the child knows.

5. Keep the personal items, such as clothes, shoes or a toy, which came with your child. Make these items available to your child.

Attachment Suggestions For an Older Child:

1. If your child appears awkward with your touch, begin by placing lots of lotion on each others' arms. Then draw pictures in the lotion, rub the lotion smooth and start drawing pictures again.

2. Make a big deal out of scrapes and hurts. Be the nurturing parent.

3. Throughout the day, pat the child on the shoulder or give him a quick hug.

4. Dress in similar clothing. Wearing the same type of T-shirt and jeans is a visual affirmation that you belong to each other.

5. Put a sticker on your face and wait until your child comments about it.

6. As you play games, add the new rule that eye contact is needed before each turn.

7. Do things together: bake cookies, sort laundry, do yard work, walk for exercise, and sit together to watch a video. Your child may not have been exposed to television or movies, so it is important to watch the child's reactions to what he sees.

8. Eye Contact Game: Turn off the lights and play with flashlights. Whenever a beam falls on you or your child, both of you look at each other and count to five. Then move and catch each other again.

9. Put matching washable tattoos on each other.

10. Spend extended time brushing or combing your child's hair.

11. Give butterfly kisses until your child is comfortable giving or receiving a kiss.

12. Play "London Bridge," "Tower of Hands," and other hand-holding games with your child.

13. Play the game, "Who can make the funniest face?" Maintain good eye contact.

14. Sleep in the same room for an initial time period. All family members can sleep in sleeping bags on the floor.

15. Play with dolls by acting out your family life. Have dolls nurture and care for each other.

16. Keep a joy journal to share with your child as he develops language.

17. Write these ideas on small note cards or Post-It notes and place the notes throughout your home to remind you.

18. Smile at your child.

19. Laugh together.

20. If your child goes to daycare or school, give your child a small laminated family picture he can keep with him all day long as a reminder of you and other family members.

At times you may be concerned that there are attachment problems in your family. Feel free to share your apprehensions with your adoption social worker. They are here to help make your adoption journey a blessing to you and your child.

This article was written by Karin Price, Midwest Regional Coordinator for Dillon International, Inc. Dillon International is a licensed, non-profit, Tulsa, OK-based adoption agency—with branch locations in Little Rock, AR, St. Louis, MO, Wichita, KS, and Fort Worth, TX—that has specialized in international adoptions since 1972. The agency provides adoption services and humanitarian aid in South Korea, India, China, Ukraine, Haiti, Guatemala, Vietnam, and a pilot program in Kazakhstan. The agency also provides post-adoption services, such as heritage camps, tours to Korea, and support services for adoptive families.

Active Waiting

by Nadine and Paul Sanche

We have been married since 1989, formed our family by adoption and by birth, and have always shared these stories with our children. We adopted Catherine and Michael as infants and gave birth to Jason. Catherine's and Michael's are open adoptions. We socialize, celebrate special occasions together, and honor the many relationships which originate and extend outward from our children.

Couples who decide to adopt face a challenging journey, marked by seemingly endless times of waiting. A couple may wait years to begin a home study, and when that is complete, wait for a baby. After placement, there are additional times such as the revocation period and the time while legal documents are being processed. These experiences can be exhausting and seem little more than endurance tests. During these periods, focusing on ways to grow as a family, and preparing for the arrival of a child, can enrich the waiting times.

BECOME INFORMED

When you are anticipating adopting a child, it is important to become knowledgeable about parenting issues as well as adoption issues. Read newsletters, articles, reports, books, and newspapers.

Access libraries, the Internet, and resource centers. Be critical of what you read. Discuss topics and issues, and concentrate on developing your philosophies about parenting and adoption. Read literature that supports your ideas, but encourages you to be open to new ones.

FIND SUPPORT.

Maximize the positive influences and resources in your life. Share your experiences and plans with your extended family and within a support group. It is reassuring when others are aware of your situation, and you may find they have had similar experiences. Friends and family members may be able to offer emotional, spiritual, financial, and material support. Often, they must help you grieve adoption-related losses so they need to be a part of your experience, as they would be if you were expecting a child by birth. Additionally, sharing with even one encouraging person is an important step. When working through grief and loss, placing trust in someone else provides a necessary start towards emotional healing. If you join a support group, keep it positive. For example, consider joining an adoption group rather than an infertility group. Focus on moving forward and being hopeful.

WRITE

Writing can clarify thoughts and feelings, and bring new understandings about complex situations. Compose a letter (not necessarily to be delivered), keep a journal (as an individual or a couple), or keep track of events on a calendar. These are all beneficial. Although neither one of us kept a journal before, we found the experience a source of comfort and affirmation during our home study. We tried to be positive and optimistic in our writing, and kept track of important dates and milestones while waiting. Documenting provided a means of gaining and keeping an accurate perspective on events and the passage of time.

APPRECIATE THE ADOPTION PROCESS

Be active participants during the home study. Pose questions and provide thoughtful answers when asked for information. When writing a letter to the birthparents, be sure the words you choose accurately represent what you wish to say. Inquire about your completed home study file on a regular basis. This keeps you informed and indicates your continued interest in adopting. If your file is selected by a birthparent, anticipate that you may need to decide if the situation will fit your expectations and commitment, or if you should wait for another opportunity to adopt a child.

PREPARE YOUR HOME

Make arrangements for the basics you will need if a child arrives on short notice. We anticipated adopting an infant, so we gathered small, essential items such as diapers, clothing, bathing items, and feeding supplies. We made arrangements to receive larger items at short notice (such as crib, highchair, car seat), and chose not to take them into our home until we needed them. Consider keeping items in storage, where they may be a hopeful reminder of what is to come (setting up a child's room can become a painful reminder of what is missing). Additionally, if you expect to adopt a child with special physical, intellectual, or social needs, prepare your family and home to welcome the child and to meet the child's needs beyond the homecoming day. If the child is school-aged, or if you are going to adopt a sibling group, investigate community support and facilities, including schools, medical centers, play groups, and family and cultural resources.

RESPECT VARIED EXPERIENCES

All families waiting to adopt need support, respect, and understanding for their experiences. Be accepting of other people on the adoption journey, and validate their experiences as you need them to do for you. Neither downplay nor exaggerate anyone else's experiences, nor your own.

EDUCATE OTHERS

Sometimes people who have not had the opportunity to learn about adoption make comments and ask questions that may seem insensitive or rude. At such times, take the opportunity to offer information, change the topic, or say nothing. Reading and sharing in a support group are two ways to learn appropriate responses. Consider practicing responses so you are more comfortable when in the actual situations. Experience will help you respond in ways that educate others and affirm yourselves.

BE A FAMILY

View yourselves as a family, with or without children. Be open to a new image of "family," especially if your original family plan included having a specific number of children by birth or adoption. Read about grief resolution to make the transition from first plans to the new reality. Defining yourselves as a family, and living fully in that context, can provide you with increased peace of mind, confidence, and pleasure.

RECOGNIZE YOUR ROLES

Just as you affirm yourselves as a family, acknowledge and nurture your other roles. Celebrate the connections you have with siblings, parents, and friends, and use your desire to care for your own child to put energy into relationships with nieces, nephews, godchildren, and other children.

Improving the quality of waiting experiences by maintaining individual, family, and community activities can enhance the relationships and lives of couples seeking children through adoption. It is encouraging to actively participate in life by continuing to learn, travel, work, volunteer, and socialize. In the future, whether you have a child, or you decide not to raise children, you will be pleased you made the most of the waiting times through your adoption journey.

Index Of Resources

The following list of resources has been compiled from the recommendations and experiences of the people who have contributed articles for this book. Also, several people who have written pieces have graciously given their e-mail addresses in the event anyone might have questions or require more information from them. Please be aware that website and e-mail addresses are very fluid and the publisher can only verify their existence as of the publication date of this book. A Personal Touch Publishing, LLC. does not endorse and has received no fees for listing these resources.

Agencies used and mentioned by our contributors:

Adoptions From The Heart
www.adoptionsfromtheheart.org
(800) 355-5500
pg. 73, 161, 169, 211

Adoption STAR
www.adoptionstar.com
716 691-3300
pg. 51

Dillon International
www.dillonadopt.com
918 749-4600
pg. 372

The Gladney Center For Adoption
www.adoptionsbysladney.com
800 GLADNEY
pg. 121

IAC
Independent Adoption Center
www.adoptionhelp.org
800-877-6736
pg. 142, 145, 328

Adoption Services Associates
www.asasatx.org
210 699-6094
pg. 26

American Adoptions
www.americanadoptions.com
800-Adoption
pg. 20, 109, 133, 257

Focus On Children
www.focusonchildrenadopt.org
307-279-3434
pg. 181

Holt International
www.holtintl.org
541 687-2202
pg. 266

MAPS
(Maine Adoption Placement Service)
www.mapsadopt.org
207-532-9358
pg. 192, 203, 247, 303

Books used and mentioned by our contributors:

The *Adoption Resource Book,* by Lois Gilman
pg. 29

The Encyclopedia Of Adoption, by Christine Adamec and William
    L. Pierce, Ph.D.
pg. 347

The Lost Daughters Of China, by Karin Evans
pg. 199

*Secret Thoughts Of An Adoptive Mother,*by Jana Wolffe
pg. 128

There Are Babies To Adopt, by Chris Adamec
pg. 29

Toddler Adoption—The Weaver's Craft, by Mary Hopkins-Best
pg. 345

E-mail addresses of contributors:

adoption@bellaonline.com
Karen Ledbetter, pg. 331

barbaburke@comcast.net
Barbara Burke pg. 231, 344

bylerbunch@yahoo.com
Beth and Dean Byler pg. 230

CybermommyLJA@cs.com
Barbara James pg. 29

Websites of contributors:

Attachment Disorder Site
www.attachmentdisorder.net.
Nancy Georghegan pg. 237

BellaOnLine
www.bellaonline.com/site/adoption
Karen Ledbetter pg. 331

BirthMom Buds,
www.birthmombuds.com
Nicole Strickland pg. 91, 333

Byler Bunch Adoption Adventures
www.bylerbunch.com
Beth and Dean Byler pg. 230

Choices Counseling And Consulting
www.choicesconsulting.com
Arlene Lev, pg. 268

Legacy Video Productions
www.legacyvideoproductions.com
Nicole Sandler pg. 180

Our "Hope" Chest
www.clanroundtable.homestead.com/hope/hope.html
Manon Bougie, Denis Benoit pg. 364

Tomorrow Is A Gift (Christian Family Website)
www/adoptionfamily.org
Barbara Burke pg. 231

Websites recommended by contributors:

Adoption.com
www.adoption.com
pg. 94, 134

Asia Threads
www.asiathreads.com
pg. 199

ATTACH
(Association for Treatment and Training in the Attachment of Children)
www.attach.org
pg. 237

Attach-China
www.attach-china.org
pg. 215, 219

Attachment Disorder Network
www.radzebra.org
pg. 214, 220

BlessedKids (Services for Adoptive Parents of Chinese Children)
www.blessedkids.com
pg. 199

The Eastern European Adoption Coalition
www.eeadopt.org
pg. 181